Postcard History Series

Missouri at War

KEMPER
MILITARY SCHOOL AND COLLEGE

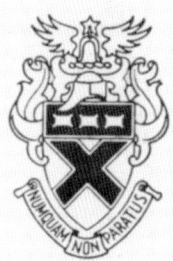

1844

BOONVILLE, MISSOURI

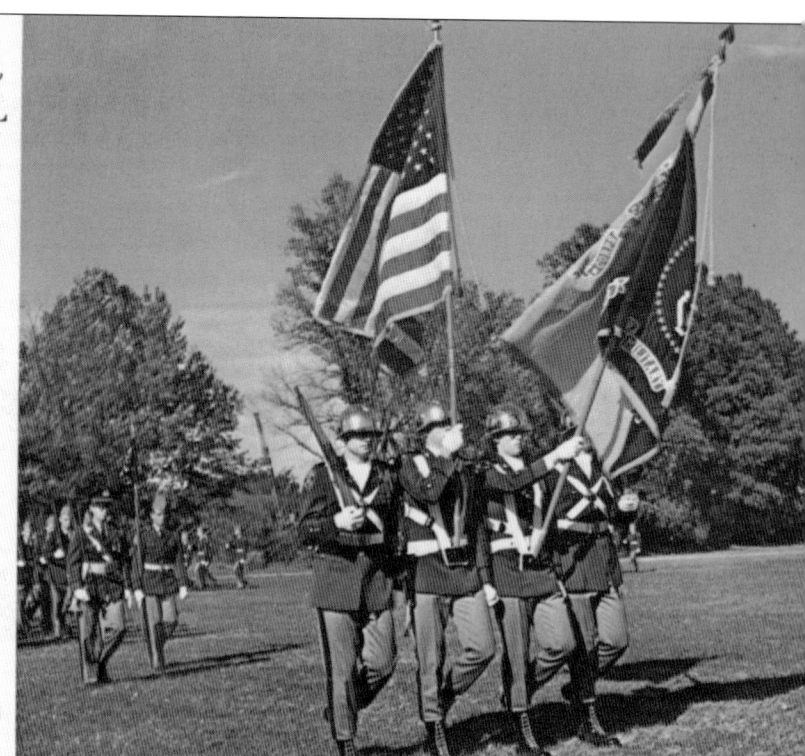

A color guard of cadets at the Kemper Military School and College is pictured in this real-photo postcard from the early 1970s. Established in the community of Boonville in 1844, the Kemper Military School survived the Mexican-American War, Civil War, Spanish-American War, World War I, World War II, Korean War, and Vietnam; however, the school eventually became insolvent because of declining student enrollment and closed its doors in 2002. (Author's collection.)

ON THE FRONT COVER: Taken on November 1, 1921, this real-photo postcard features the five Allied military leaders of World War I who attended the dedication of the site of the Liberty Memorial in Kansas City. From left to right are Gene. Baron Jacques of Belgium, Gen. Armando Diaz of Italy, Marshal Ferdinand Foch of France, Gen. John J. Pershing of the United States, and Adm. Earl David Beatty of Great Britain. (Author's collection.)

ON THE BACK COVER: *The Call of Missouri* was a painting by muralist Edwin Howland Blashfield featured on this postcard. The painting cost $20,000 and was a gift to the Public Library of Kansas City, Missouri, in 1918 by the Kansas City Chapter of the Daughters of the Missouri Revolution. In the painting, Blashfield symbolizes Missouri as a seated woman watching her troops depart for service overseas in World War I. Over her should are trumpeters representing France, Spain, Union, and Confederate forces. (Author's collection.)

Postcard History Series

Missouri at War

Jeremy Paul Amick

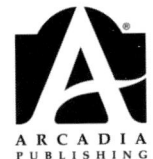

Copyright © 2017 by Jeremy Paul Amick
ISBN 978-1-4671-2656-4

Published by Arcadia Publishing
Charleston, South Carolina

Printed in the United States of America

Library of Congress Control Number: 2017930861

For all general information contact Arcadia Publishing at:
Telephone 843-853-2070
Fax 843-853-0044
E-mail sales@arcadiapublishing.com
For customer service and orders:
Toll-Free 1-888-313-2665

Visit us on the Internet at www.arcadiapublishing.com

I cannot express enough thanks to all veterans—past and present—whose service and sacrifice has inspired me to preserve the military history of Missouri.

Contents

Acknowledgments		6
Introduction		7
1.	Military Bases, Camps, and Air Fields	9
2.	Military Academies and Educational Institutions	43
3.	Memorial Sites and Tributes	61
4.	Armories, Buildings, and Service Organizations	85
5.	People, Events, and Naval History	111
Bibliography		127

Acknowledgments

There are many historical societies and organizations whose knowledge and resources have in some way contributed this book. I must thank the Jefferson Barracks Historic Site and the Museum of Missouri Military History for being quite responsive to the barrage of questions I fired in their general direction regarding the history of both Jefferson Barracks and the Missouri National Guard. Also, thank you to the staff at the Macon County Historical Society and Wentworth Military Academy for the time you have dedicated to me in recent interviews and bequeathing me historical details that were beneficial in compiling sections of this book. Without your assistance, my research for this book would have been much more complicated. Also, I give a "tip of the hat" in acknowledgment to all the publishers who, whether motivated by profit or for more preservationist-minded reasons, helped maintain the legacy of much of our state's military history through the printing of several different types of postcards. Many of the postcards featured in this book are of sites and buildings no longer in existence; however, because they were printed on postcards, we can peer into history and envision how they once appeared. Unless otherwise noted, all postcards are from the author's personal collection.

INTRODUCTION

Prior to becoming the 24th state in 1821, Missouri had already begun to demonstrate an integral purpose in the annals of the nation's military history. Evidence of this comes in many forms, and often there is little left to verify the existence of this role; such is the case through sites such as the former Fort St. Carlos that was built in downtown St. Louis in 1780. Though the remains of this Spanish fort have long since disappeared, several miles to the south, another military garrison provides a link to the past and continues to demonstrate the state's military role. Established in 1826, Jefferson Barracks was named to perpetuate the memory of Pres. Thomas Jefferson. Though many of the original buildings on site have been demolished and replaced by newer structures, there is still evidence of the post's role in conflicts such as the Civil War and the Spanish-American War. Thanks to the efforts of the local historical societies, preservation-minded individuals, and companies that produced various types of postcards, many of these long-forgotten structures can now be remembered in their original form.

Nearly 250 miles to the west in Kansas City, indications of the honor that was extended to local veterans who fought and died in the First World War can be witnessed in the Liberty Memorial—an Egyptian Revival-style monument that rises 217 feet above the main courtyard of this historic site. The memorial was completed in 1926 and dedicated by Pres. Calvin Coolidge during a ceremony attended by an estimated 150,000 people. In later years, the site of the Liberty Memorial became home to the National World War I Museum. A few miles to the northeast in the community of Sibley is the reconstructed site of a fort that once helped establish a fledgling US military presence in her western boundaries. Now operated by the Jackson County Parks and Recreation, Fort Osage remains one of several military landmarks near Kansas City whose memory has been preserved through postcards.

Many types of postcards, including real-photo and linen, have been integral in maintaining the historical impact of the military academies within the Show-Me State, one of which continues to operate. This includes the oldest military academy—Kemper Military School and College—which was established in 1844. Located in Boonville, the school remained in operation until filing for bankruptcy and closing its doors in 2002. The Blees Military Academy in Macon was founded by the late Col. Frederick Wilhelm Victor Blees, a Prussian immigrant that came into a veritable fortune following the death of his father and then chose to dedicate both his resources and efforts to build the academy and improve the standing of his adopted Missouri community. In Lexington, the Wentworth Military Academy was founded in 1880 and has on its list of notable former cadets two Medal of Honor recipients—George B. Turner, a Texas native who served with the 14th Armored Division during World War II, and William Edward Adams, a Wyoming native who was killed while serving with the Army during the Vietnam War. Sadly, Wentworth closed its doors in the spring of 2017. Still in operation is the Missouri Military Academy in Mexico, which has trained cadets since its opening in 1889.

Several of the state's past and present military posts and bases have also been preserved through the publication of postcards. This includes Fort Leonard Wood near Waynesville—an Army installation founded in 1940 that was initially designated as an infantry division training area but that later became an Engineer Replacement Training Center. Named for Gen. Leonard Wood, a Spanish-American War veteran and recipient of the Congressional Medal of Honor, the post now serves as home to the US Army Military Police School and the Chemical, Biological, Radiological, and Nuclear School. On the aviation side of the state's military history, the Sedalia Glider Base was activated on August 6, 1942; weeks later the site was renamed Sedalia Army Air Field and used as a training site for glider tactics and paratroopers. Although the base closed at the end of World War II, it acquired new life as Sedalia Air Force Base during the Korean War when it became part of the Strategic Air Command. On December 3, 1955, it was renamed Whiteman Air Force Base to honor the memory of 2nd Lt. George A Whiteman—a Sedalia area native who trained as a pilot with the Army Air Corps and became the first Missourian killed in World War II when the Japanese attacked Pearl Harbor.

Postcards have also served as an integral format in sharing much of the history related to the Missouri State Militia, which later became known as the Missouri National Guard. This includes several armories throughout the state, some of which were built using state and federal funds, while others were constructed solely through public donations. Additionally, much information about many of the training sites used by the National Guard can be acquired by perusing postcards and includes locations such as Camp Crowder. Named for Maj. Gen. Enoch Crowder, a Missouri native who gained a level of notoriety for his work in developing the Selective Service Act during World War I, the Army broke ground for Camp Crowder on August 30, 1941, in an area located a few miles southeast of Neosho. During World War II, the camp became home to the Midwestern Signal Corps School while also being used as an internment site for nearly 2,000 Axis prisoners of war. In later years, much of the property was deemed surplus and sold, although a portion of the camp has been retained by the Missouri National Guard for use as a training site. Other locations, such as Camp Clark in Nevada, also have rich histories and continue to be used by the National Guard.

Each of the state's historic sites, memorials, military bases, etc., makes up the patchwork of the quilt that has become Missouri's military legacy, and the common thread that ties each separate piece together are the postcards that define important events and places pertinent to this shared military past. As you sift through pages filled with postcards covering people, places, and events from throughout the state, you will come to understand the role each community played in various national and international conflicts and acquire an appreciation for all the brave men and women who have given of themselves to support *Missouri at War*.

One

MILITARY BASES, CAMPS, AND AIR FIELDS

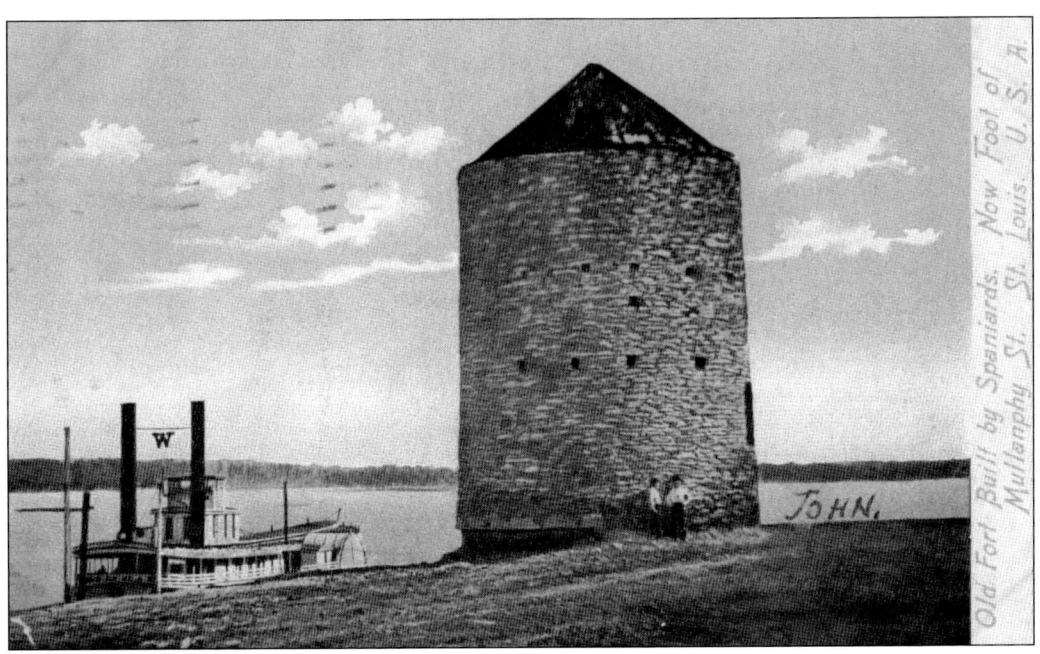

Postmarked 1908, this postcard shows the old Spanish fort that once stood in what has become downtown St. Louis. Named Fort St. Carlos, it was built in 1780 to defend Spanish troops and French Creole settlers. Though the fort is long gone and lies somewhere beneath the area of Busch Stadium, there is a memorial bronze plaque explaining the significant role the fort played in the history of St. Louis.

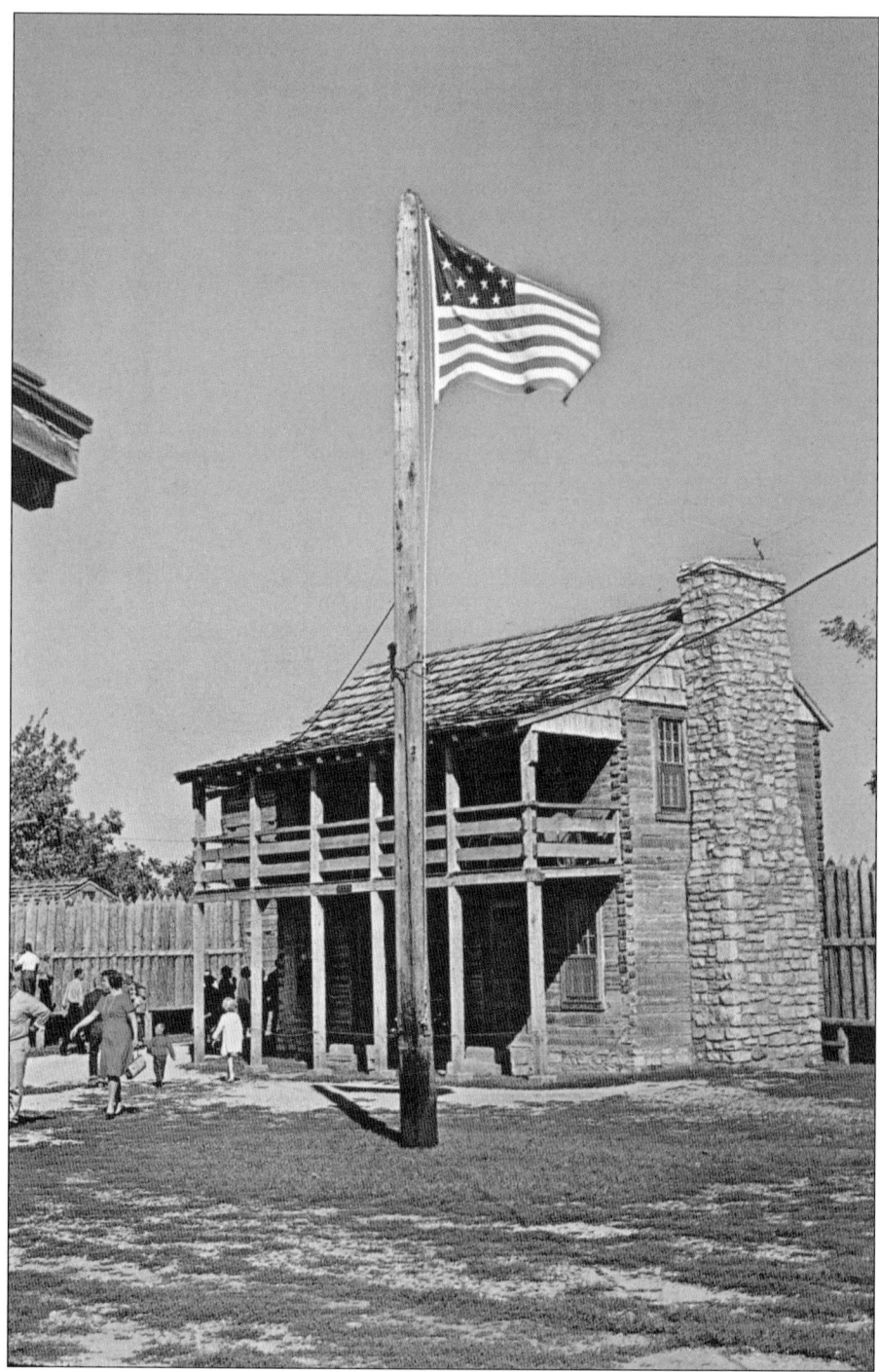

Fort Osage was established in 1808 as an outpost in the Louisiana Territory and under the guidance of William Clark, of the famed Lewis and Clark Expedition. Located near the community of Sibley, the fort was built with the purpose to affirm the United States' intent to protect its territories and to help form relations with Native American populations in the area. The fort is now a park owned and operated by Jackson County Parks and Recreation.

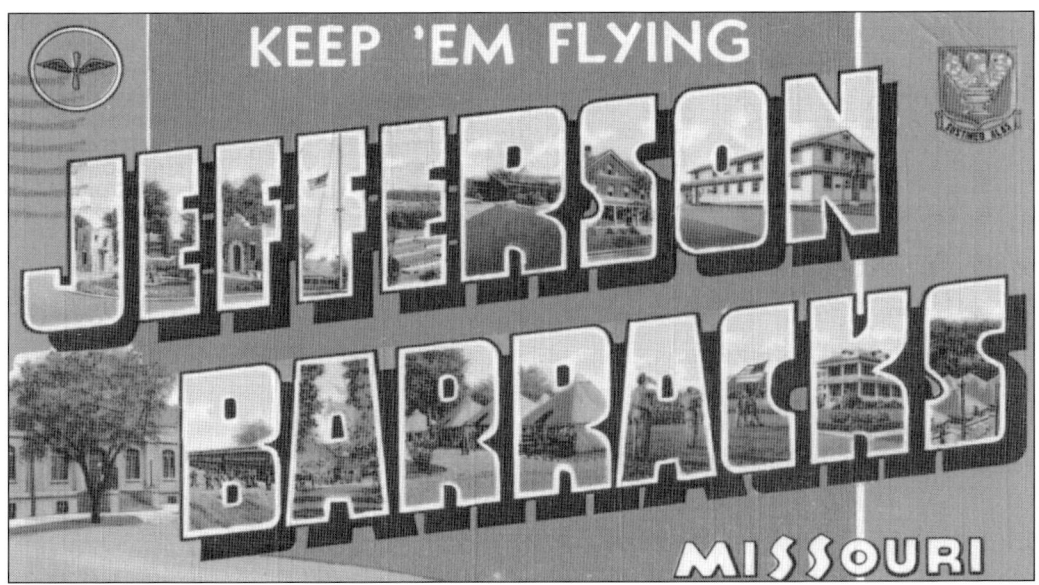

Established in 1826 and named in honor of Pres. Thomas Jefferson, Jefferson Barracks has the most extensive military history out of all the current military bases and posts in Missouri. This postcard, printed during World War II, highlights the important role the base played during the war by serving as an induction and separation center, basic training site, internment site for prisoners of war, and an Air Corps Replacement Training Center. Former presidents Zachary Taylor, Ulysses S. Grant, and Dwight Eisenhower all served at Jefferson Barracks at some point during their military careers.

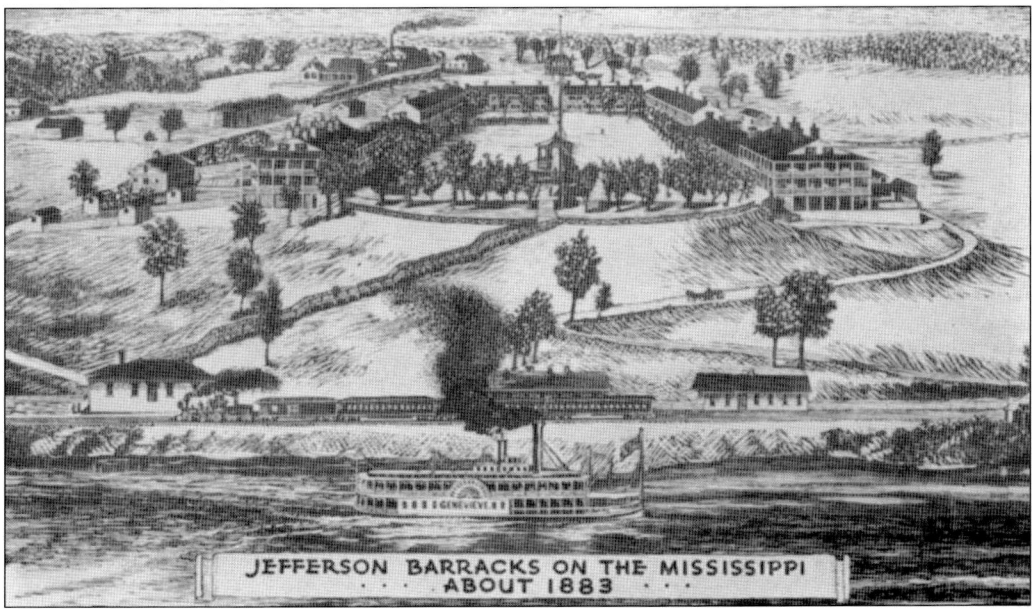

Located south of St. Louis along the Mississippi River, Jefferson Barracks is pictured in this postcard view, looking west, in 1883, which was 57 years after its founding. In the foreground is the steamboat *Genevieve*, which served as a troop transport to the post in the early 1880s. In the upper-center section of the postcard are the flagpole, fountain, and bandstand, all of which were once situated on the site of the current post headquarters.

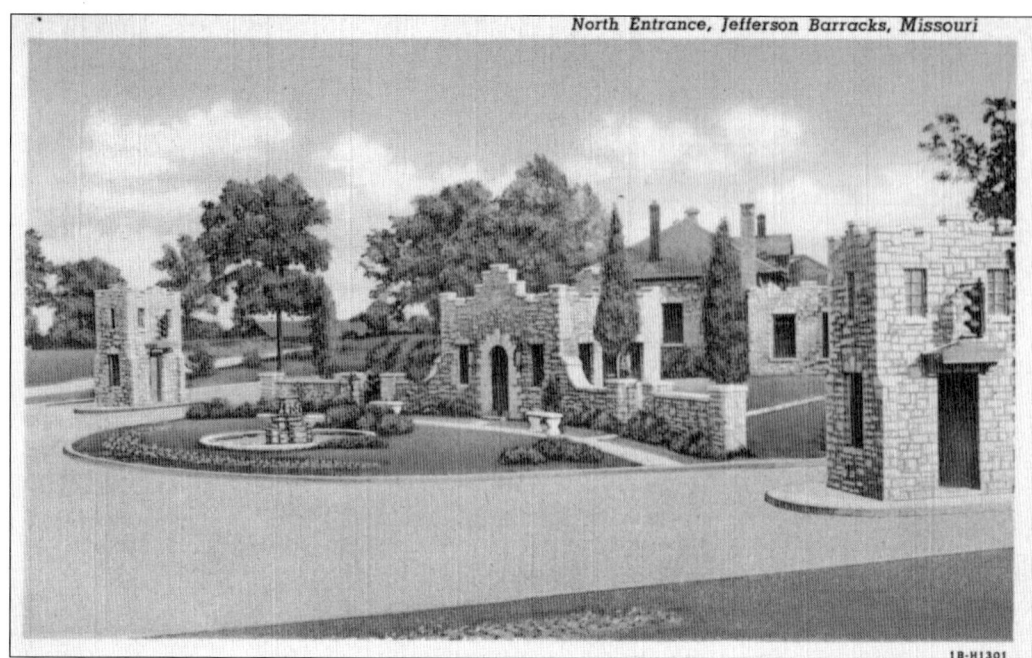

The north entrance to what is now Jefferson Barracks Park is located off South Broadway in St. Louis and was built in the late 1930s as part of a major Works Progress Administration project that employed more than 3,000 workers at the Army post. At the entrance is a stone guardhouse with gardens and two cannons on display.

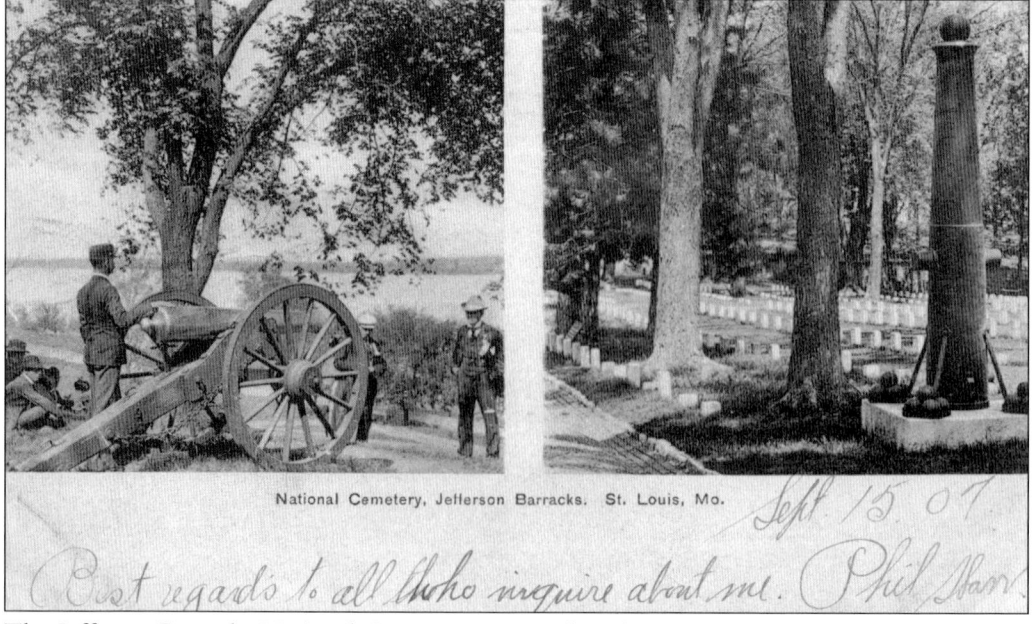

The Jefferson Barracks National Cemetery received its designation as a national cemetery in 1866, although the first burial is believed to have occurred on August 5, 1827, one year after the founding of the Army post. The photograph on the right section of the postcard shows one of the eight original artillery guns displayed vertically throughout the cemetery as a type of monument to those who served.

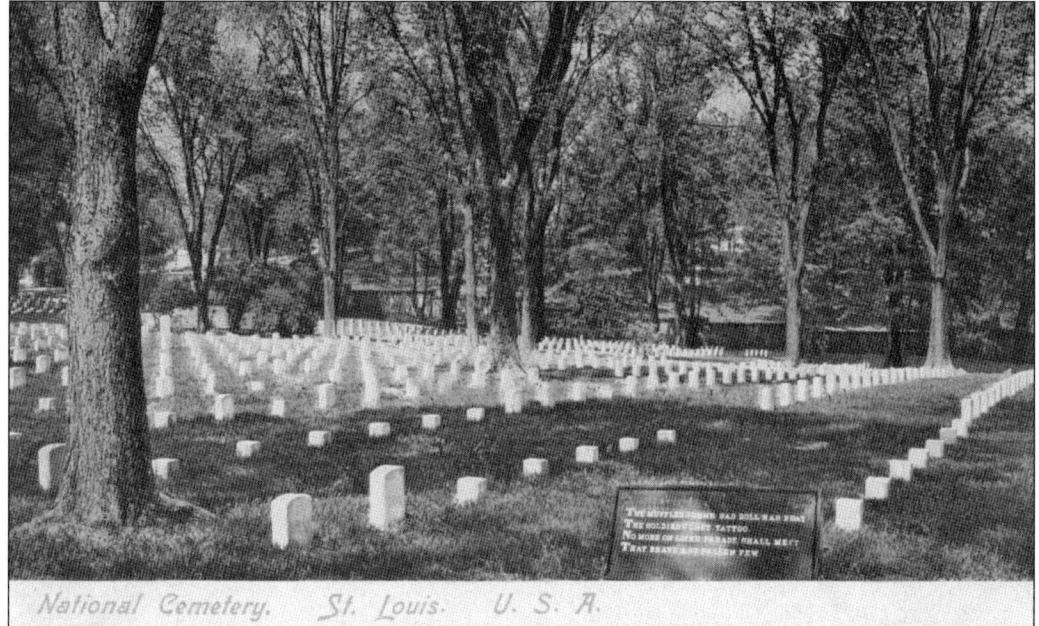

The Jefferson Barracks National Cemetery has become a burial site for military members from all wars in which the United States has been involved. The old section of the cemetery is comprised of approximately 20,000 grave sites, and the cemetery has undergone several expansions throughout the years. In addition to the graves of 3,255 "unknowns," the cemetery includes the graves of both German and Italian prisoners of war from World War II. In 1998, the cemetery was added to the National Register of Historic Places.

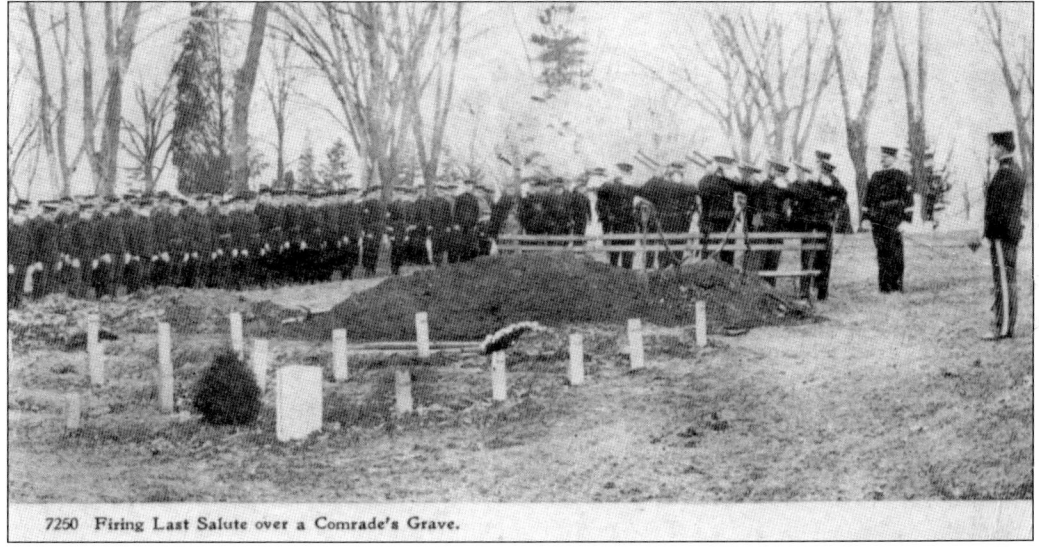

As shown in this real-photo postcard by the Adolph Selige Publishing Company of St. Louis, the ceremonies to bury deceased service members at the Jefferson City National Cemetery have often included what is called the three-volley salute. During this ceremony, an honor guard consisting of seven military members fires a volley of three rounds in unison, thus resulting in a total of 21 shots being fired. The term "21-gun salute" is often used interchangeably; however, this tradition refers to the use of cannons or artillery to honor the deceased veteran.

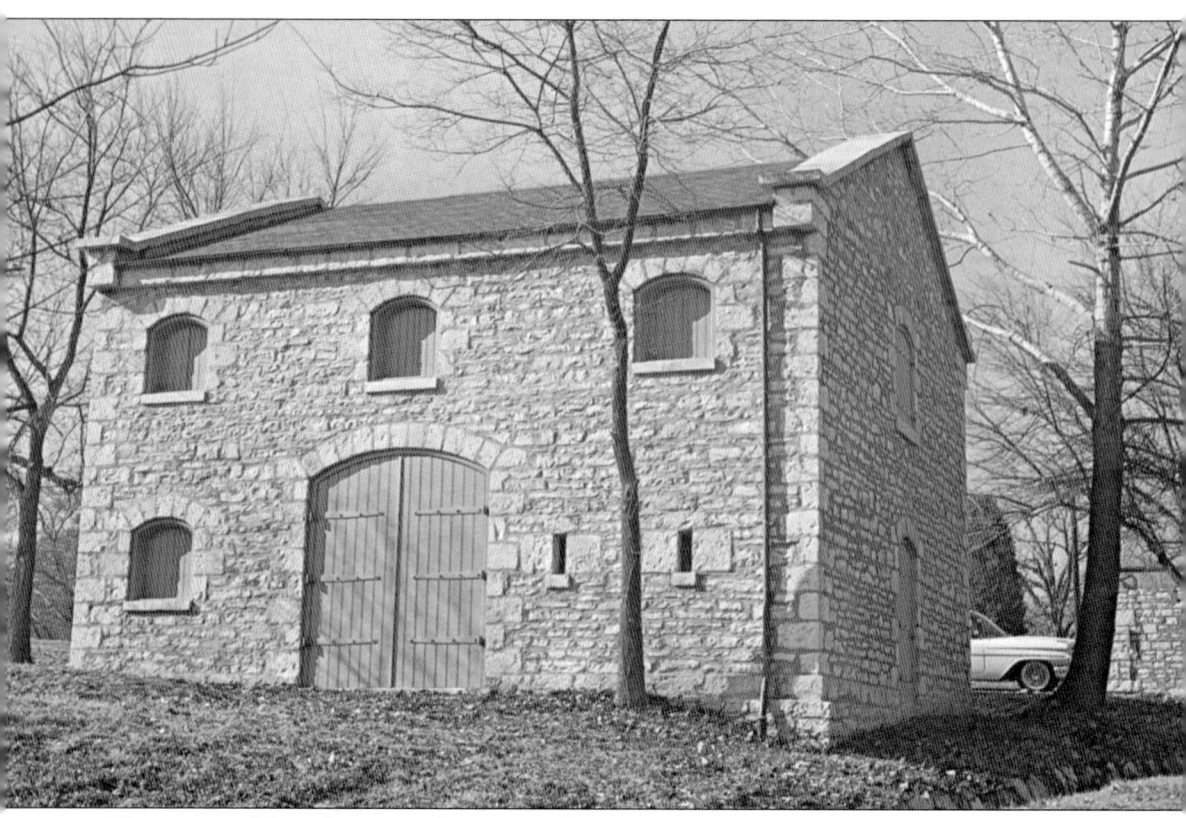

The stone stable and carriage house at Jefferson Barracks was built in 1851 with the capacity to house four horses and two wagons. At one time, it was used as an icehouse and, in 1959, underwent a restoration as part of St. Louis County's program to preserve the Jefferson Barracks Historic Site and exhibit items related to the US Cavalry.

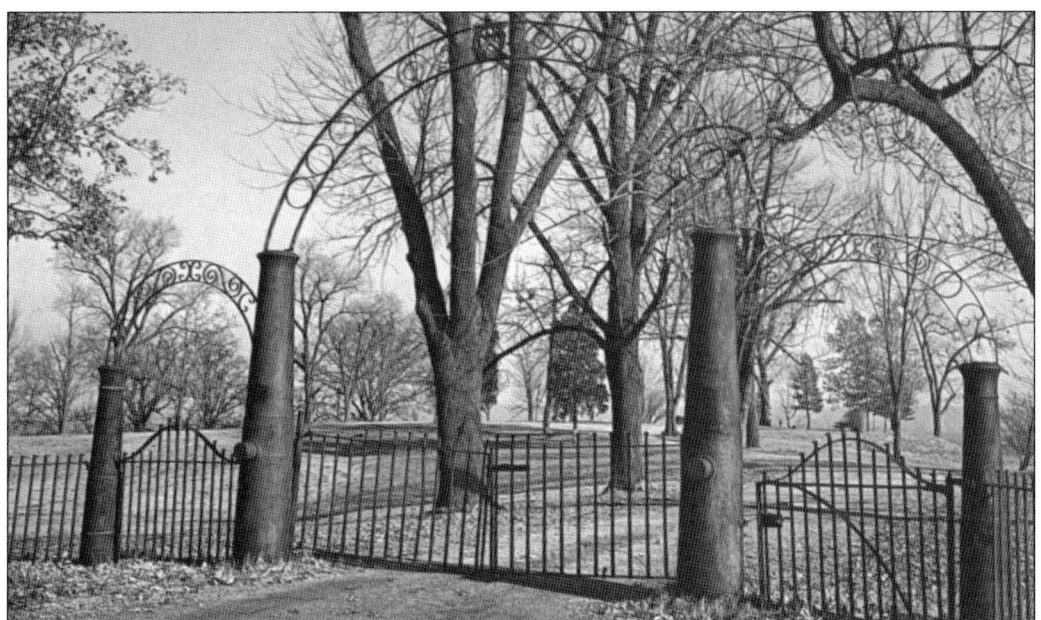

Once part of the military post, this fence made of Civil War cannons and rifle barrels was constructed in 1858 and has been preserved as part of the legacy of the Jefferson Barracks Historic Site. This fence at one time led to the home of the commanding officer of the Ordnance Department of the post and was controlled by a system of levers. In 1942, a large portion of this fence was removed and sold for scrap as part of the effort to provide steel for new armament during World War II.

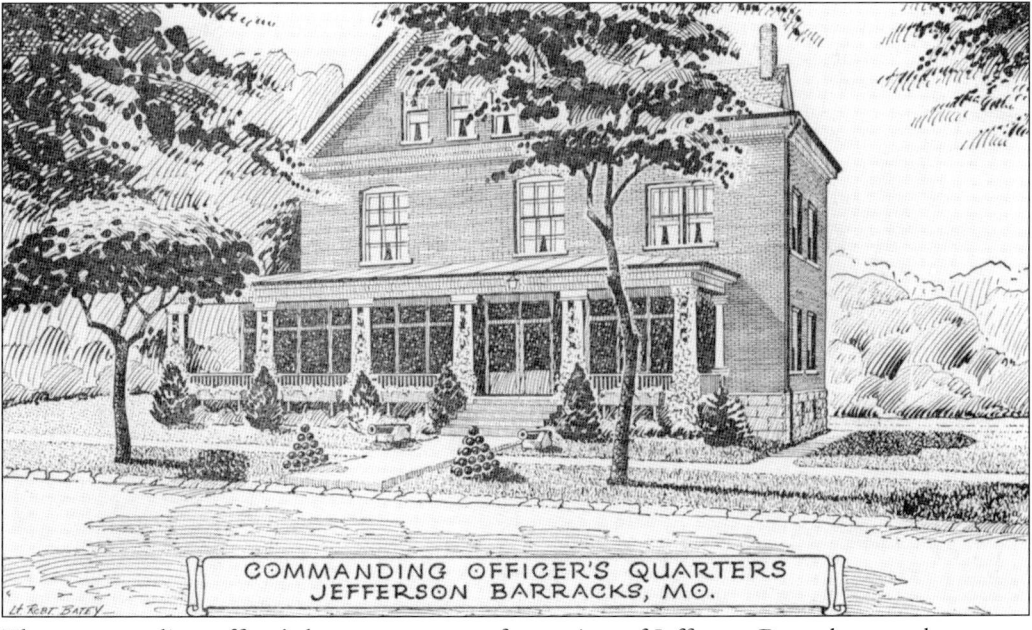

The commanding officer's house was part of a section of Jefferson Barracks once known as Officer's Row. This house was torn down by the US Army prior to the site being turned over to the St. Louis County Parks. There are now only two buildings remaining in Officer's Row—one houses the Jefferson Barracks Phone Museum and the other the POW/MIA Museum.

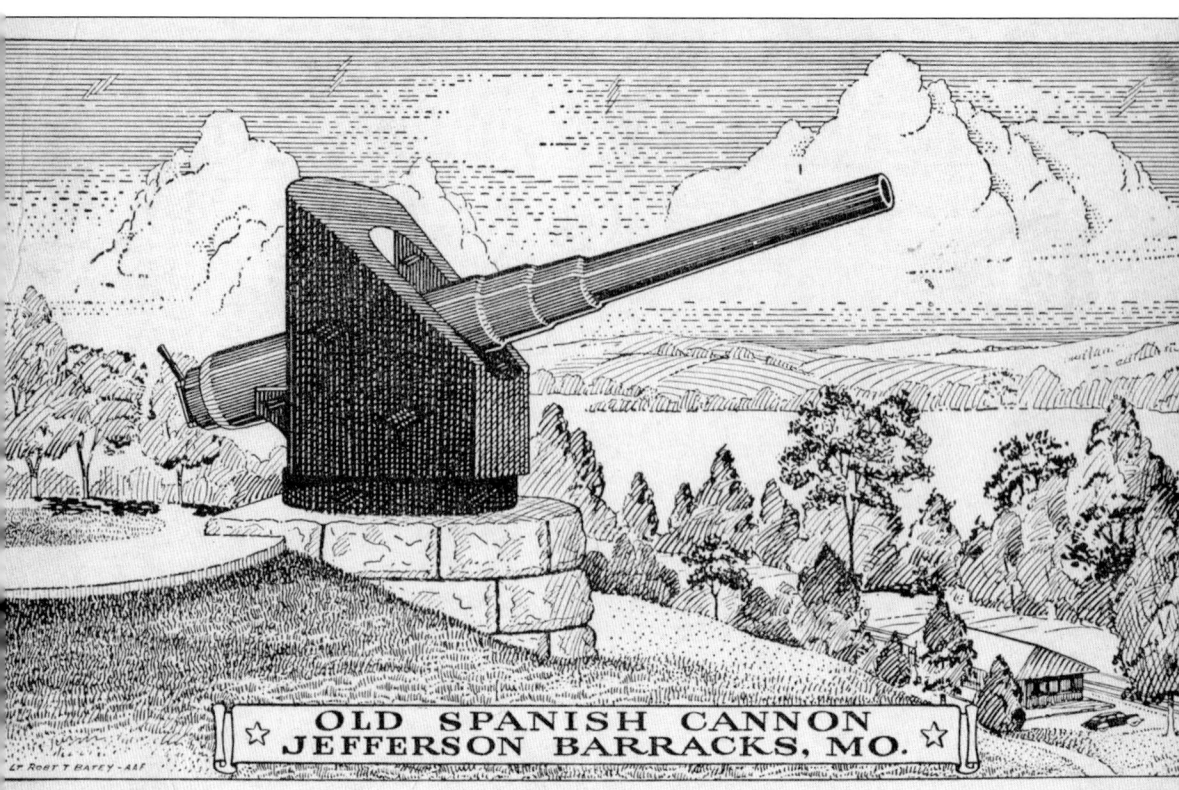

Situated on the east side of the post headquarters at Jefferson Barracks and overlooking the Mississippi River is a large relic of the Spanish-American War. This 20-foot-long cannon was recovered from the Spanish battleship *Oquenda* that was sunk in Santiago Bay on July 3, 1898. The cannon was presented to Jefferson Barracks in 1900 by the mayor of St. Louis. Several other municipalities and locations in Missouri received Spanish cannons after the war, including the state capitol in Jefferson City.

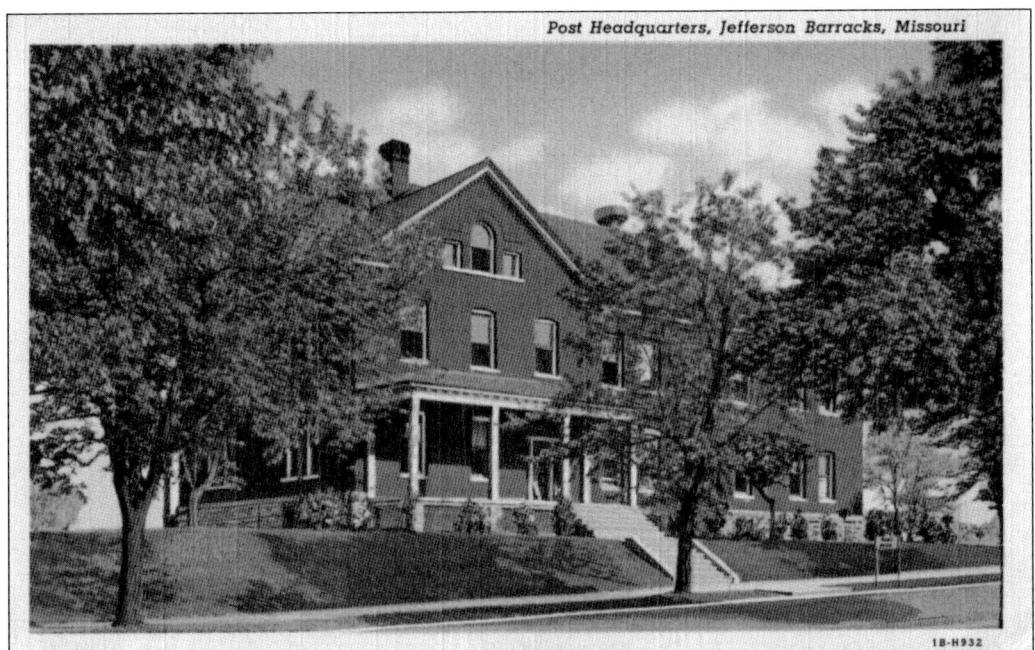

Pictured is the headquarters building located on the eastern edge of the post overlooking the Mississippi River. The three-story post headquarters was built in 1900 after the War Department ordered the expenditure of $39,000 for improvement of the post. The headquarters building contains a large room on the south end of the second floor that was once used as a ballroom.

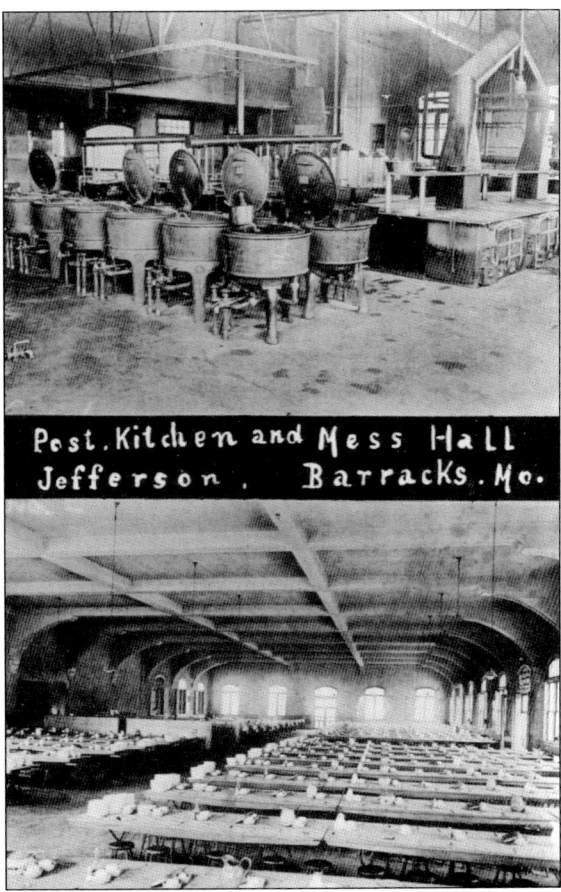

Pictured is one of the mess halls that once existed at Jefferson Barracks in the early 1900s. Based upon the architecture seen in the photograph, this appears to have been the mess facility and kitchen once located in Building 36, which was later replaced by a dining facility in Building 78. Building 36 was significantly remodeled in the late 1990s for use as office and meeting space by the Air National Guard.

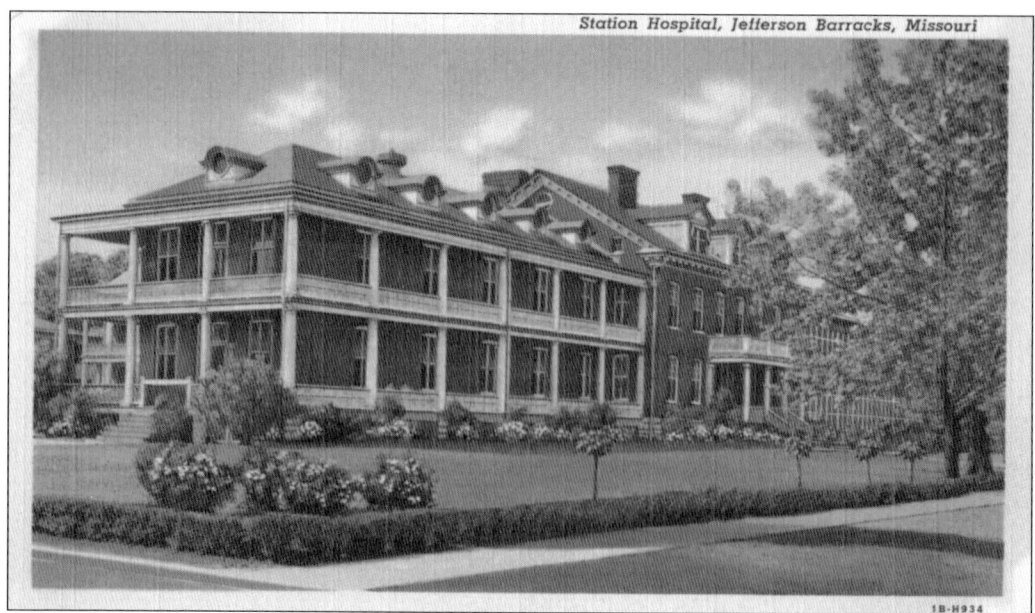

The station hospital at Jefferson Barracks was built around 1909 as part of the Office of the Surgeon General's plans for new hospital construction. The hospital was later classified a "station" hospital after the Veterans Administration built a hospital nearby to care for veterans of World War I. Following its closure in 1946, the hospital became the property of Mehlville School District and is still utilized by the district's maintenance team.

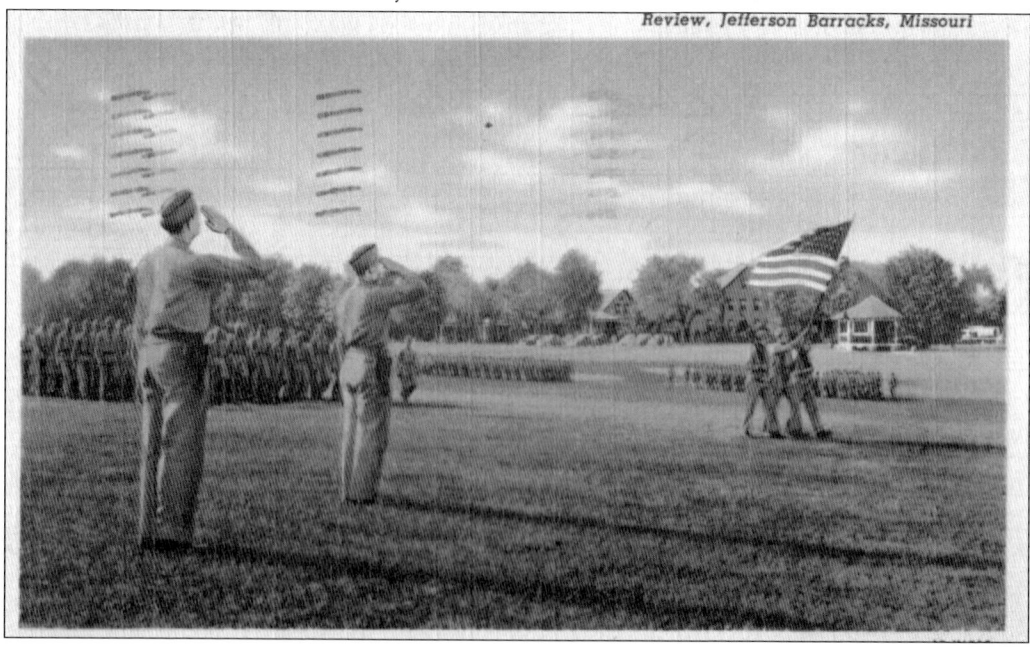

The parade grounds at Jefferson Barracks have undergone many changes in size and layout throughout the post's extensive history. Between 1998 and 2008, a section of the parade grounds was sectioned off for use as baseball fields but have since been removed and returned to something reminiscent of the days of World War II when reviews of troops, such as the one pictured in this postcard, were a regular occurrence.

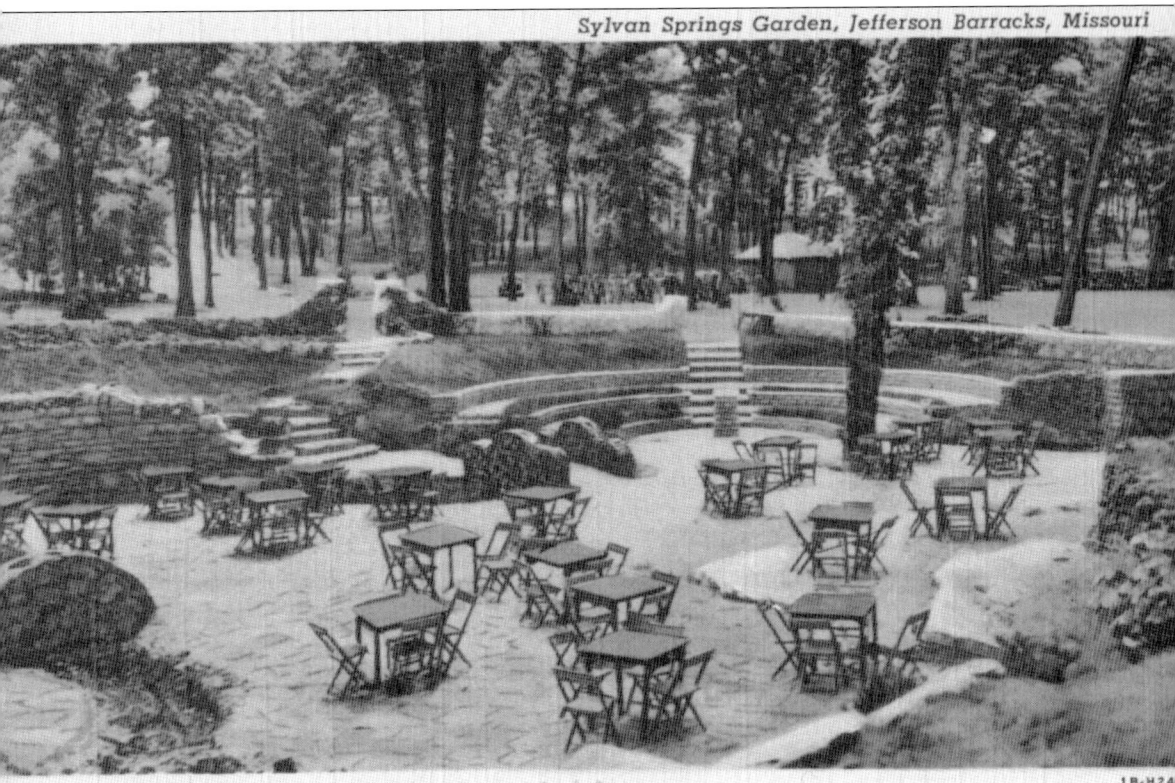

Sylvan Springs Park was originally known as Rock Springs and was the site of the first bivouac of troops to occur at Jefferson Barracks. In 1941, enlisted soldiers from the post built an amphitheater, dance floor, and football and baseball fields at the site. In addition to a variety of social events, United Service Organizations (USO) shows took place at the park; however, the property was conveyed to St. Louis County by the federal government in 1950.

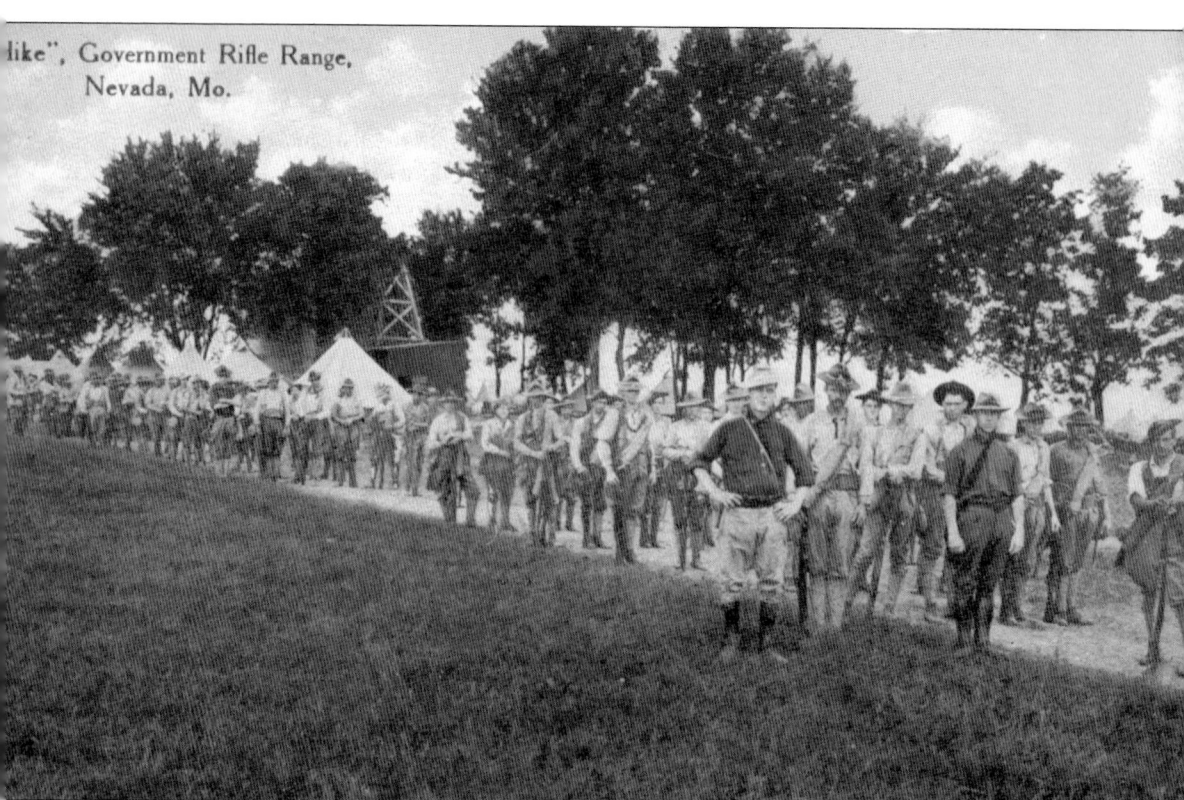

like", Government Rifle Range, Nevada, Mo.

The State Rifle Range in Nevada, Missouri, was purchased in 1908 from funds allotted by the federal government to promote rifle practice. The year following its establishment, the state's adjutant general gave permission to the military academies in Missouri to send cadet companies to utilize the range for an annual encampment. Additionally, the Missouri National Guard began using the range for annual encampments during the summer months. In June 1916, an electrical storm swept through an encampment, killing Maj. V.O. Williams and blowing down many of the soldiers' tents.

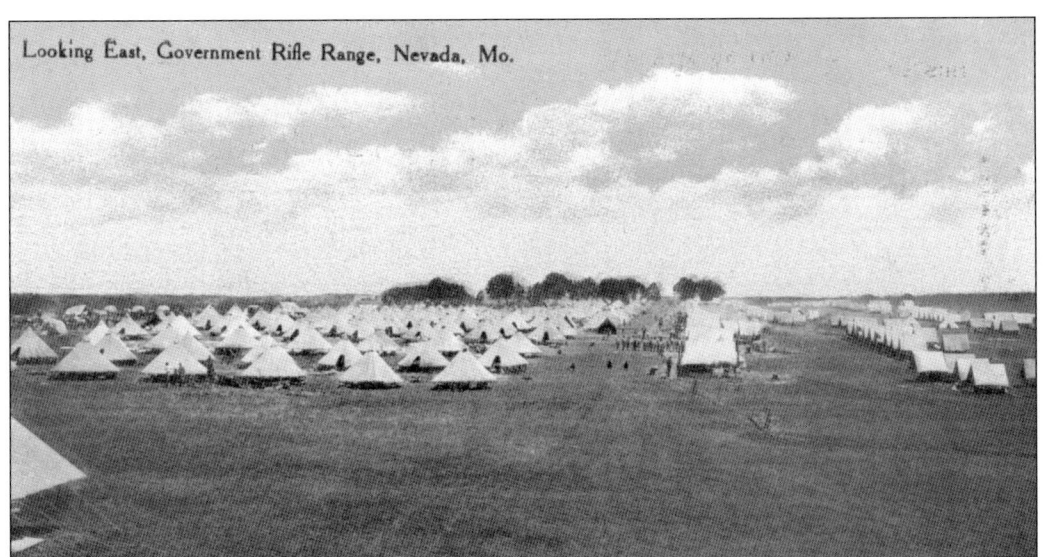

Scenes such as the one pictured here could often be witnessed as scores of tents went up during the annual encampments of the state's National Guard companies. At times, during the early years of using the State Rifle Range, more than 3,000 soldiers could be found in the area performing a variety of military maneuvers. Departing from towns throughout the state, the various companies, once arriving by rail in the town of Nevada, would depart their trains and march the three miles to the rifle range to set up camp.

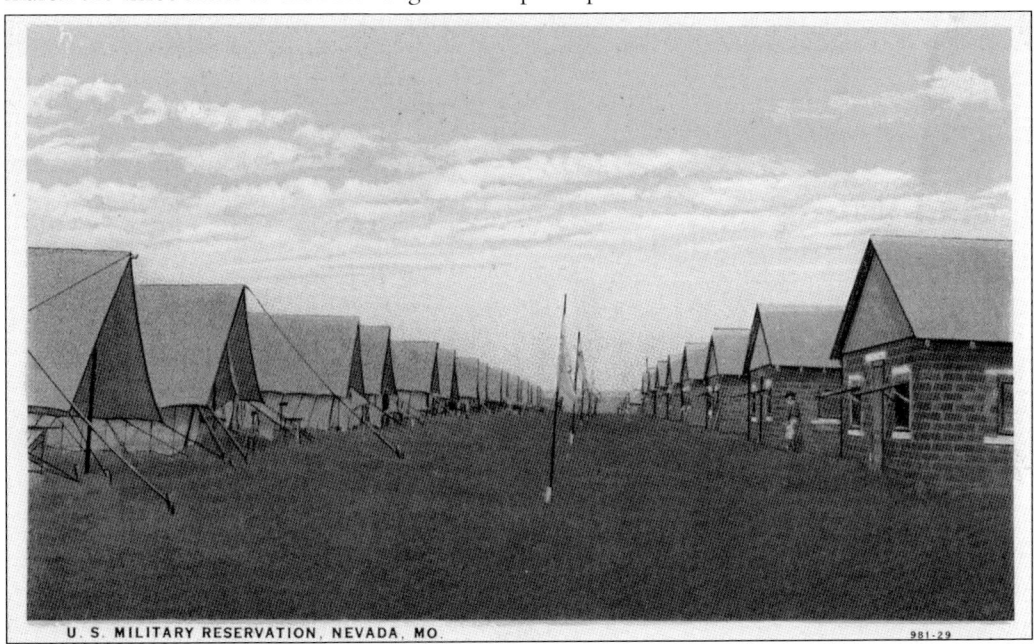

Prior to the establishment of the rifle range, the Missouri National Guard trained in other locations, such as Swope Park in Kansas City and at Fort Riley, Kansas. In later years, more permanent barracks and structures were erected at the State Rifle Range in Nevada, such as the brick buildings seen at right. As early as 1916, the State Rifle Range began to assume the title in newspaper articles and among the soldiers as "Camp Clark," named for Gen. Harvey C. Clark, a former adjutant general and commander of the Missouri National Guard.

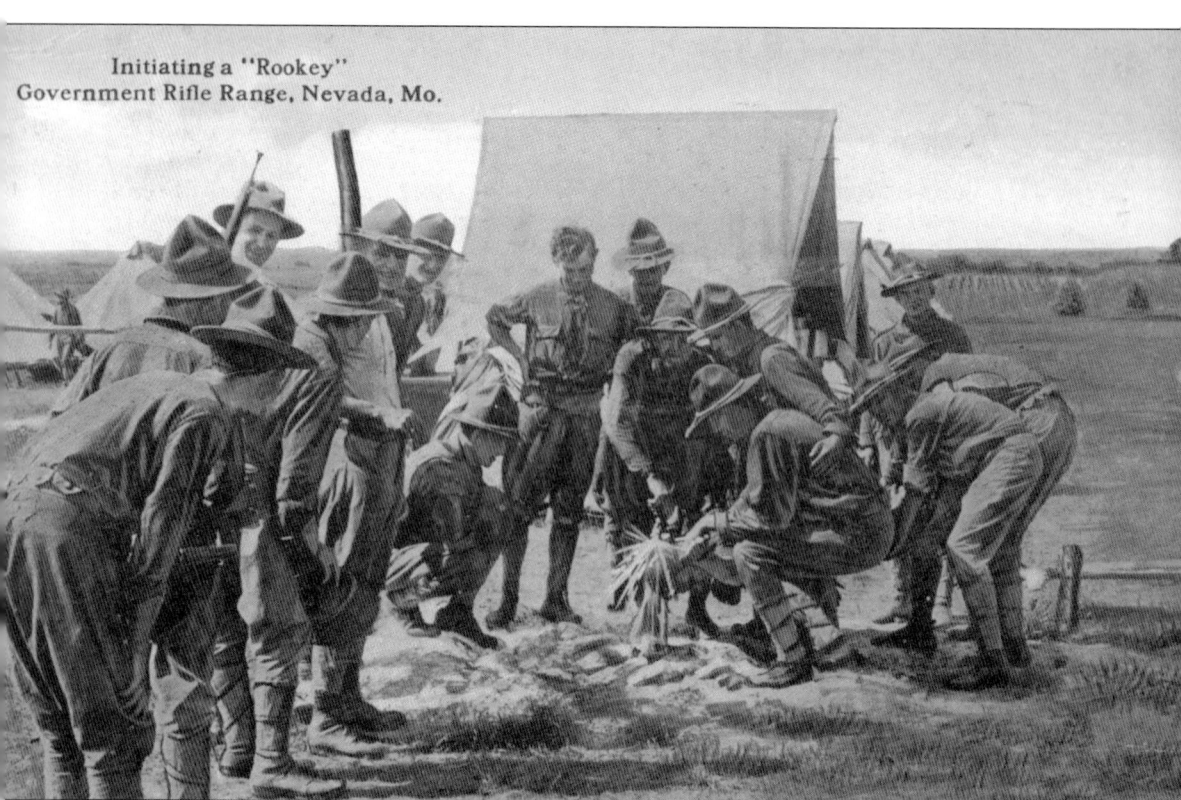

Initiating a "Rookey"
Government Rifle Range, Nevada, Mo.

Soldiers continued to train at Camp Clark, and in later years, it became an assembly point for Missouri National Guard troops mobilized for the Punitive Expedition to Mexico in 1916. Months later, it again became a mobilization site during World War I. It also served as a prisoner of war camp for Italian and German soldiers in World War II. To this day, Camp Clark carries forth its historic legacy by serving as a training site for the Missouri National Guard.

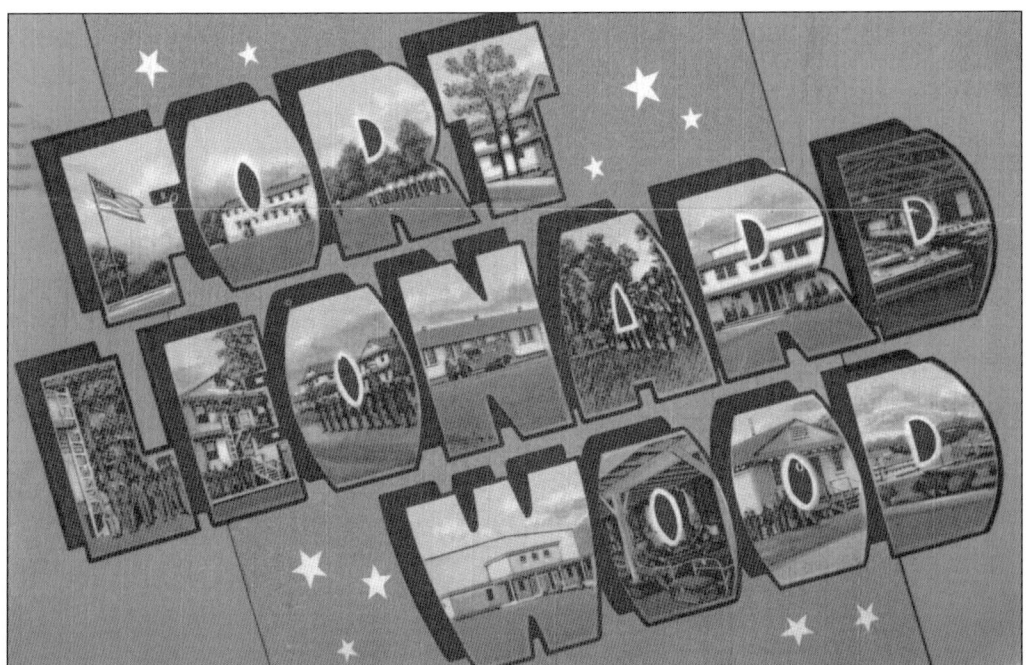

In December 1940, a year prior to the attack on Pearl Harbor, ground was broken in rural Pulaski County for what was initially known as the Seventh Corps Area Training Center. The following month, the installation was named Fort Leonard Wood in honor of Maj. Gen. Leonard Wood, who was awarded the Congressional Medal of Honor for valor during the Apache Indian Wars, served with Teddy Roosevelt in the Rough Riders during in the Spanish-American War, and served many years as Army chief of staff, to name but a few of his accomplishments.

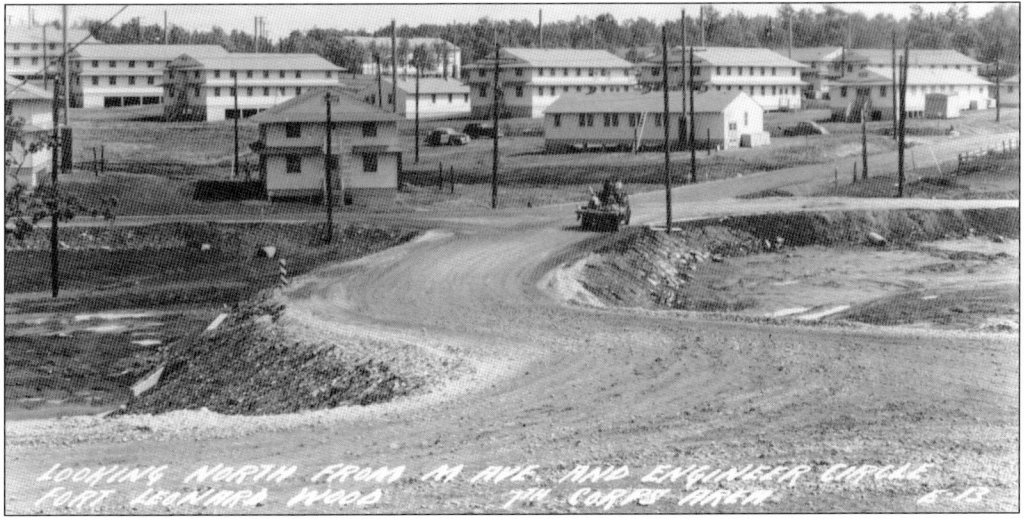

This postcard shows the early months of Fort Leonard Wood's existence when the Ozark terrain was still rough and unforgiving and the roads unpaved. Although the layout of the site for the post presented many challenges, such as a lack of adequate housing for the thousands of construction workers flooding into the area for work and a rail service located several miles away, crews overcame these obstacles, and the initial elements of construction were completed six months later, in June 1941.

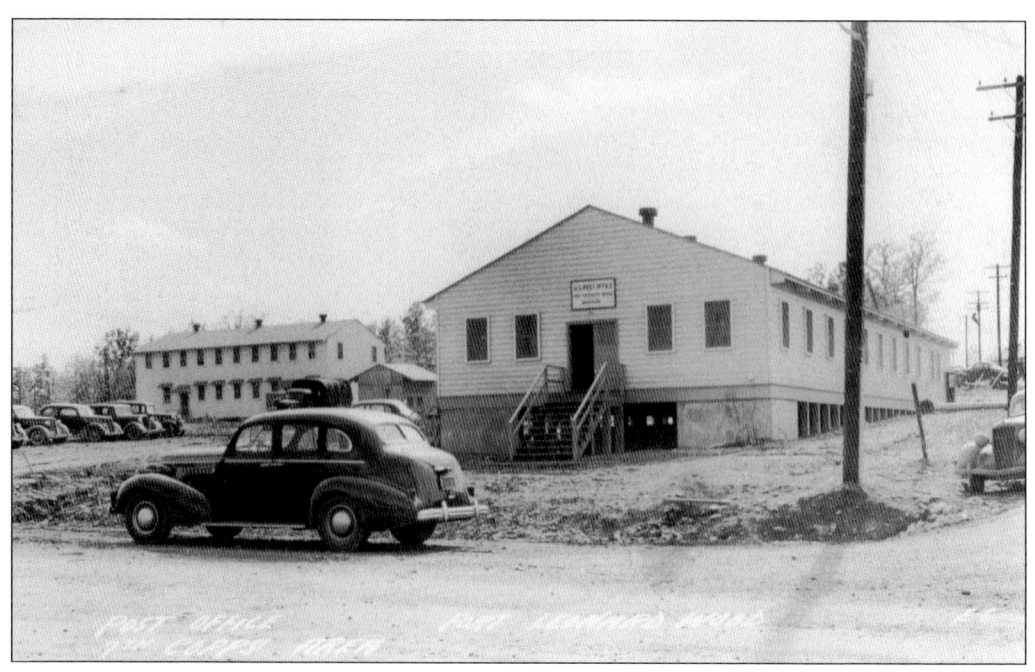

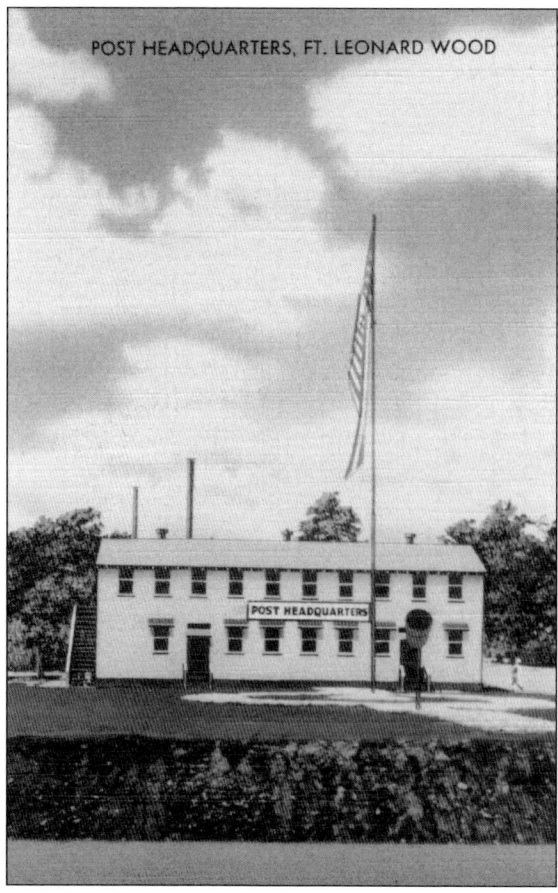

This base post office was one of nearly 1,600 buildings constructed at Fort Leonard Wood during its first six months of existence. In its infancy, the post was designated to serve as the home of the 6th Infantry Division, with four other infantry divisions and various other units arriving to train at the post during World War II. In early spring 1941, the post assumed an engineer training mission as well, but it would be more than five decades later, in 1985, that the US Army Engineer School was moved from Fort Belvoir, Virginia, to Fort Leonard Wood.

The old post headquarters at Fort Leonard Wood was constructed during the early months of 1941 along Missouri Avenue. German POWs later constructed a 600-foot, stone-covered embankment in addition to retaining walls, steps, walkways, and ditches adjacent to the headquarters building. The building was demolished in 2012, but the site is now part of Veteran's Park, where the flagpole and courtyard of the original post headquarters can be seen.

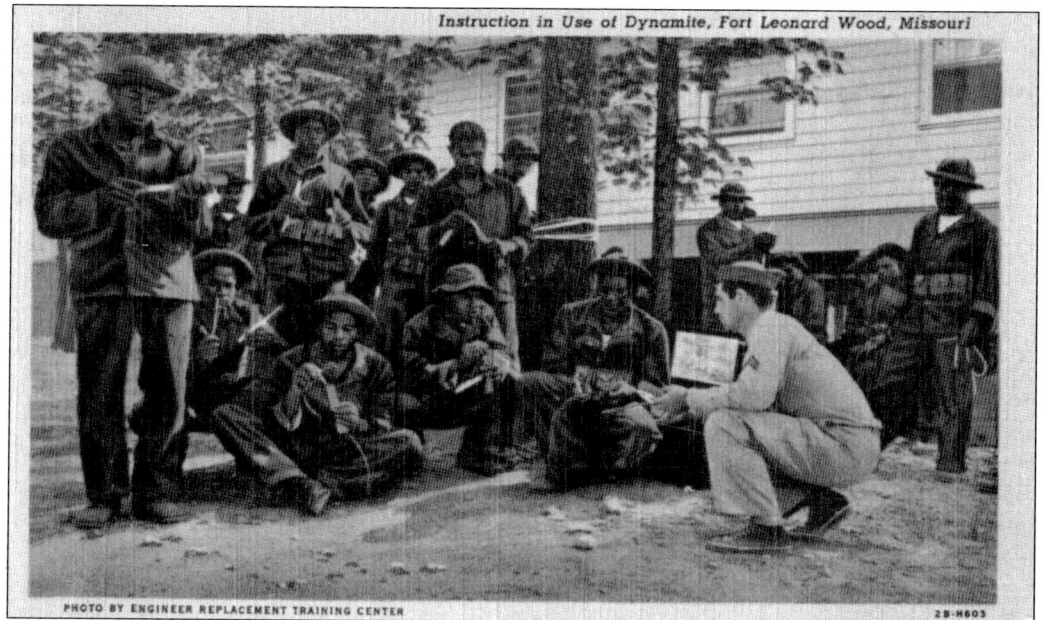

Fort Leonard Wood housed, trained, and mobilized more than 300,000 troops during the Second World War, many of whom were black soldiers who were placed into segregated training groups. This linen postcard, postmarked 1942, shows a group of black soldiers assigned to the 7th Training Group receiving instruction on the use of dynamite through the Engineer Replacement Training Center.

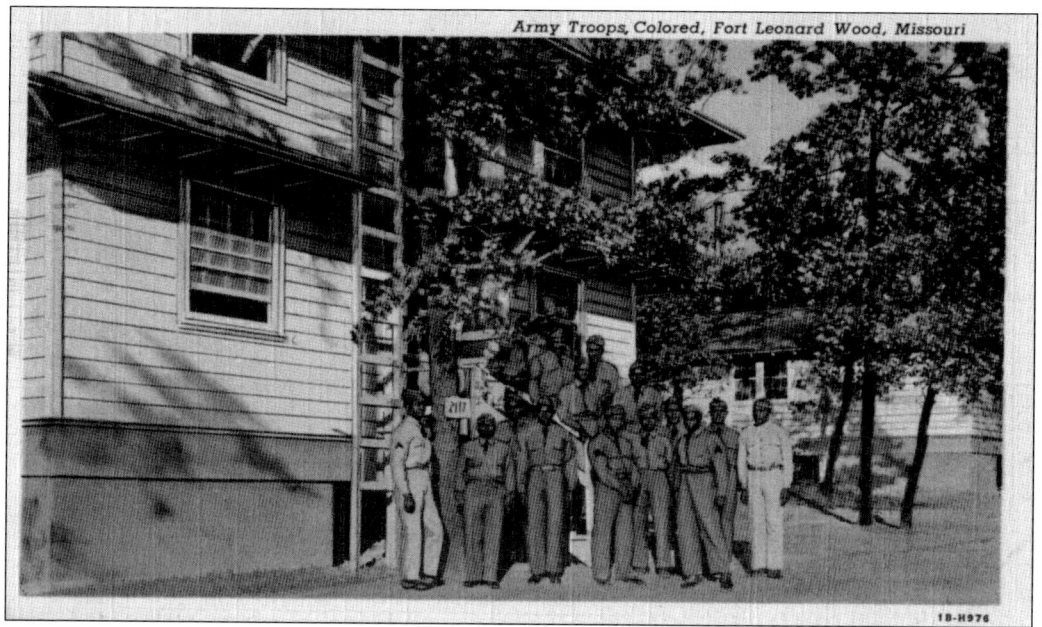

During World War II, many black soldiers at Fort Leonard Wood lived and often trained on a segregated section of the post. Building 2101 was an administrative building that was converted into a service club for black officers after white officers denied them entry into another service club during World War II. This building is now in the National Register of Historic Places and contains a painting by a black soldier once stationed on the post.

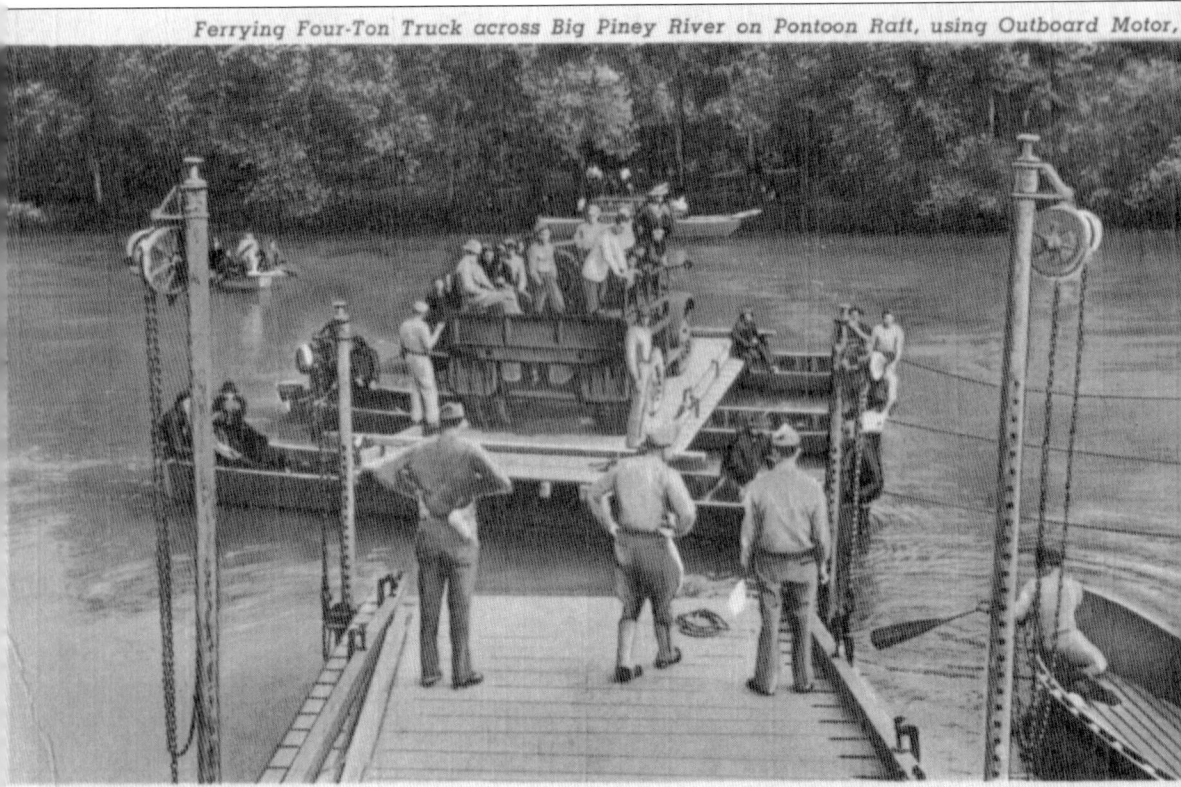

Ferrying Four-Ton Truck across Big Piney River on Pontoon Raft, using Outboard Motor, Fort Leonard Wood, Missouri. PHOTO BY ENGINEER REPLACEMENT TRAINING CENTER

River crossings have long been an important aspect in training soldiers, and the training at Fort Leonard Wood was certainly no exception. Located along the Big Piney River, the post has taken advantage of their surroundings by establishing a Pontoon Training Area to train soldiers in the safest and most expeditious manner to transport troops, supplies, and equipment across a river or waterway.

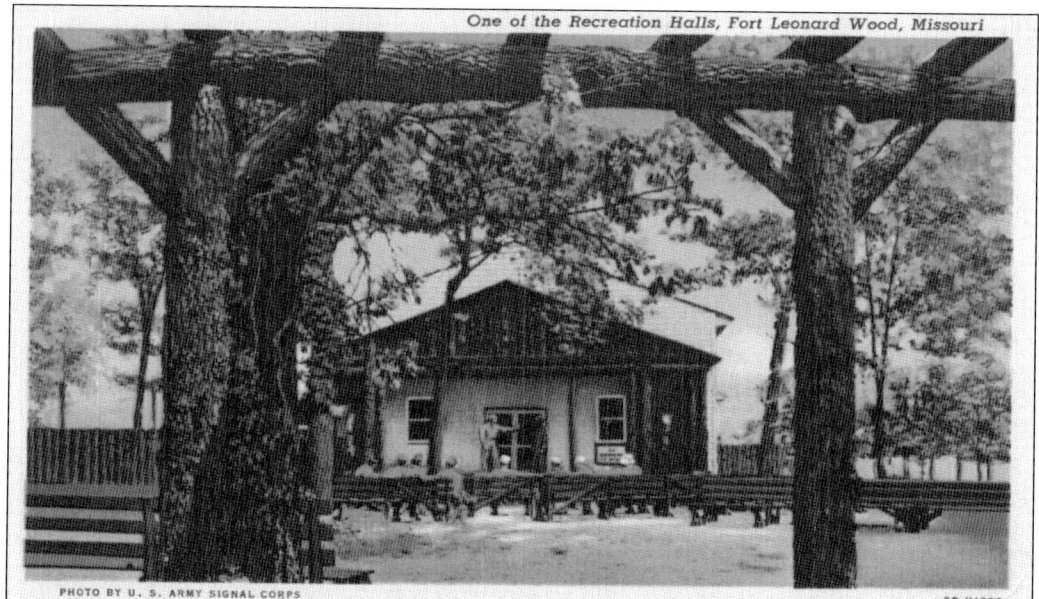

In the early days of Fort Leonard Wood, there were few opportunities for rest and relaxation considering the remoteness of the post. Though "Fort Lost in the Woods," as many soldiers refer to it, has grown and prospered over the years, recreational halls, such as the one pictured in this postcard, once provided those stationed on the post a place to listen to music, play games, and visit with friends and fellow soldiers.

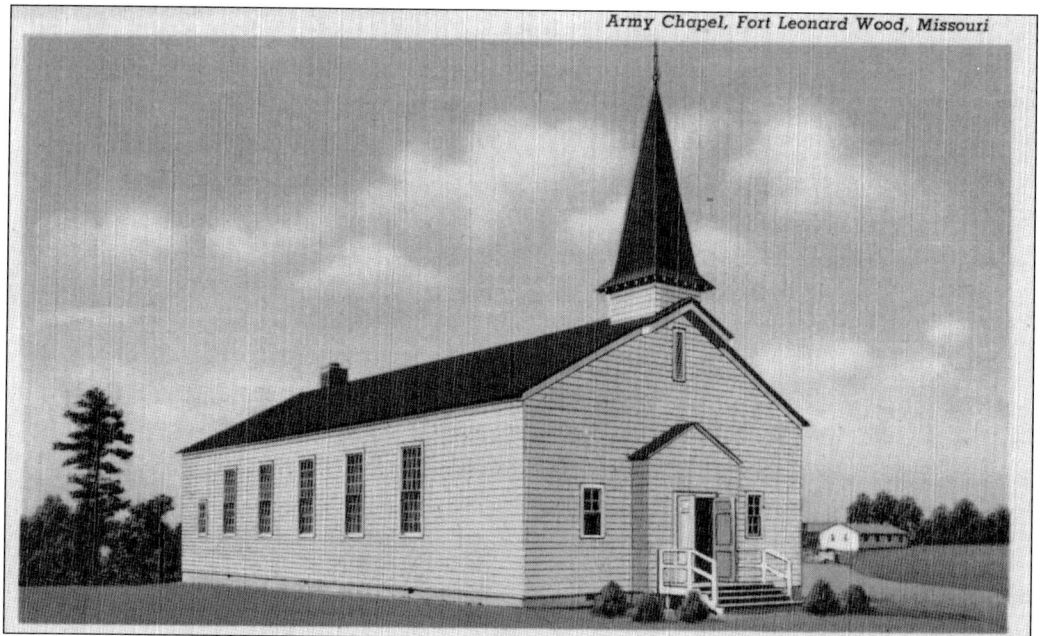

Like many of the buildings on post, the Old Post Chapel at Fort Leonard Wood was essentially identical to many that were constructed at Army posts during World War II and which were initially intended to be temporary in nature. This chapel was moved to its present location in 1999 and is now the World War II Museum Chapel, beautifully situated among a complex of restored and preserved World War II–era buildings.

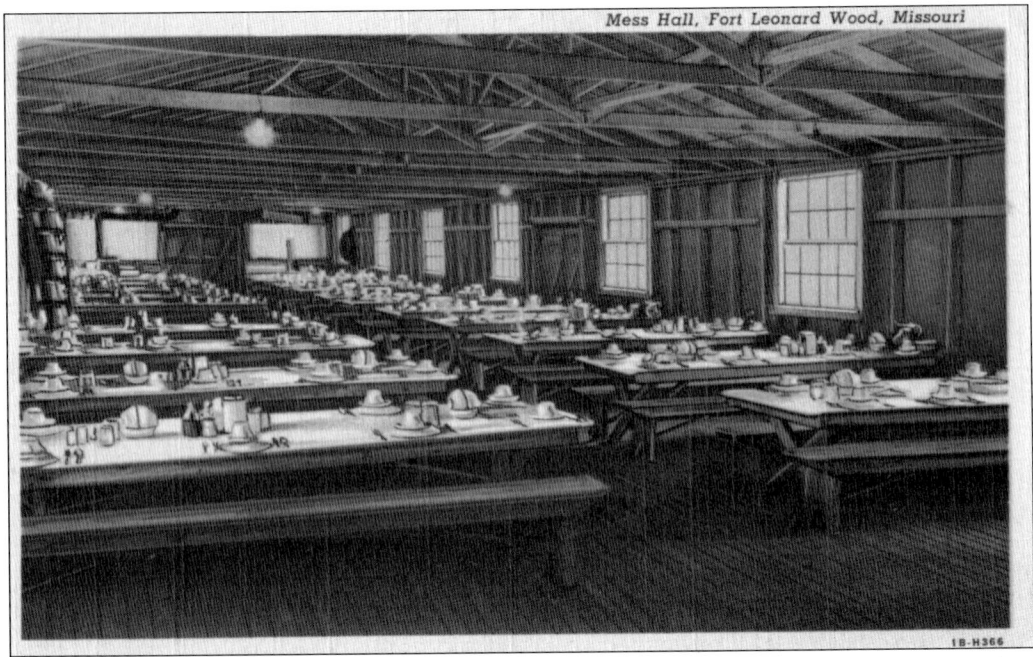

Mess Hall, Fort Leonard Wood, Missouri

With more than 300,000 troops passing through Fort Leonard Wood during the Second World War, mess halls had to be constructed to feed the soldiers. Visitors to the post can still tour one of these early mess halls as part of the John B. Mahaffey Museum Complex, which serves as a replica of a World War II camp.

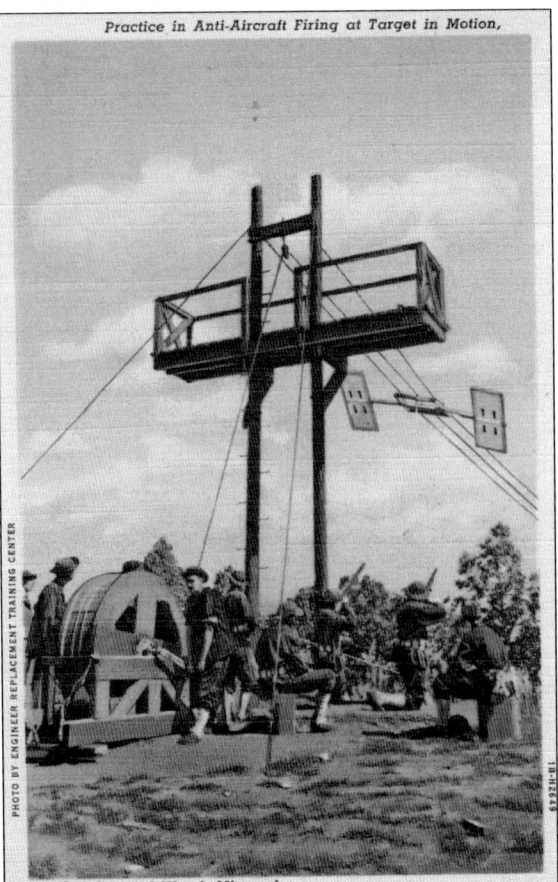

Practice in Anti-Aircraft Firing at Target in Motion, Fort Leonard Wood, Missouri

The Engineer Replacement Training Center at Fort Leonard Wood trained engineer recruits not only in a variety of construction specialties, but also established a curriculum that included exercises involving antiaircraft firing. Ranges on the post were established, such as the one pictured here, which were structured to assist the recruits in developing the marksmanship skills necessary to effectively fire on a moving aerial target.

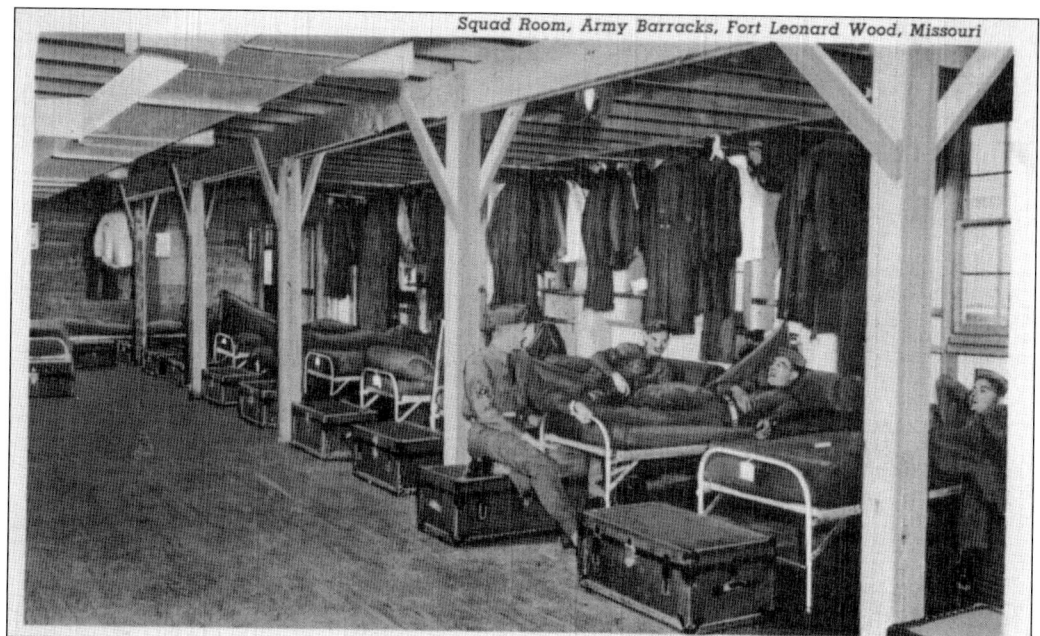

This postcard provides a glimpse into barracks life during the mid-1940s and early 1950s. The World War II barracks were often built using a standard set of blueprints consistent among several Army bases, providing more than 4,700 square feet of space with rooms on two floors. Additionally, the buildings were designed to provide living quarters for 63 enlisted men and noncommissioned officers.

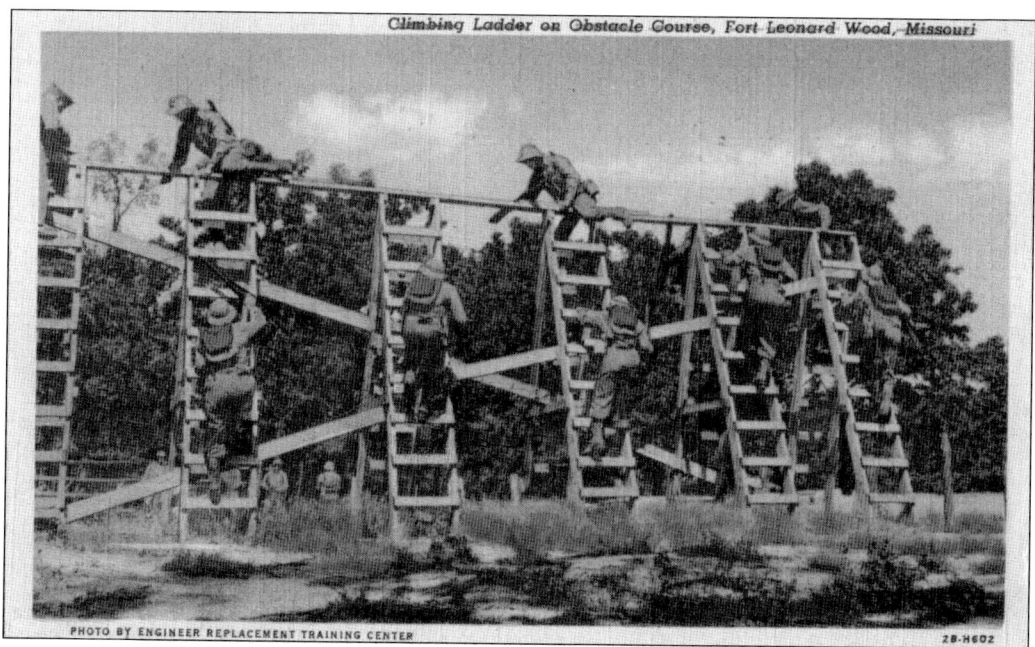

Obstacle courses quickly became an important component of the frenetic training cycle during World War II. Though employed at Fort Leonard Wood and other military bases, the initial concept for the obstacle course is reputed to have been first developed at the Engineer Training Replacement Center at Fort Belvoir, Virginia, sometime during the Second World War.

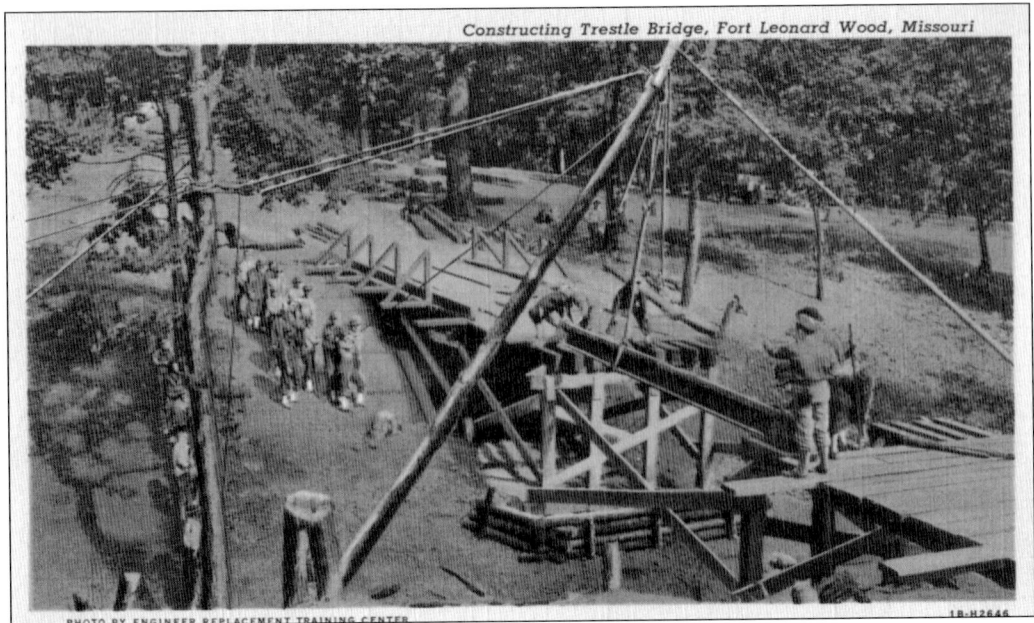

Trained in several aspects of construction, recruits undergoing instruction with the Engineer Replacement Training Center during World War II learned such skills as the assembly of a trestle bridge. The techniques for constructing bridges would serve the US Army well in Europe during the war, since many such structures were often destroyed by German forces to prevent access to strategic locations.

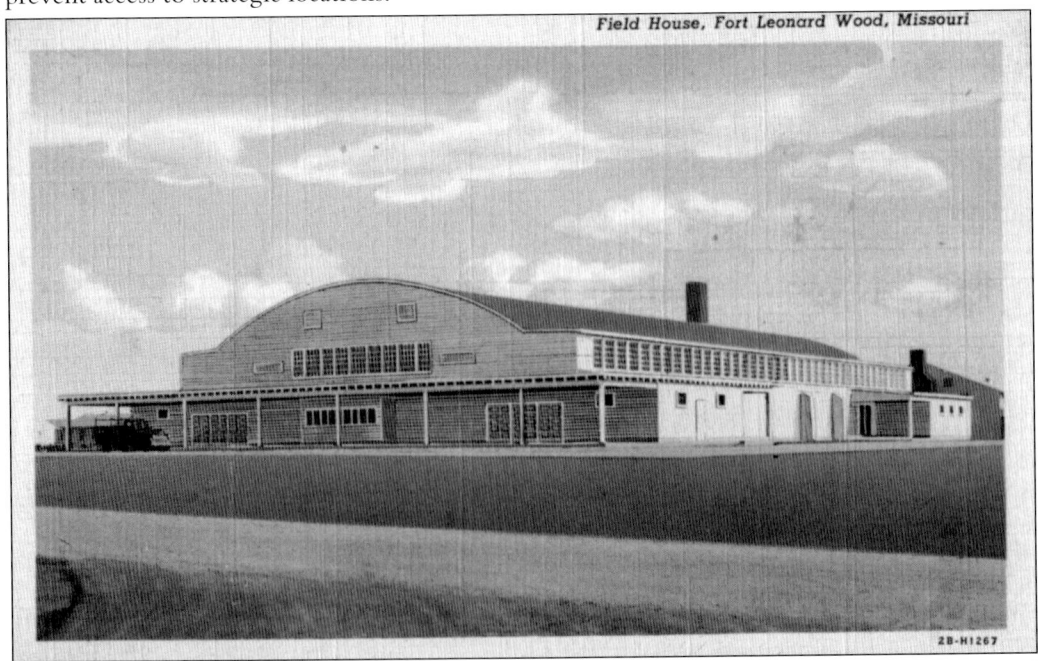

Built in 1942, this field house provided recreational facilities for soldiers serving at Fort Leonard Wood. In 1954, the field house was bestowed the name Nutter Field House in honor of Wisconsin native Daniel L. Nutter, a 24-year-old infantry officer who was killed on November 11, 1944, while serving with the 25th Armored Engineer Battalion, 6th Armored Division in France.

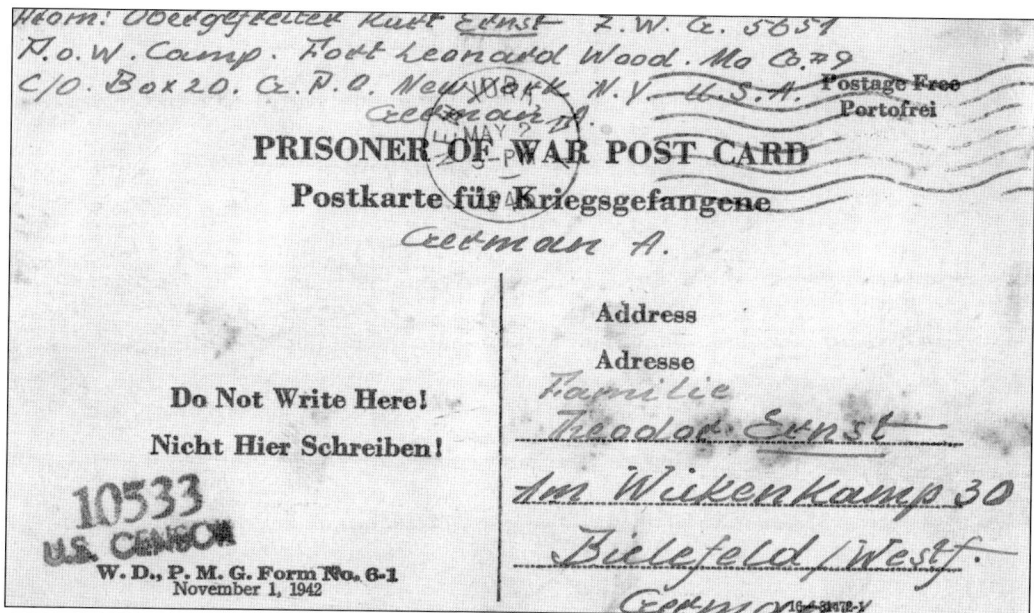

More than 15,000 German and Italian POWs were held in Missouri camps during World War II. Pictured here is a "Prisoner of War Post Card" sent from Kurt Ernst—a German POW held at Fort Leonard Wood—to his family in the town of Bielefeld in the state of Westphalia, Germany. A block of Ernst's communication on the back of the card is censored as it likely violated established rules of communication.

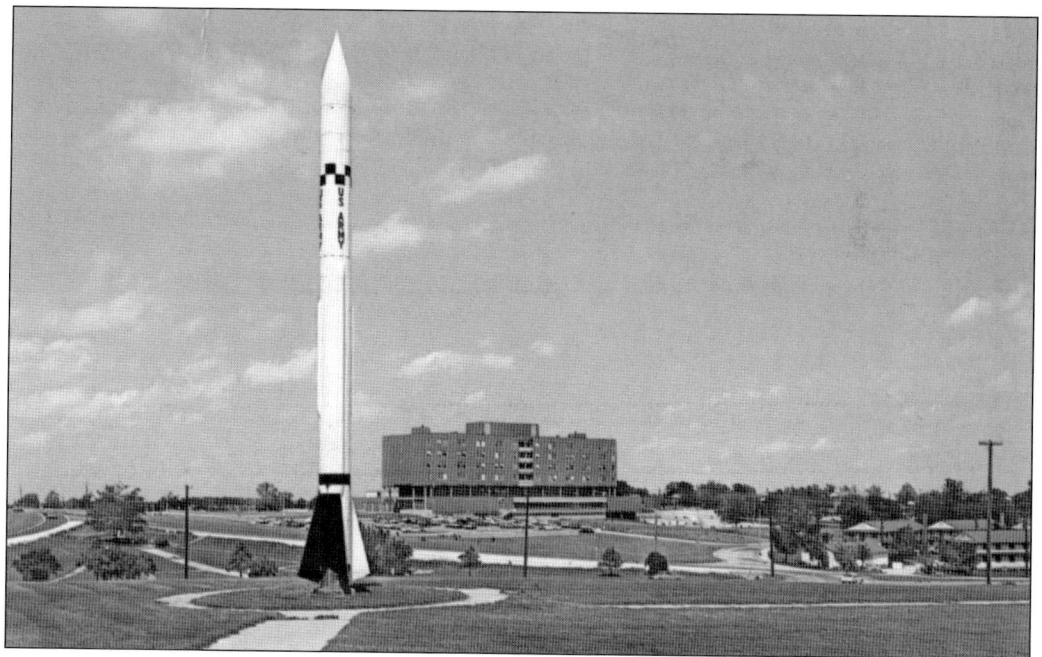

Many military display pieces have come and gone throughout the years at Fort Leonard Wood, such as this deactivated Corporal missile—America's first operational guided missile. Though the missile is no longer on display, the General Leonard Wood Army Community Hospital visible in the background continues to serve the post just as it has from its current location since 1965.

This postcard from an Italian prisoner of war held at Camp Weingarten was transferred to the District Postal Censor in New York, New York, in 1944 before being sent to the intended recipient. Located in Weingarten on Highway 32 between St. Genevieve and Farmington, the camp had the capacity to hold 5,800 POWs and remained in operation until October 1945.

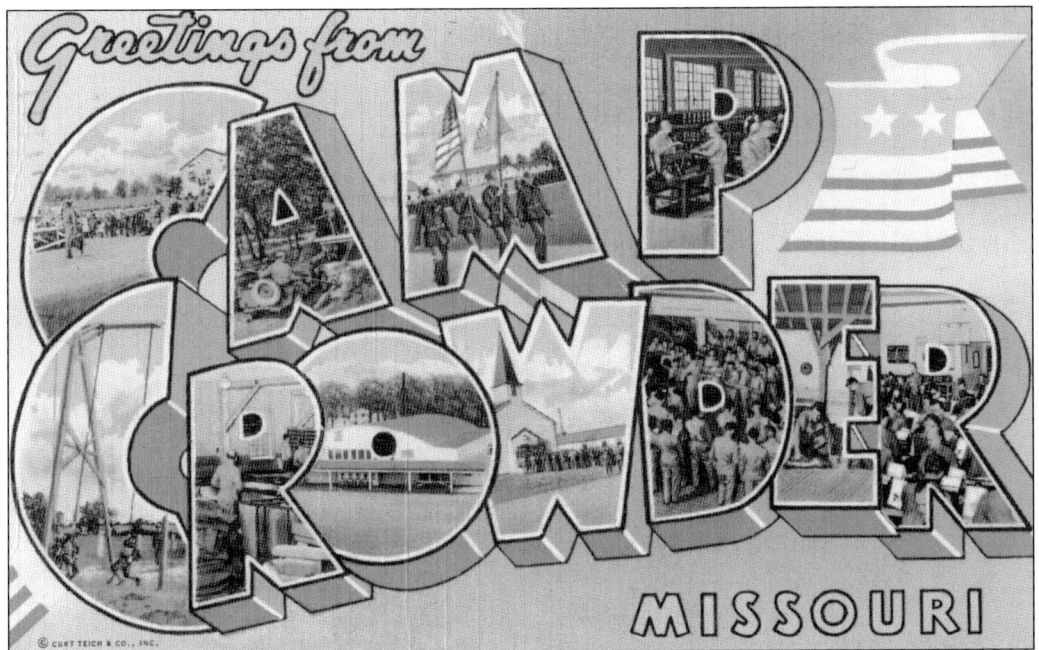

It was announced in May 1941 that a site near Neosho, Missouri, which would soon be named Camp Crowder, had been selected to become an additional training camp for the US Army. A civilian survey crew was dispatched to the area and quickly began the process of laying out the plans for the camp, which was followed by the acquisition of properties in the area in order to begin construction on the 66,650-acre site.

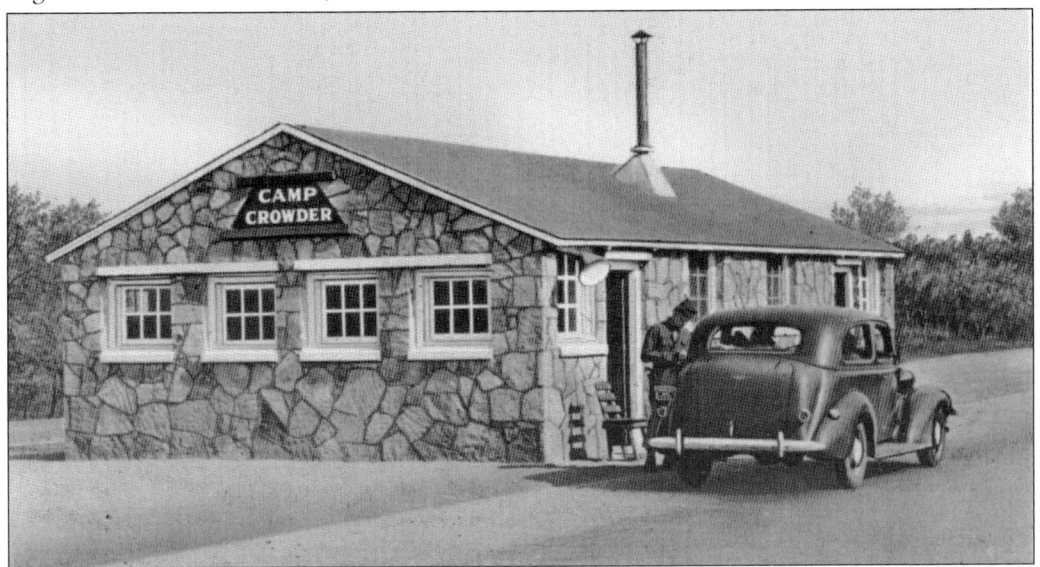

An initial award of $12.5 million was announced in August 1941 for two companies, both of which had already built Camp Robinson in Arkansas, to begin work on the new Army camp a few miles southeast of Neosho. As construction began, Lyon Gate, as pictured in this postcard, was established as the main gate for the post and named in honor of Gen. Nathaniel Lyon—a Union general who was killed in the Battle of Bloody Hill near Springfield, Missouri, on August 10, 1861.

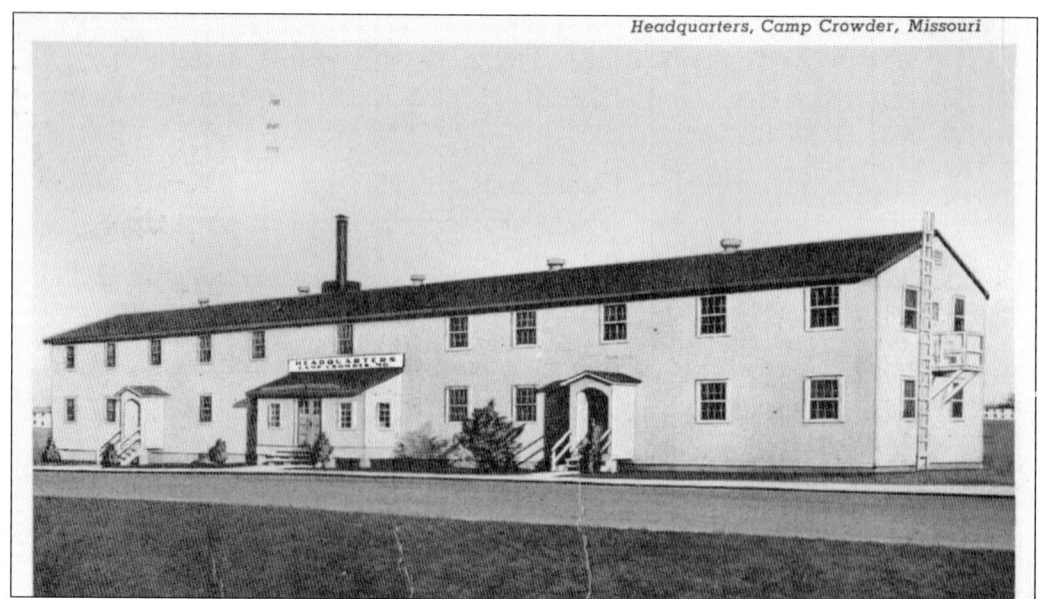

As construction progressed into the latter part of 1941, buildings such as the post headquarters began to dot the landscape on the new, sprawling Army post. Though it went several months without a name, it was announced by the War Department in September 1941 that the post would be called Camp Crowder in honor of the late Maj. Gen. Enoch Crowder—a Missouri native who is most notable for implementing the Selective Service Act during World War I.

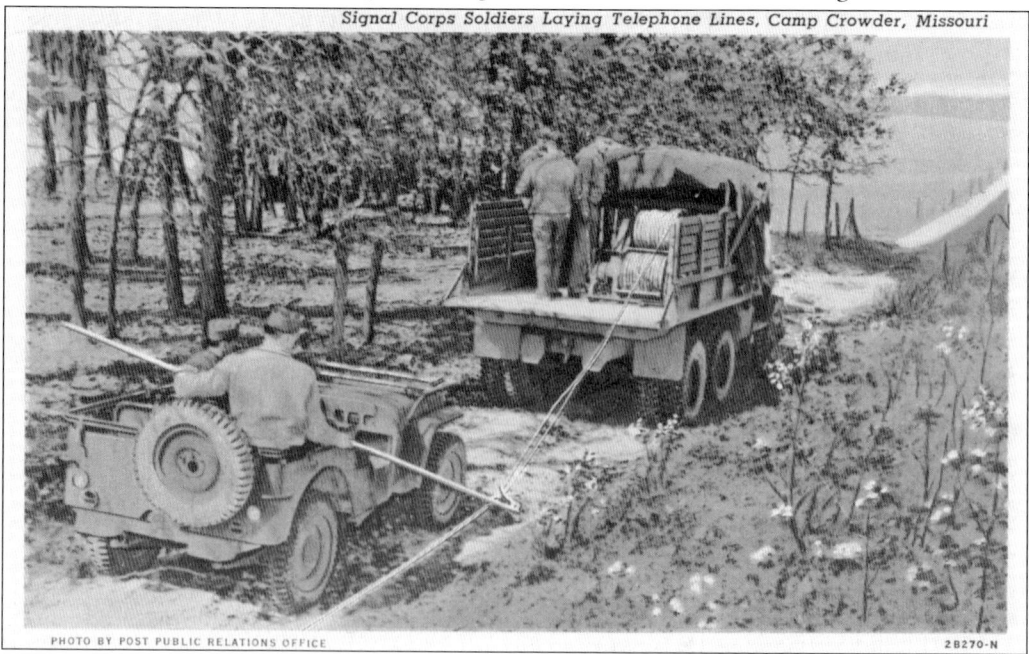

Camp Crowder dedicated the Midwestern Signal Corps School on August 11, 1942, a month after opening their first classes. The Signal Corps is a technical branch of the US Army responsible for establishing, controlling, and maintaining communications. Pictured are Signal Corps trainees laying telephone lines during their communications training at Camp Crowder sometime during World War II.

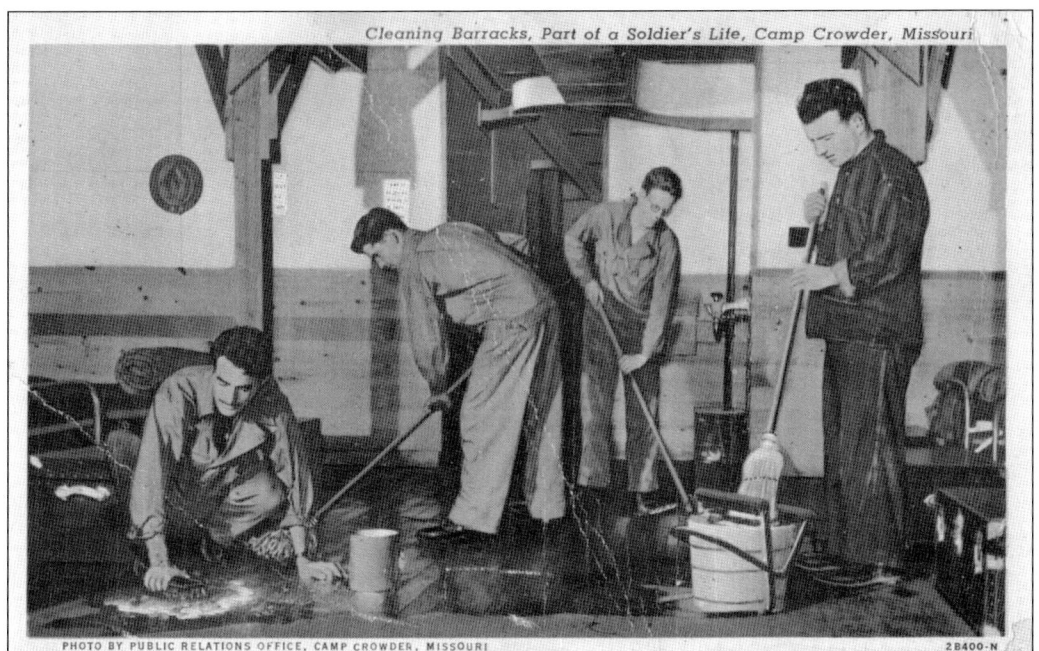

As this postcard aptly demonstrates, not every aspect of a soldier's life while living and training in an Army camp is filled with excitement and glory. Maintaining the barracks in which they resided was a daily routine of a soldier's existence at Camp Crowder and other Army posts and required one to learn such basic—yet necessary—skills as sweeping, scrubbing, and mopping floors.

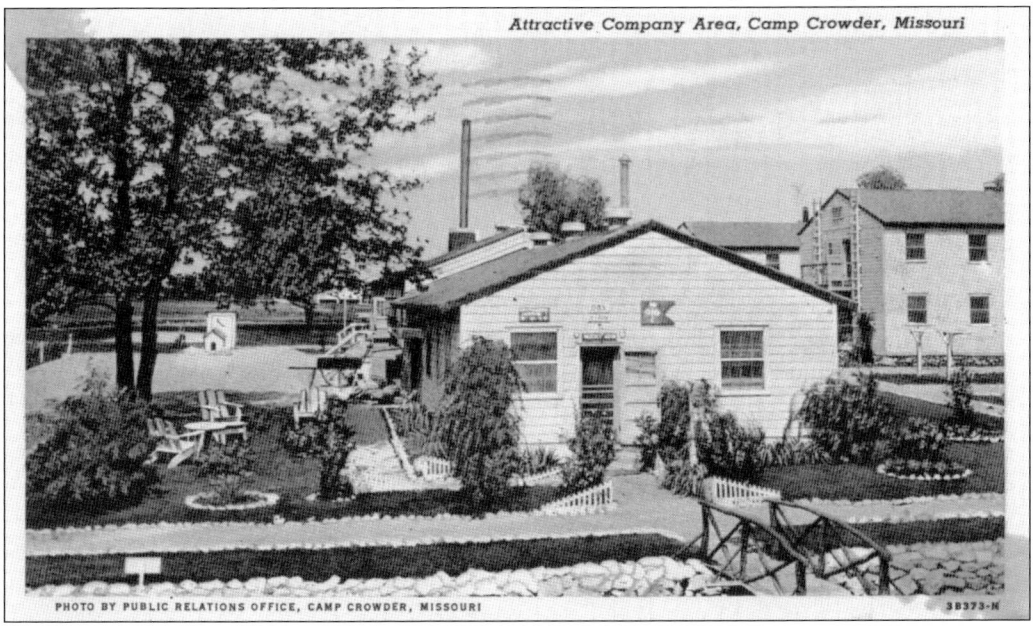

Not only did the US Army and other branches of the military stress upon the troops the importance of maintaining the cleanliness and order of their indoor environments, but the exterior areas of a military post received much care and attention as well. Visible in this postcard of a company area on Camp Crowder during World War II are paths that are bordered with painted white rocks, as well as well-manicured lawns surrounding the barracks and administrative offices.

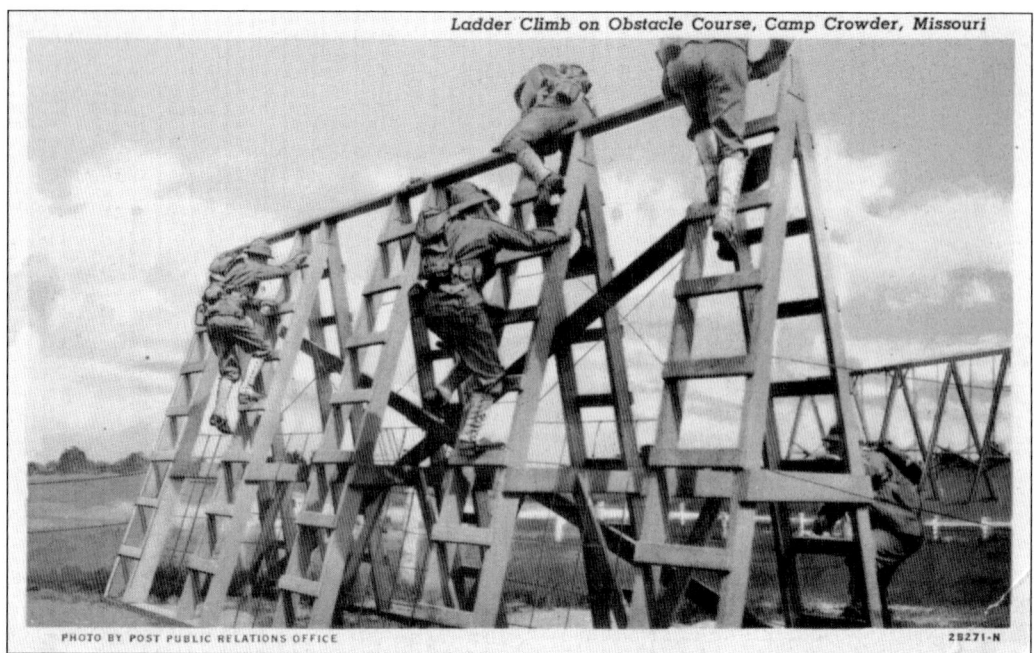

While engineer trainees at Fort Leonard Wood prepared to perform their assigned tasks in difficult overseas environments, so too did the Signal Corps trainees at Camp Crowder by undergoing strenuous exercises on the obstacle course. In this postcard, Signal Corps trainees toughen up their bodies while at Camp Crowder by negotiating an obstacle course somewhere on the camp, all while burdened with a full pack of gear.

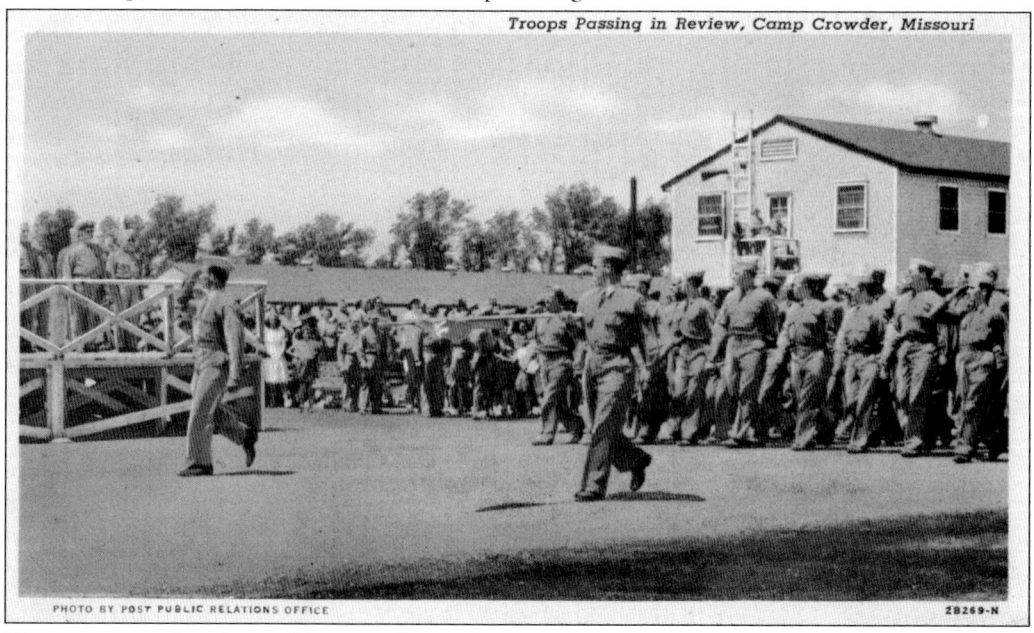

The pass in review is a military tradition during which a company (or companies) of troops pass by a reviewing party for inspection purposes. This postcard depicts one such review on the parade grounds at Camp Crowder during World War II. Officers can be seen on the reviewing stand at left looking over the troops in formation.

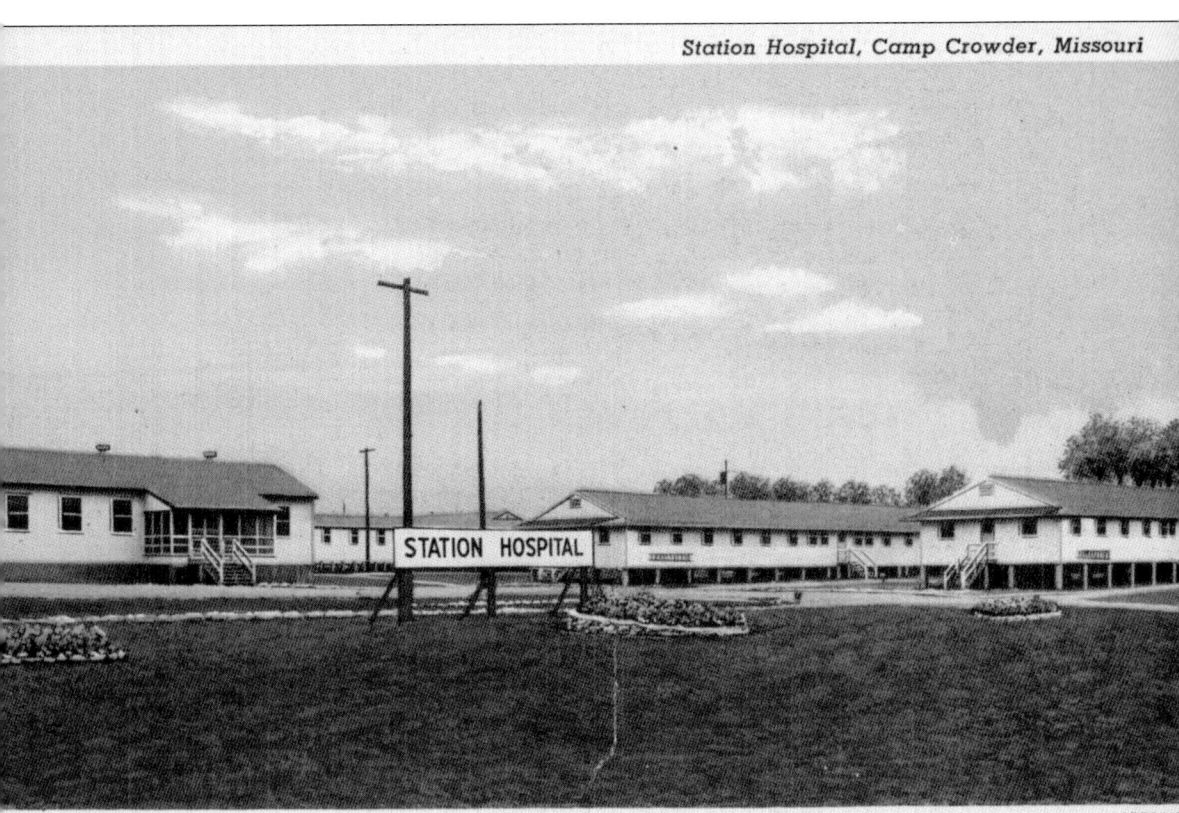

Station Hospital, Camp Crowder, Missouri

With an average population of 45,000 during the period of World War II—which included soldiers, civilians, and members of the Women's Army Corps—medical care was an important aspect of maintaining physical readiness at Camp Crowder. In addition to the station hospital complex pictured in this postcard, there were 15 infirmaries and three dental clinics once situated throughout the camp.

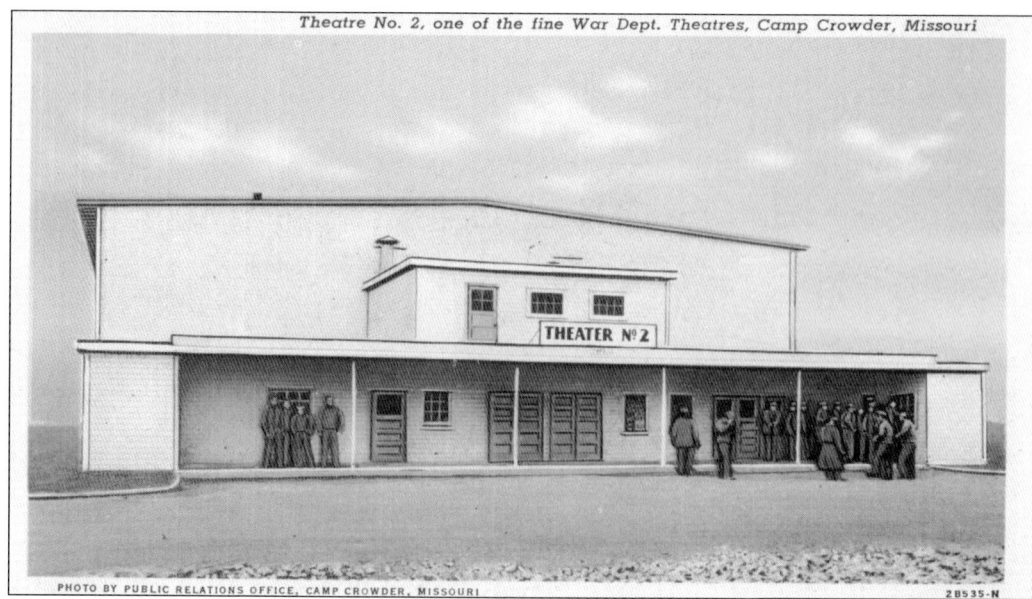

With very limited venues in nearby Neosho to provide adequate entertainment for the thousands of soldiers flooding into the area during World War II, the US Army built theaters for soldiers to enjoy movies while they were off duty. During the war, there were six movie theaters located at Camp Crowder that were similar in design and layout to Theater No. 2, which is pictured on this postcard.

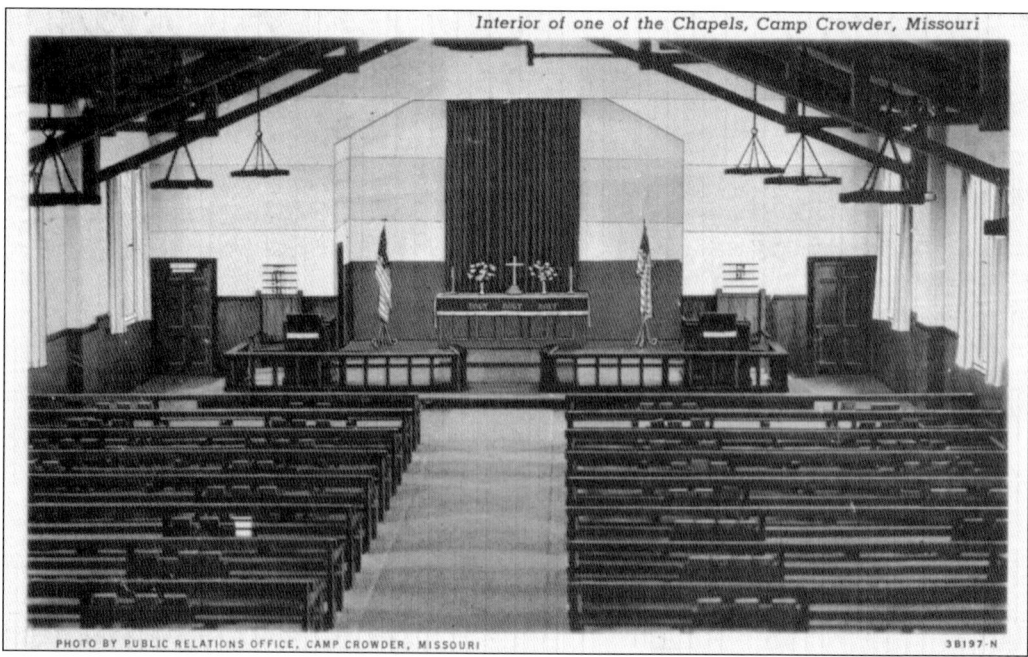

The US Army constructed 16 chapels at Camp Crowder in the early 1940s to tend to the spiritual needs of the soldiers in training. As the war progressed, the camp became a temporary home to more than 2,000 German prisoners of war who, in addition to performing such tasks as painting, landscaping, and working in the kitchens, were frequently extended the opportunity to attend religious services at one of the post chapels on Sunday.

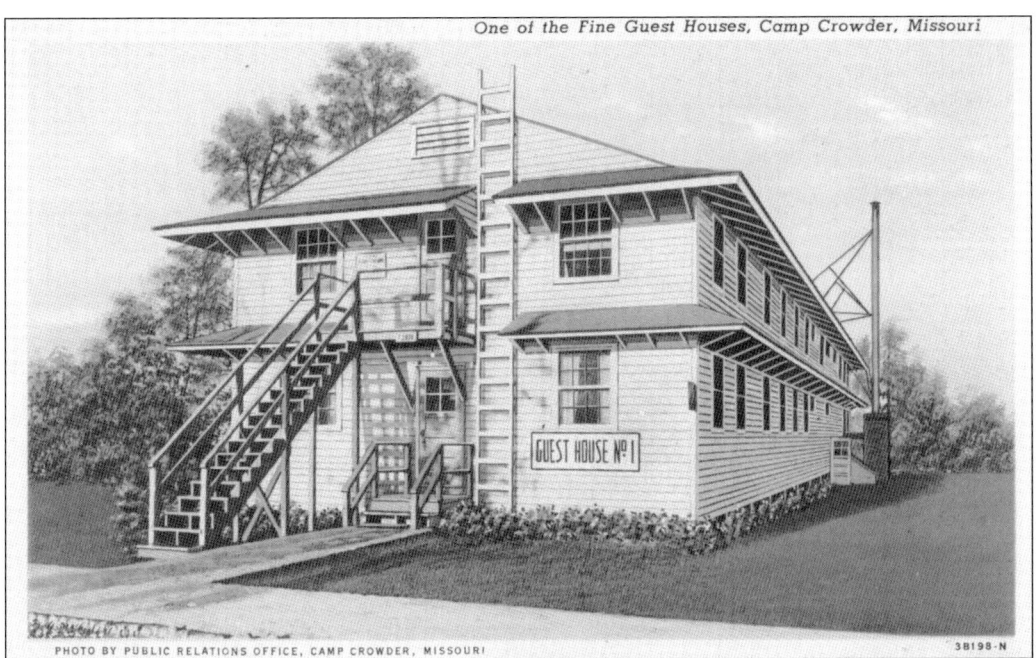

One of the Fine Guest Houses, Camp Crowder, Missouri

During the war, an estimated 1,600 buildings, such as the guesthouse pictured in this postcard, were constructed on Camp Crowder; however, only a handful of these original structures survive today, some of which are being used by Crowder College. In the years following World War II, some of the original property was deemed surplus and sold to private interests, but the Missouri National Guard continues to utilize a large section of Camp Crowder as a training site.

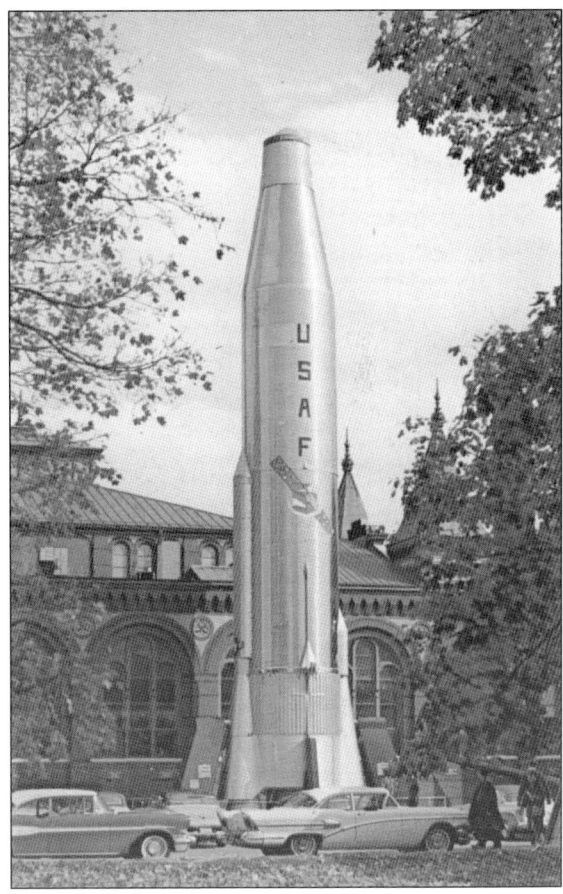

During the height of the Cold War in the 1950s, the Army transferred a section of Camp Crowder to the Air Force to build a manufacturing plant for rocket engines. It was known as Plant 65. For many years, the plant built engines for such rockets as the Thor, Saturn, and Atlas, the latter of which is pictured on this postcard printed by the Smithsonian Institution.

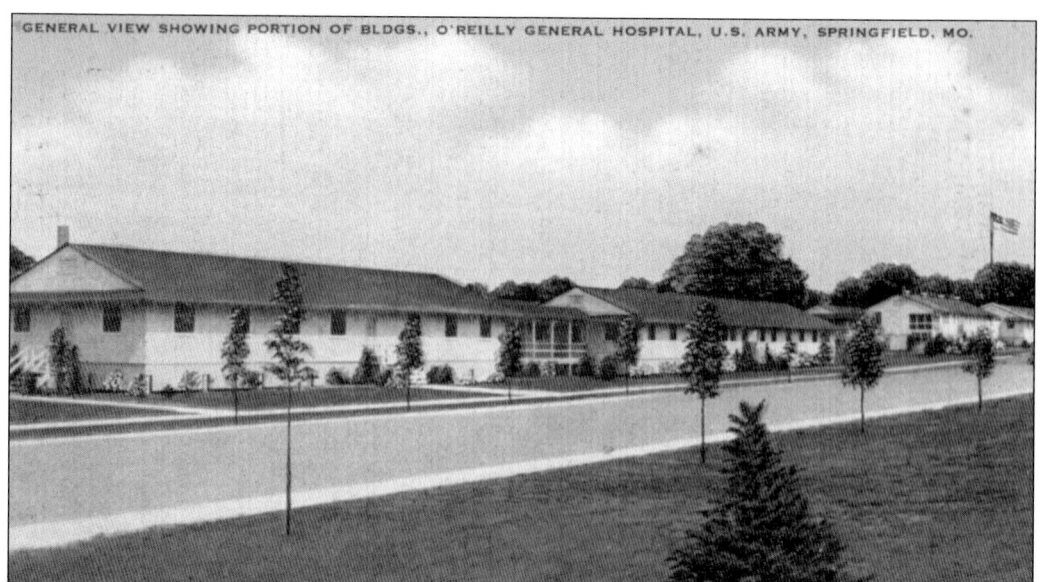

A site in Springfield, which is now home to Evangel University, was selected in 1941 to become O'Reilly General Army Hospital. Named in honor of Gen. Robert Maitland O'Reilly—whose service spanned from that of a hospital cadet during the Civil War to a field surgeon in the Indian campaigns and the Spanish-American War and later as surgeon general of the Army—the hospital complex sat on a site nearly 155 acres in size with an estimated 250 buildings.

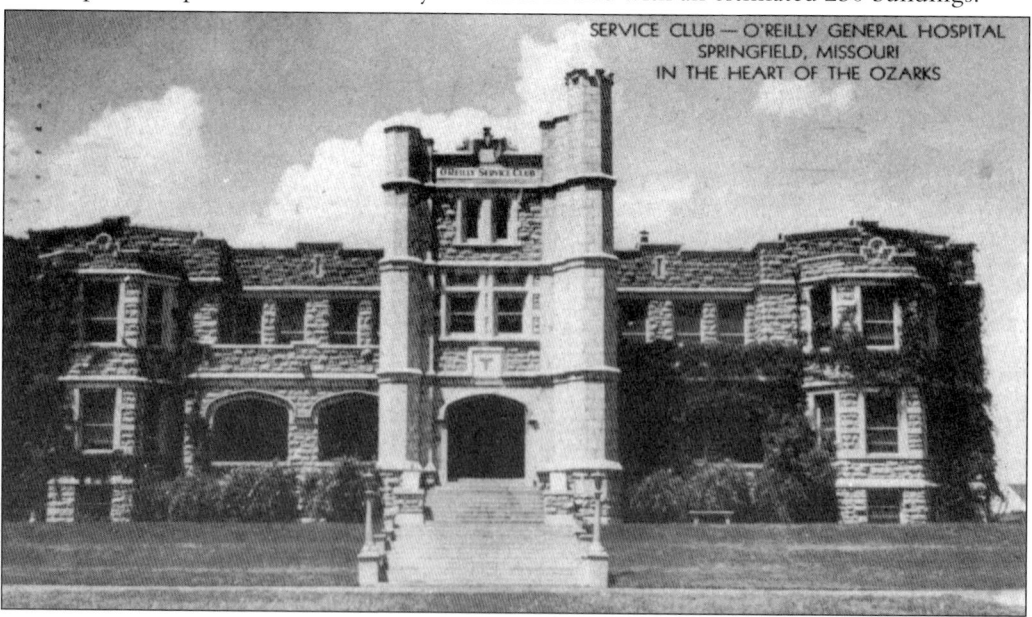

The Enlisted Men's Service Club, on the grounds of O'Reilly General Army Hospital, began its life as a home for widows and orphans of deceased members of a society known as Knights of Pythias of Missouri. The structure was built from Carthage stone and was first dedicated on June 14, 1914; however, it was purchased by the US Army in 1942 and became part of the hospital property. This building, now referred to as Pythian Castle, is listed in the National Register of Historic Places and is privately owned but offers tours to the public and can be rented for special events.

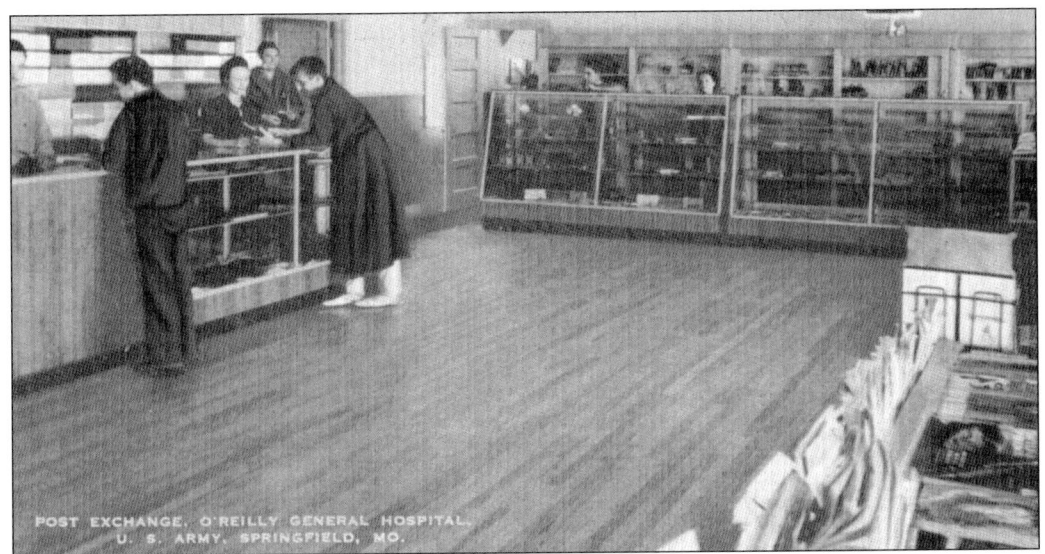

The post exchange at O'Reilly General Army Hospital was very similar to other Army facilities in that it offered various amenities and gifts for purchase by the soldiers who were recuperating from their injuries. Following closure of O'Reilly in 1946, it served briefly as a Veterans Administration hospital and then became Evangel University in the mid-1950s. The post exchange has since been removed along with most of the buildings that once covered the hospital landscape.

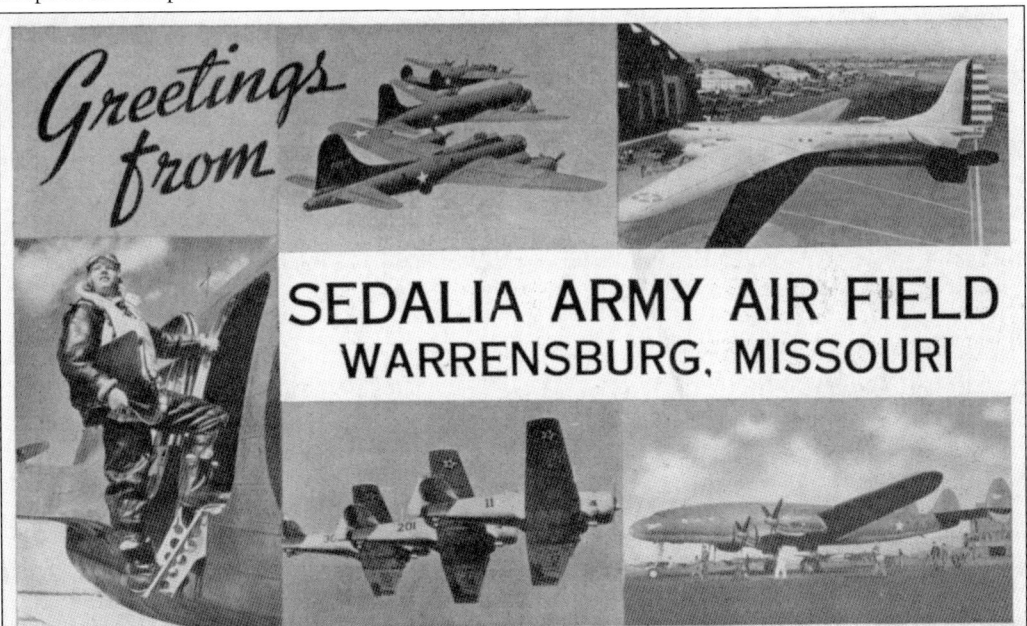

The Sedalia Glider Base was activated in August 1942 but was renamed the Sedalia Army Air Field three months later, becoming a training site for glider tactics and paratroopers. The base closed after World War II but reopened as Sedalia Air Force Base in mid-1951 as part of the Strategic Air Command. In 1955, it was renamed Whiteman Air Force Base in honor of Lt. George A. Whiteman, a Sedalia native who became Missouri's first casualty of World War II when he was killed during the Japanese attack on Pearl Harbor.

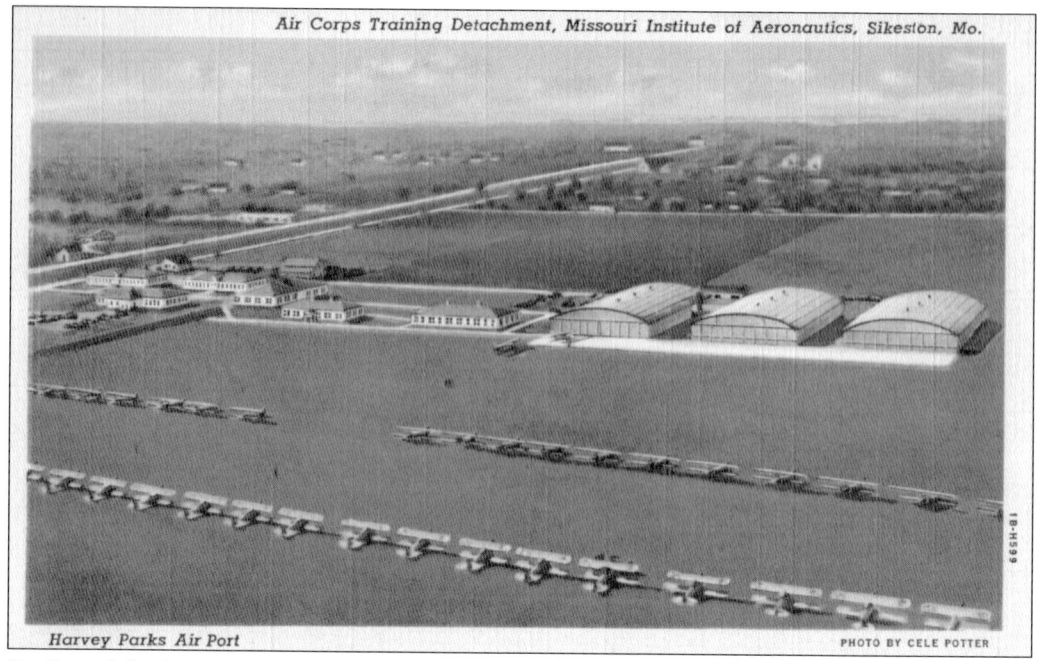

Harvey Parks Air Port

Dedicated during a ceremony on May 25, 1941, the Harvey Parks Airport in Sikeston became home to the Missouri Institute of Aeronautics and was also used to train aviators and mechanics for service in the Army Air Corps during World War II. Harvey Parks was killed in 1936 when his monoplane crashed shortly after takeoff from airfield at Parks College, which at the time was the largest civilian training school for pilots in the world. The Harvey Parks Airport is now the Sikeston Municipal Airport.

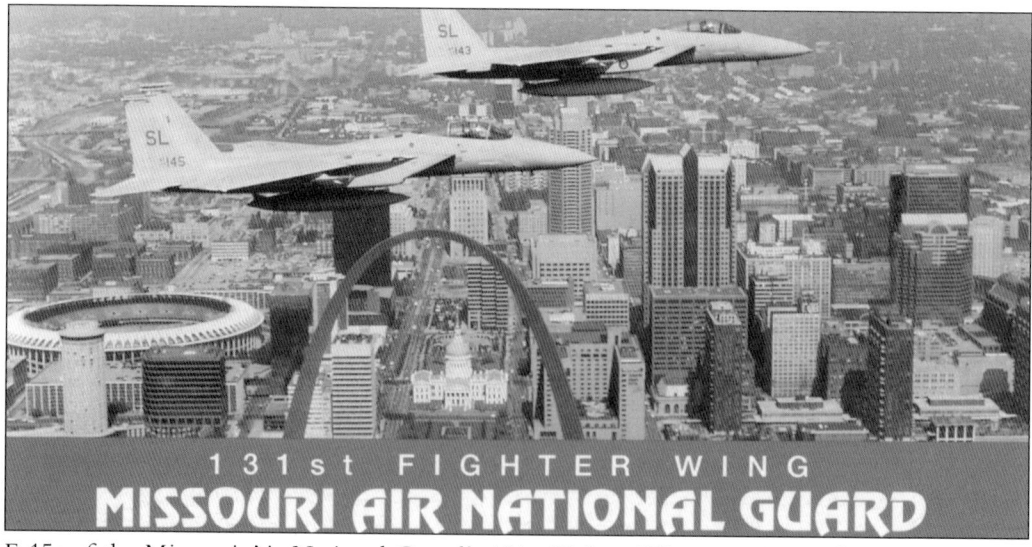

F-15s of the Missouri Air National Guard's 131st Fighter Wing are pictured passing over the Gateway Arch in downtown St. Louis. Once located at Lambert Airport in St. Louis, the 131st Fighter Wing transferred their F-15s to other Air Force sites because of a recommendation of the Base Realignment and Closure Commission (BRAC) in 2005. Because of the same BRAC recommendation, the 131st Fighter Wing was transferred from Lambert to Whiteman Air Force Base, where they now support the B-2 Stealth Bomber mission as the 131st Bomb Wing.

Two

MILITARY ACADEMIES AND EDUCATIONAL INSTITUTIONS

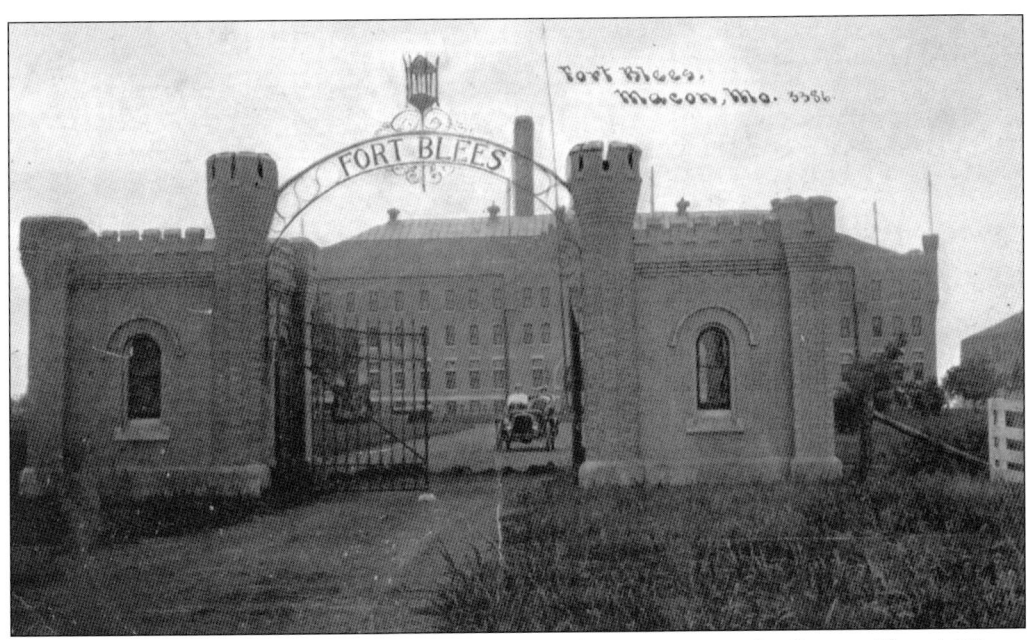

This real-photo postcard, postmarked 1912, shows the entrance to the former Blees Military Academy in Macon. Founded in 1899 by Col. Frederick Wilhelm Victor Blees—a Prussian immigrant who later inherited an estate from his father that was worth millions—historians with the Macon County (Missouri) Historical Society note that the academy was often referred to as Fort Blees on area maps.

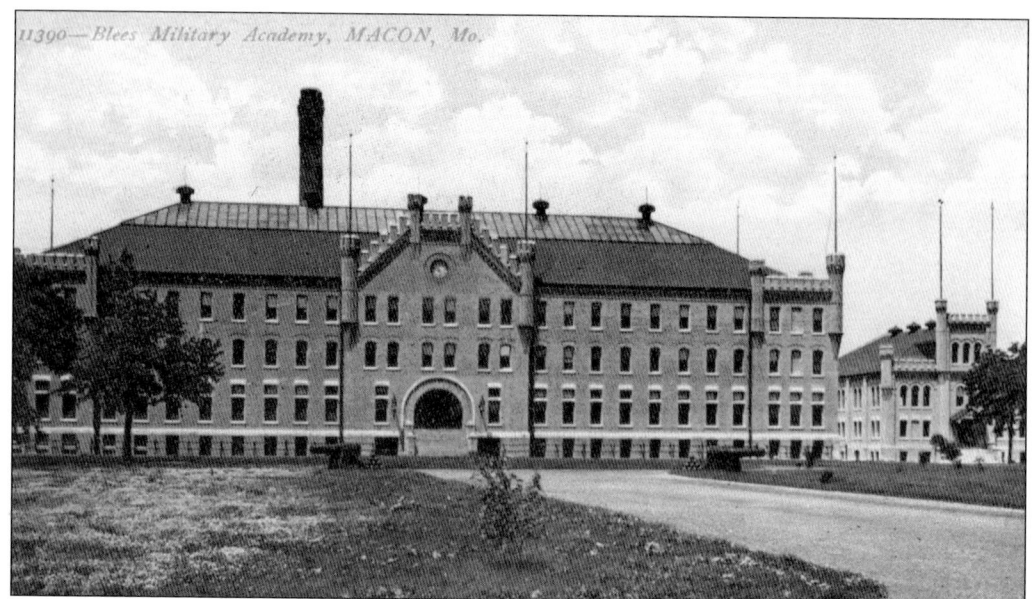

The Blees Military Academy was highlighted by the main academic hall pictured on this postcard. The hall was constructed in a variant of the Romanesque Revival style, measured 224 feet in length by 88 feet in width and had three floors and a basement. Following the closure of the academy in 1909, the hall became the Still-Hildreth Osteopathic Sanatorium for several decades, and since the 1980s it has been a senior residential living facility.

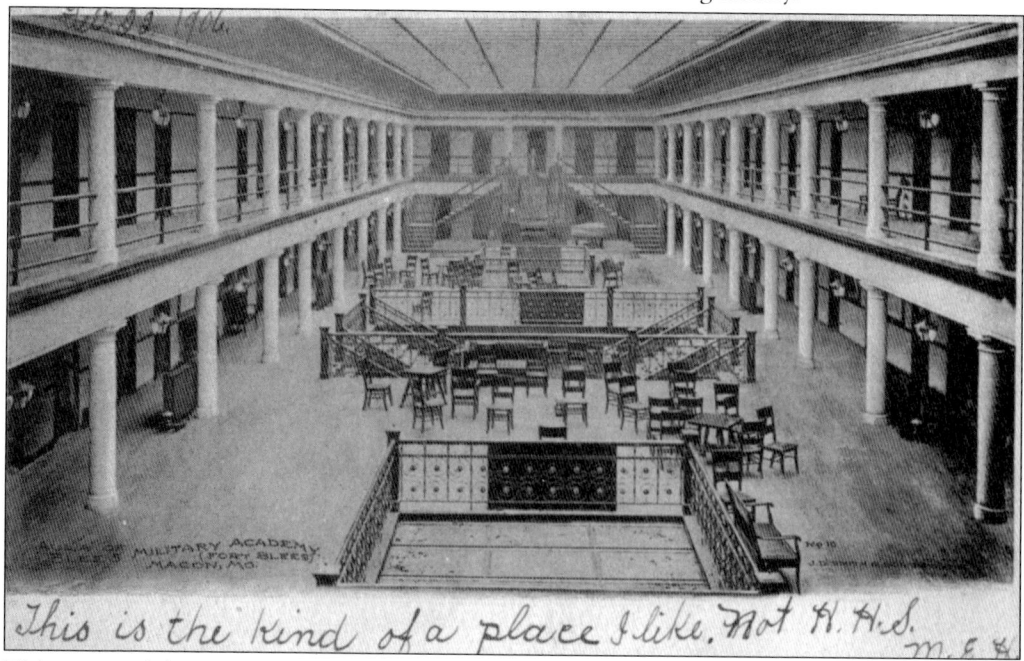

This postcard shows the second-floor area of the main residential hall as it appeared during its operation as a military academy. In the center of the room is the wrought iron staircase leading up from the first floor. The skylights in the ceiling provided daylight for the academy students, and galleried apartments can be seen on both the second and third floors surrounding the large open area.

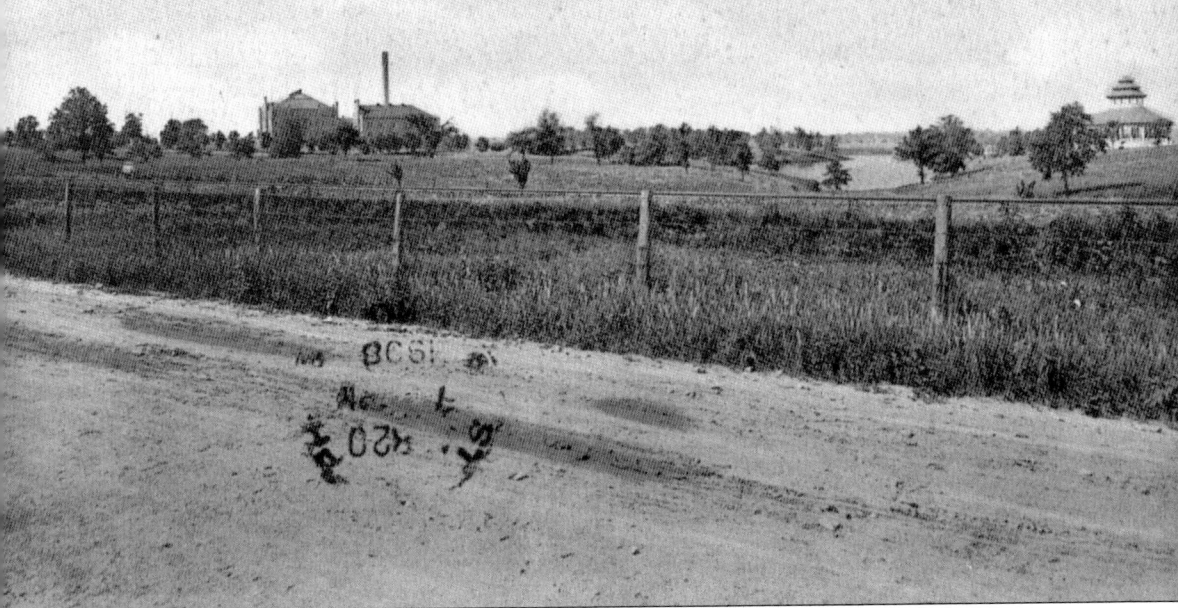

Blees Military Academy Grounds, Macon, Mo.

Although most of the area around the Blees Military Academy is now largely populated with several buildings, when it was first constructed, the academy was quietly surrounded with 400 acres that included orchards, gardens, a dairy, and a working farm. The dirt road seen in the foreground is now situated near what has become the four lane Highway 63.

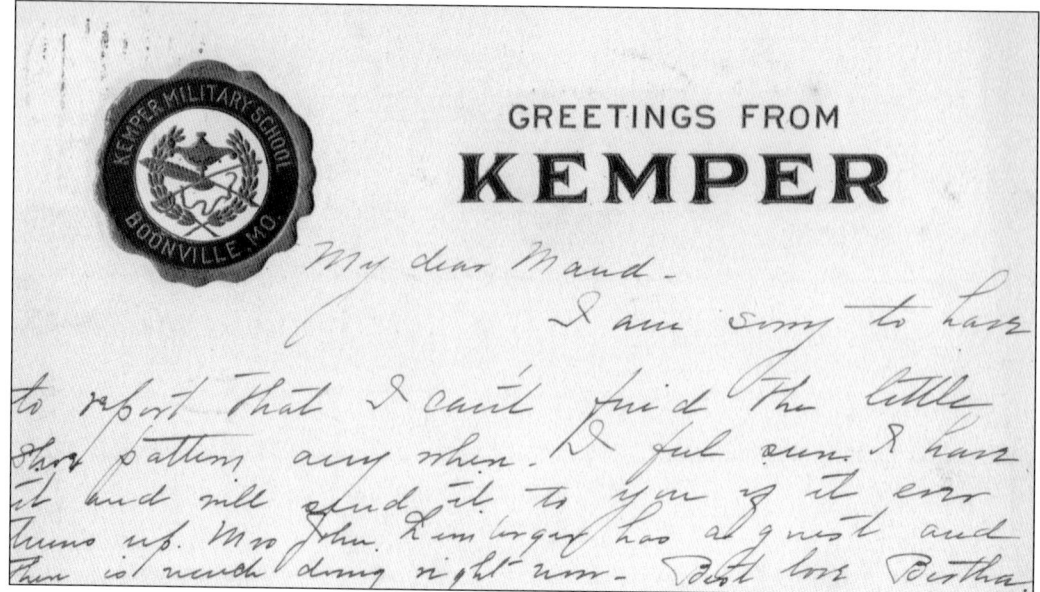

Bates Jackson & Company published this simple postcard, with a postmark of 1911, for the former Kemper Military School in Boonville. Founded in 1844 by Frederick T. Kemper, the school had a grand reputation throughout the United States and was once the oldest military school located west of the Mississippi River. The school remained in operation until 2002, at which time it filed for bankruptcy and closed its doors because of financial difficulties resulting from a decline in student enrollment.

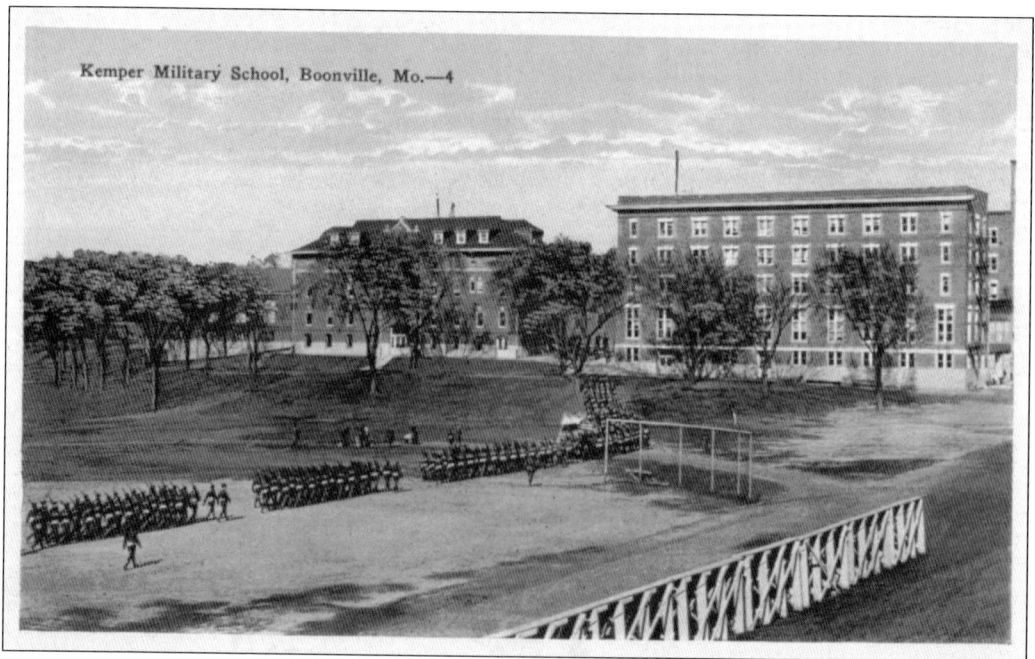

This postcard by the E.C. Kropp Company shows a view of the parade grounds on the 46-acre site of Kemper Military School sometime between the 1920s and 1930s. One of the most notable individuals to attend Kemper was cowboy philosopher Will Rogers, who later helped share the school's claim of being the "West Point of the West."

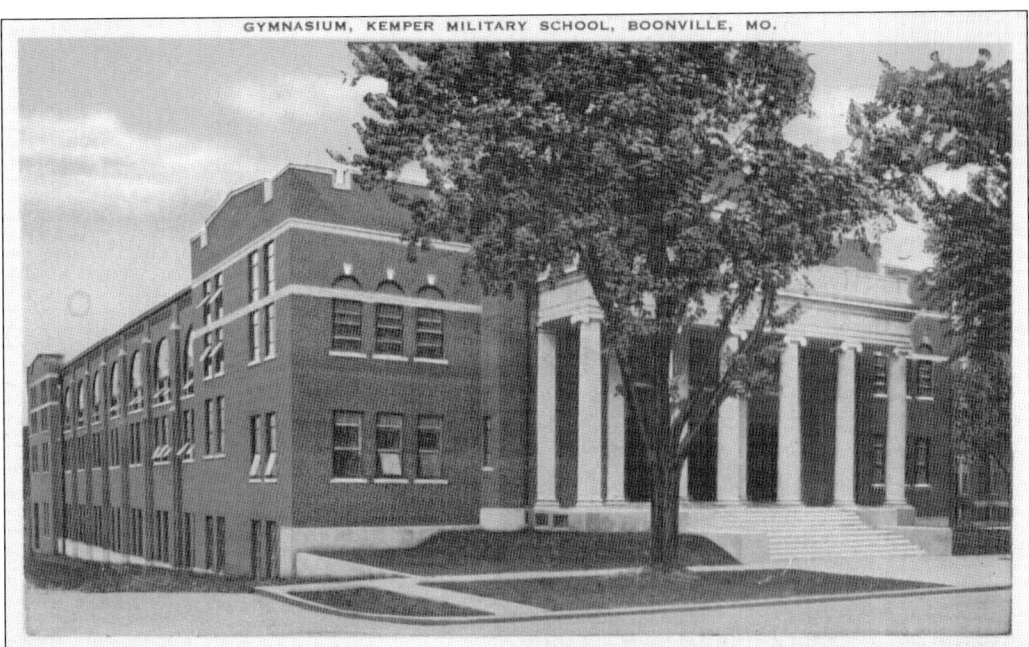

Johnston Gymnasium on the campus of Kemper Military School was constructed in the early 1920s and named for Col. Thomas A. Johnston, a former superintendent of the school. The gymnasium measured 100 feet wide by 200 feet long and was once the largest gymnasium in the state of Missouri. In addition to an open area that was used for various sports and activities, the basement included an indoor running track, shooting galleries, locker rooms, showers, and handball courts.

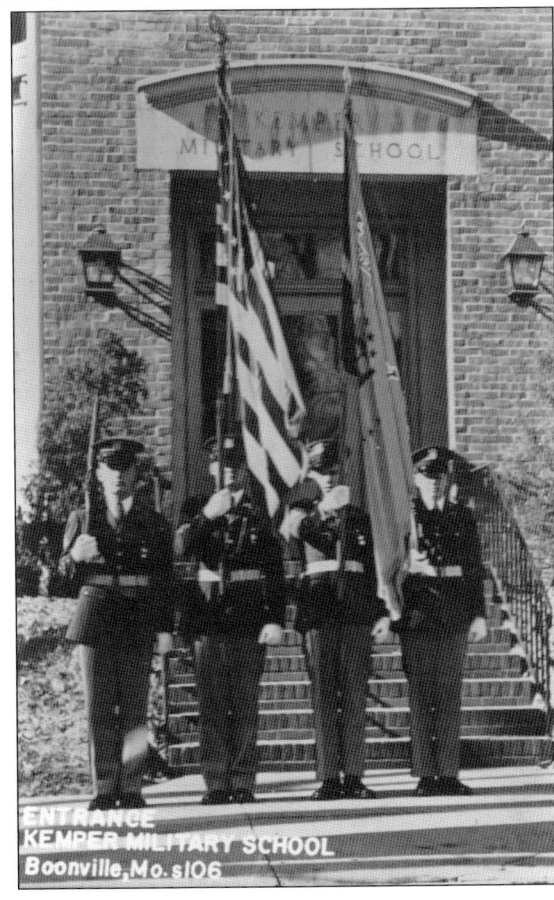

This real-photo postcard shows a color guard standing at attention in front of the administration building at Kemper Military School. With a legacy dating as far back as 1845, the building was deemed unsafe and vacated in 2001. A tower atop the administration building collapsed in 2010, and, sadly, for many historians and former students, the structure was finally demolished in 2016.

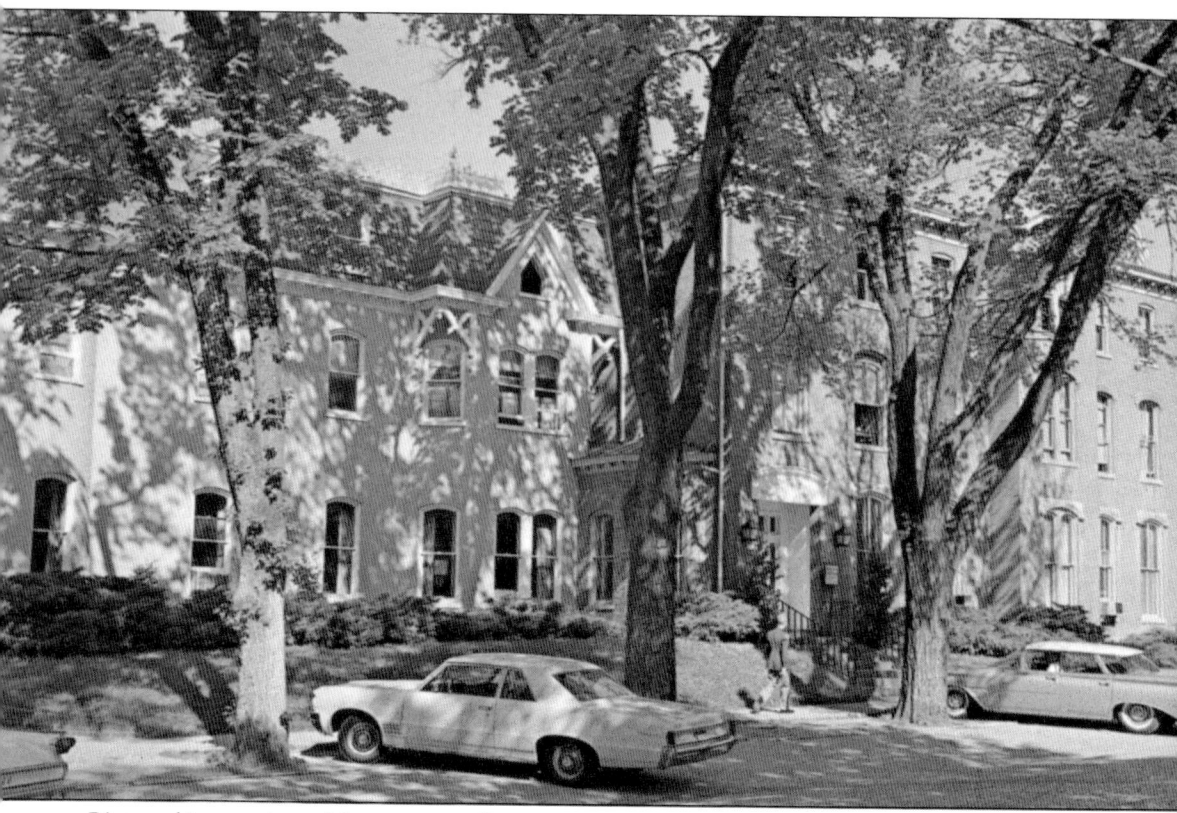

Pictured is a section of the campus of Kemper in the early 1960s, when it was known as Kemper Military School and College. Following the closing of the school in 2002, the property was purchased by the City of Boonville, a section of which has become the Frederick T. Kemper Park to honor the legacy of the school's founder. Though some demolition has occurred, other buildings have found new a new purpose, such as a satellite campus for a local college.

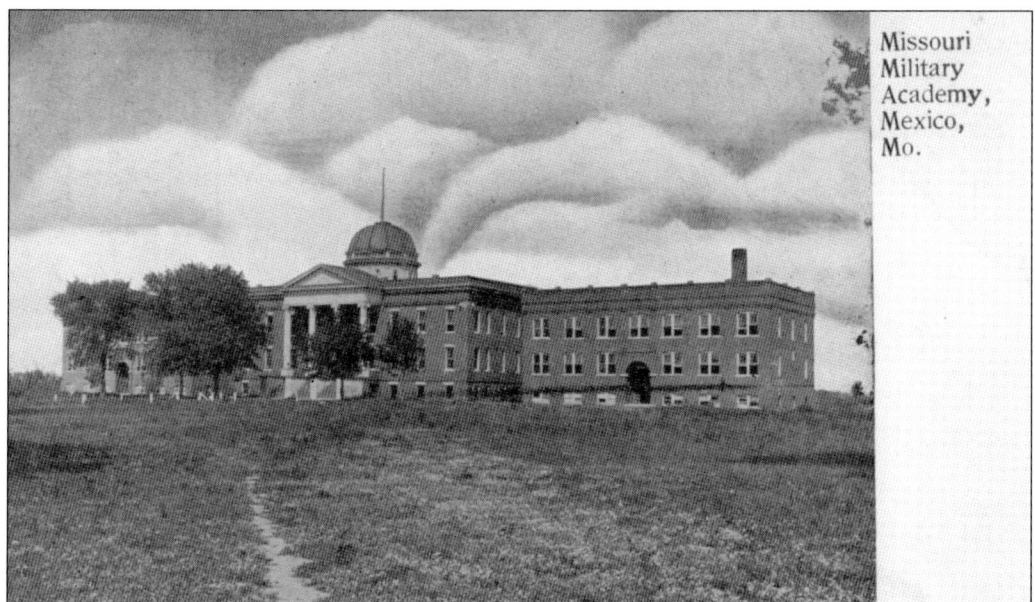

The Missouri Military Academy was established in Mexico in 1889 on a 20-acre site purchased for $2,700. The funds that initially led to the creation of the academy came from pledges from local community members, which included a substantial $1,000 donation from Charles H. Hardin—the founder of Hardin College (1858–1931) who also served as governor of Missouri from 1875 to 1877.

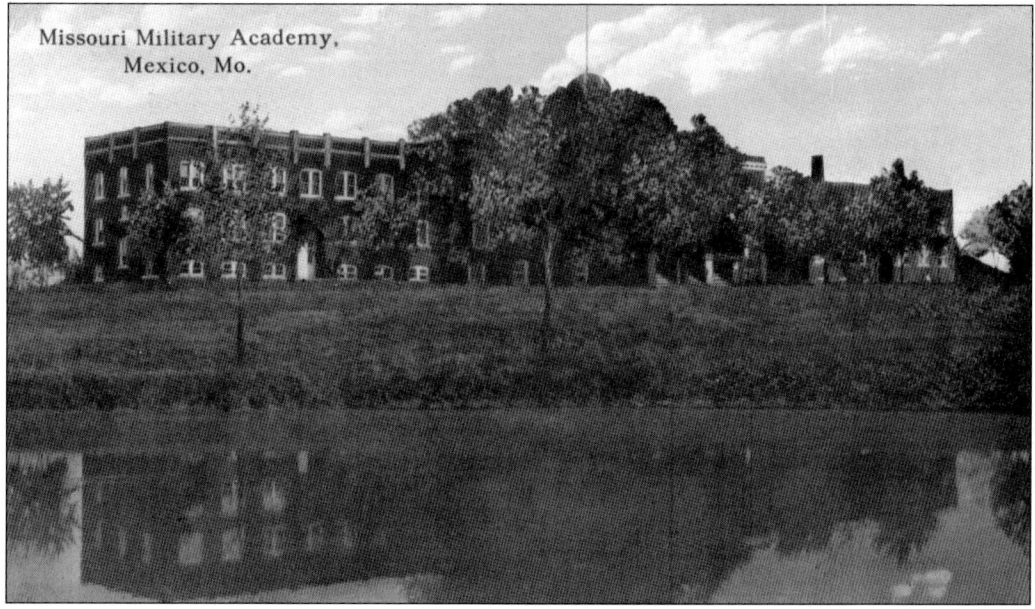

On the night of September 24, 1896, a fire swept through the Missouri Military Academy and left the academy's buildings in a state of smoldering ruin. Though it took some time, the academy gained new life when it grew to 106 acres in 1900 and moved to a location on the eastern end of Mexico. Several buildings went up, including the administration building, which is pictured behind Teardrop Lake on this postcard by W.L. Craddock & Sons—a stationery company in Mexico.

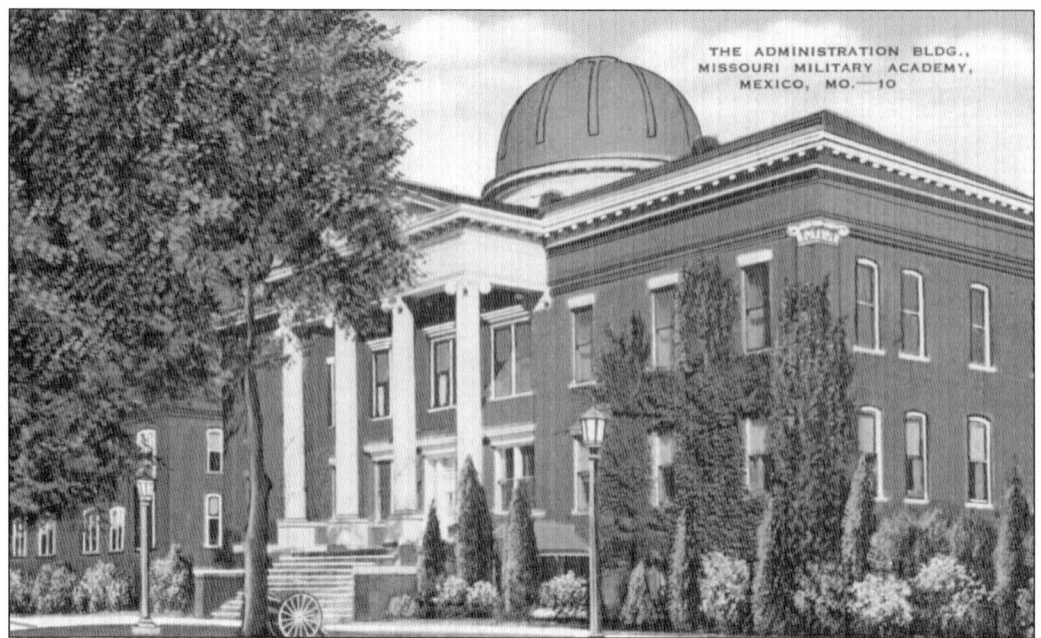

The administration building at the Missouri Military Academy, which was renamed Stribling Hall in 1981 in honor of former academy president Col. Charles Stribling, is prominently featured on this postcard published by the E.C. Kropp Company of Milwaukee, Wisconsin. The 111-year-old Stribling Hall was demolished in 2011 to make room for the new administration building on campus. Construction of the new Stribling Hall was completed the following year and is similar in design to its predecessor.

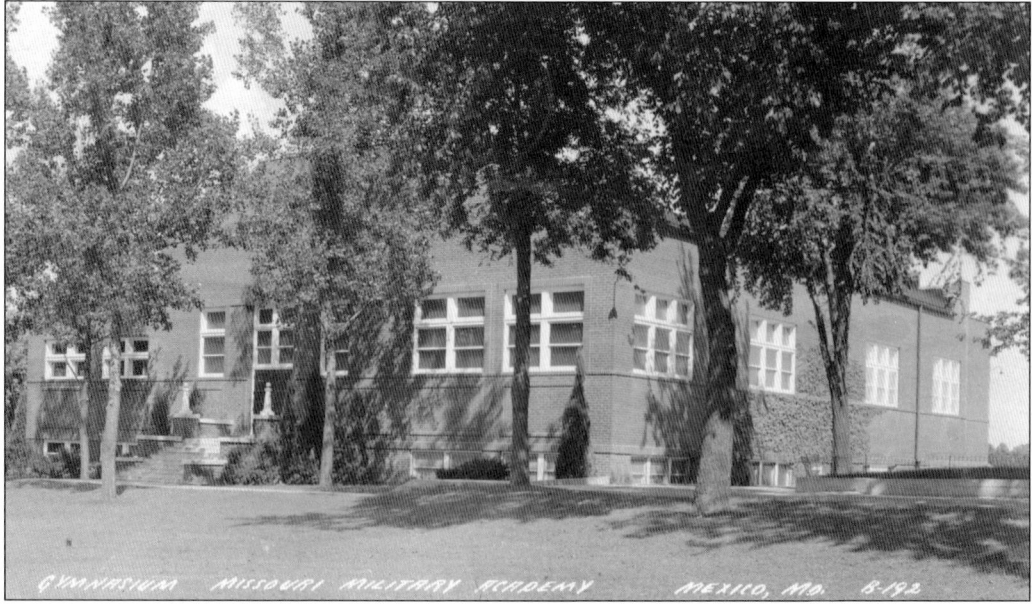

During the fall of 1914, a new gymnasium of brick veneer, as seen on this real-photo postcard, was built on the campus of the Missouri Military Academy. The main floor of the gym was used as a basketball court and in the case of inclement weather was converted to a drill floor. The gym burned down in the spring of 1934 but was rebuilt the following year on its old foundation.

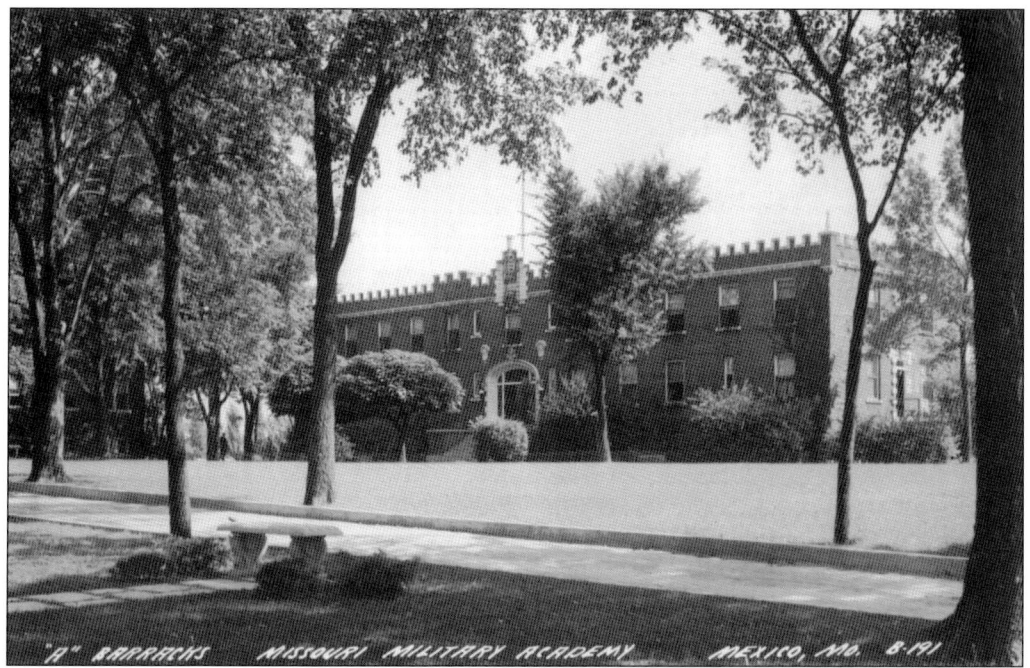

This real-photo postcard features a building once known as "A" Barracks, constructed in 1917 on the campus of the Missouri Military Academy. This three-story brick structure was demolished in 2008 to make room for Barnard Hall—a 43,350-square-foot facility that houses a student commons, library spaces, and numerous classrooms.

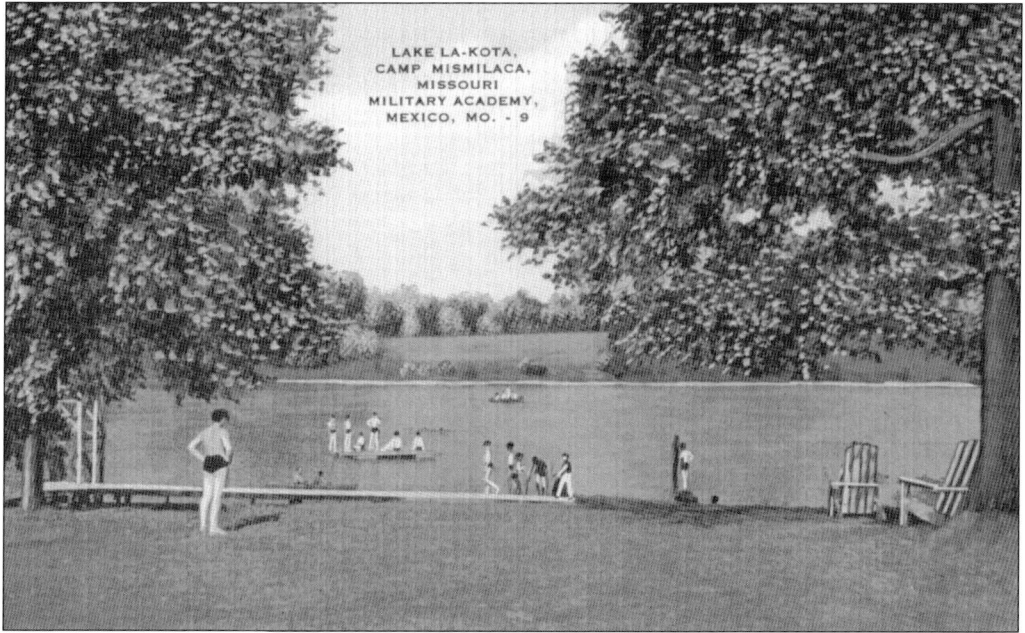

Pictured in this linen postcard by the E.C. Kropp Company is Camp Mismilaca on Lake La-Kota near Mexico, which was purchased by the Missouri Military Academy in the mid-1930s. The academy soon built a dock and a lodge on the site and began using it as recreational facilities, hosting various events such as cookouts, camping, and boating and fishing trips.

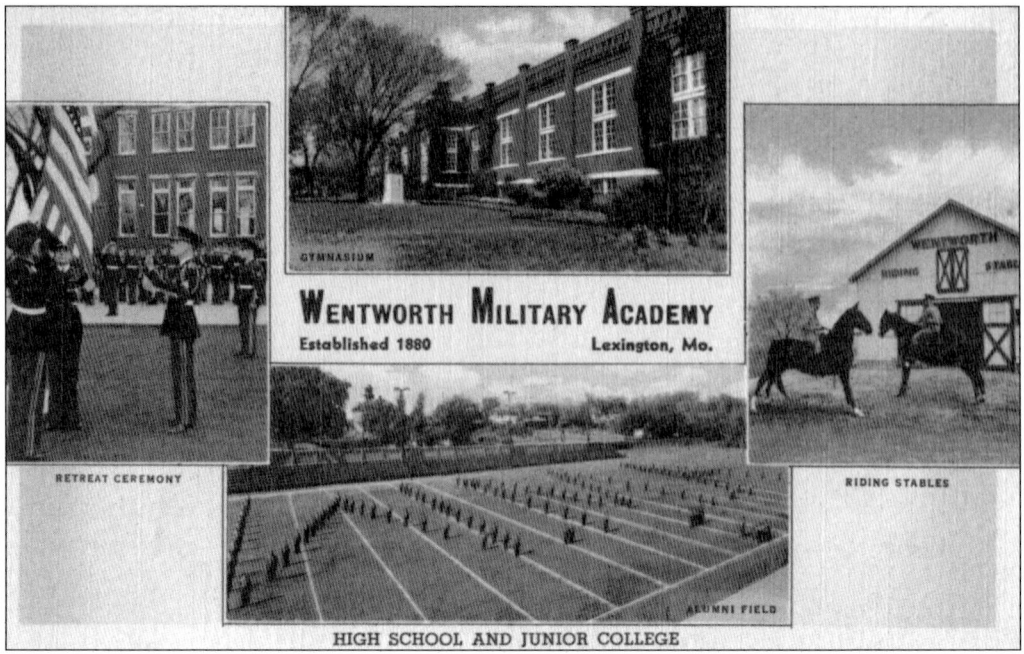

Wentworth Military Academy and College in Lexington was founded in 1880 by Stephen Girard Wentworth as a memorial to his son, who died when only 27 years of age. Though initially established as a male academy, Wentworth became a military school in 1882 after the principal saw students marching in formation while conducting the military manual of arms with broomsticks borrowed from local citizens. Wentworth closed its doors because of financial distress in the spring of 2017.

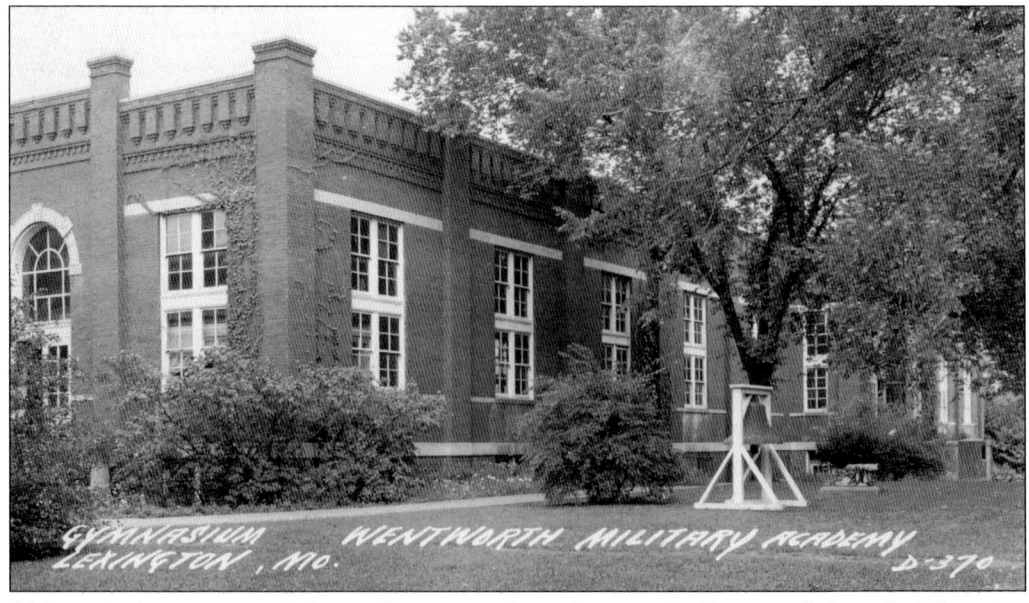

This real-photo postcard shows the gymnasium that was built east of the administration building in 1915. The gym was later renamed Groendyke Hall in honor of John Groendyke—Wentworth alumnus; CEO and chairman of the board of Groendyke Transport, Inc.; and Wentworth board member at one time.

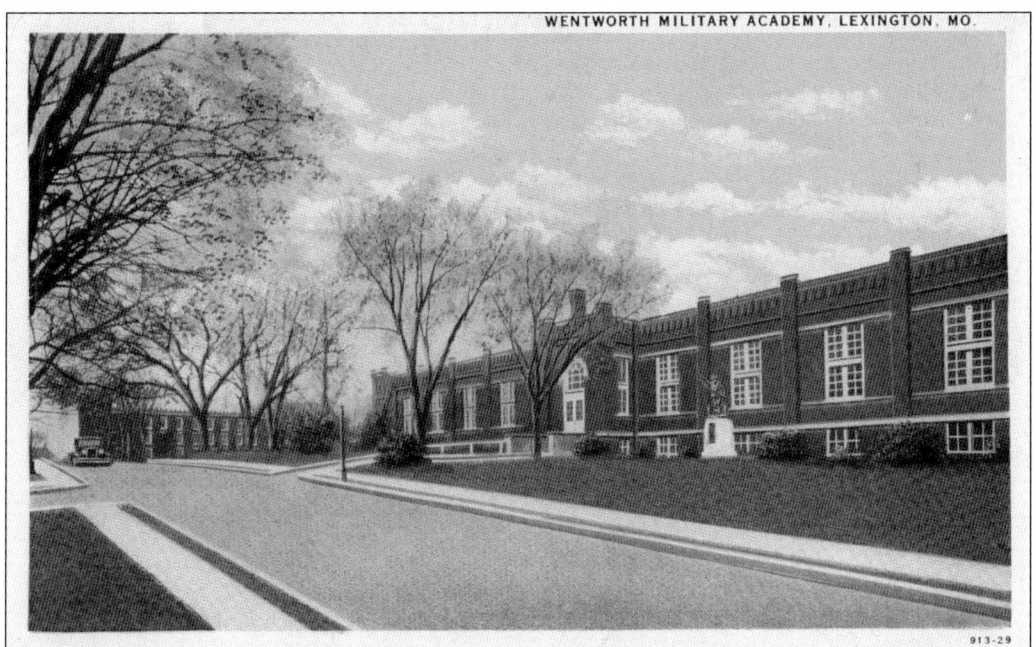

This Curtis Teich postcard shows the gymnasium of Wentworth Military Academy and College as viewed from the southeast. Visible to the right of the entrance is the World War I memorial erected by the academy's alumni and unveiled at ceremonies on June 10, 1923, during the commencement season. The statue is based upon the widely produced *The Spirit of the American Doughboy* design by sculptor E.M. Viquesney.

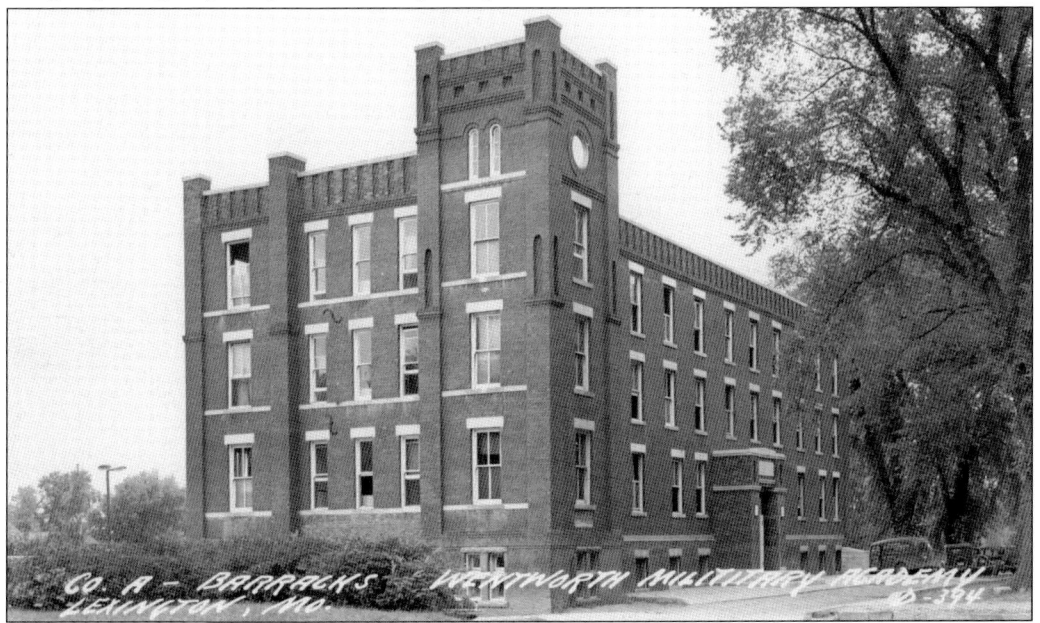

The Company A Barracks at Wentworth Military Academy and College, as seen in this real-photo postcard, was built in 1907 at a cost of $21,292.74. Measuring 180 feet by 30 feet, the barracks is three stories tall with a basement that included a furnace and recreation room and was designed to house 64 cadets.

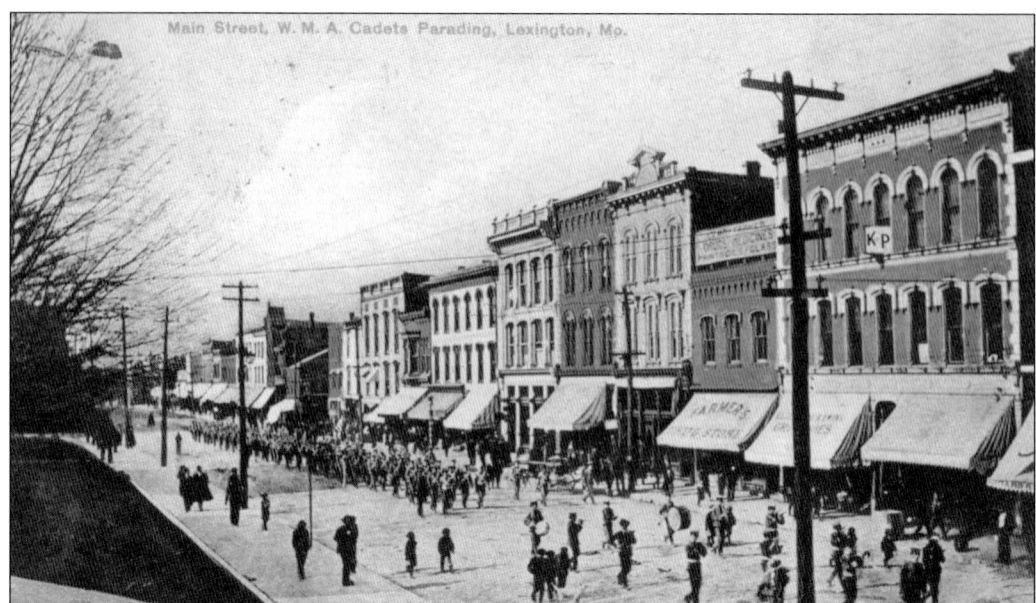

This postcard, which was made in Germany for the Picture Shop in Lexington, is postmarked 1908 and shows cadets from Wentworth Military Academy and College participating in a parade along Lexington's Main Street. The early 1900s were a period of expansion for the academy as enrollment reached 135 cadets during the 1904–1905 session, necessitating the construction of additional barracks.

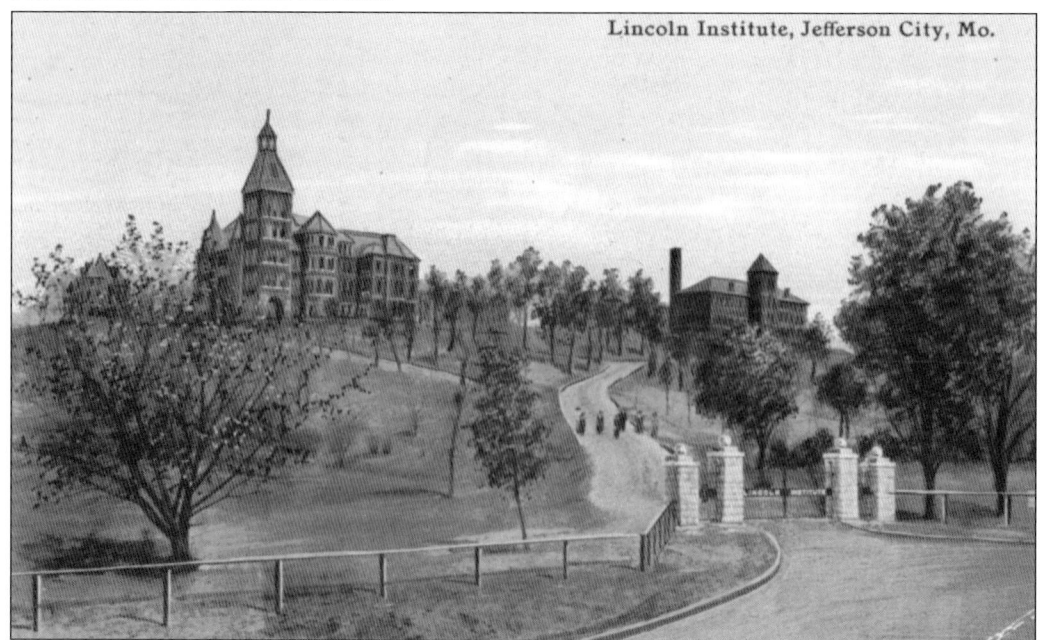

This postcard, printed by the R. Dallmeyer Dry Goods Company, is postmarked 1911 and shows Lincoln Institute in Jefferson City, which became Lincoln University in 1921. The school was originally founded in 1866 after soldiers of the 62nd and 65th US Colored Infantry donated funds collected during their Civil War service to establish an institution to educate freed African Americans.

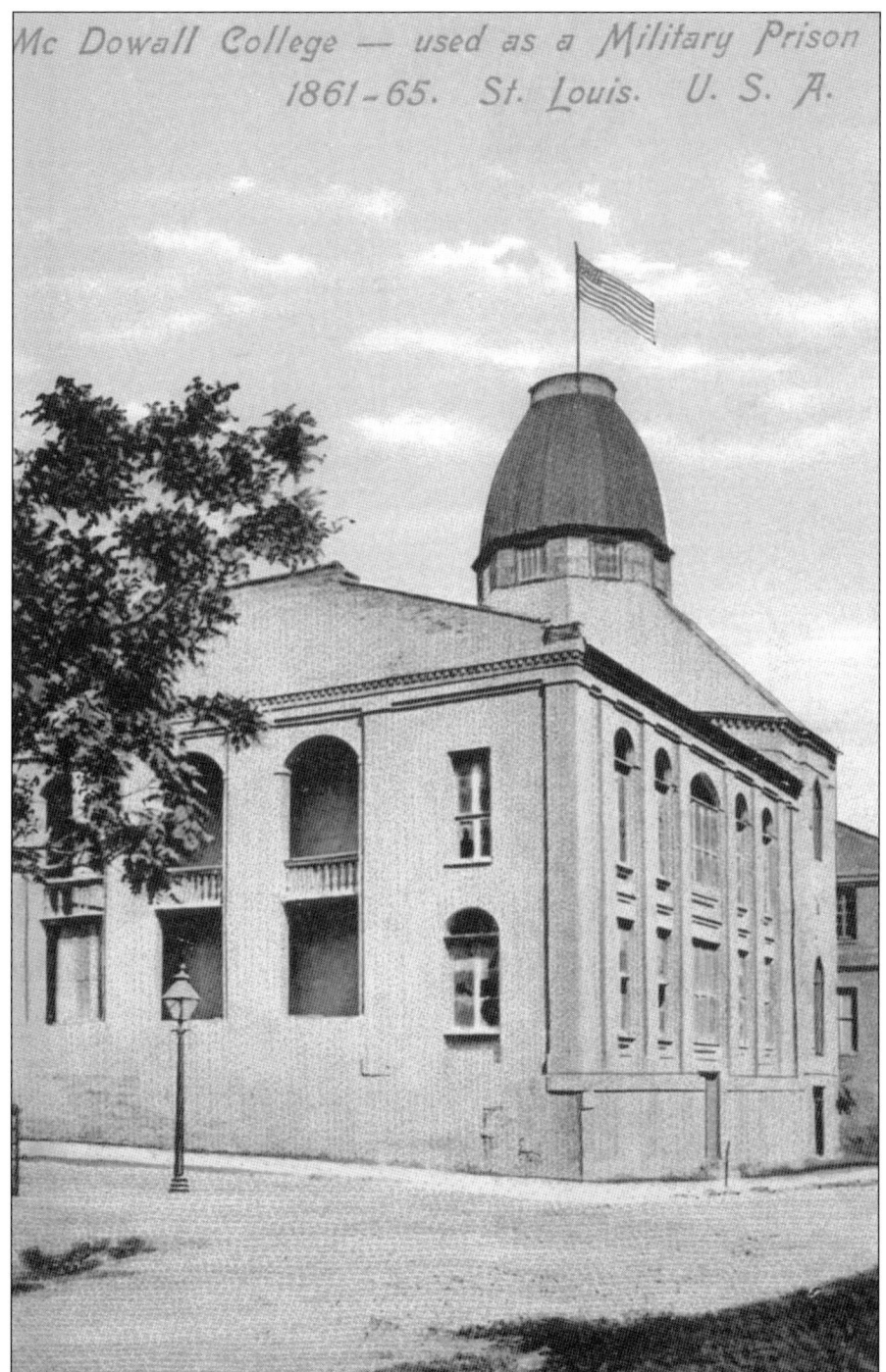

In December 1861, McDowell Medical College in St. Louis was converted into Gratiot Street Prison. During the period of the Civil War, the makeshift prison held not only Confederate prisoners of war, but was also used to detain those sympathetic to the Southern cause, as well as Union deserters. The building was demolished in 1878 and has been replaced by a parking lot for the headquarters of Ralston-Purina.

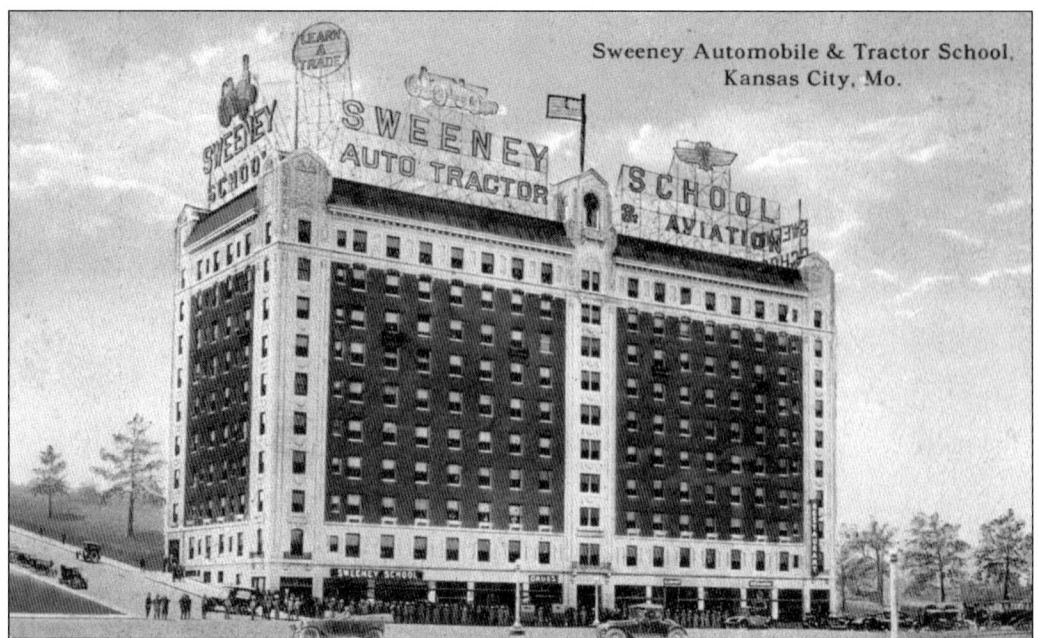

The Sweeney Automotive and Tractor School in Kansas City was established in 1908 by Emory Sweeney and quickly grew to an enrollment of more than 7,100 students in 1919. During the First World War, Sweeney secured a government contract to teach mechanical skills to enlisted soldiers; however, the school's end essentially arrived with the stock market crash of 1929. The original 10-story building can still be seen south of Union Station.

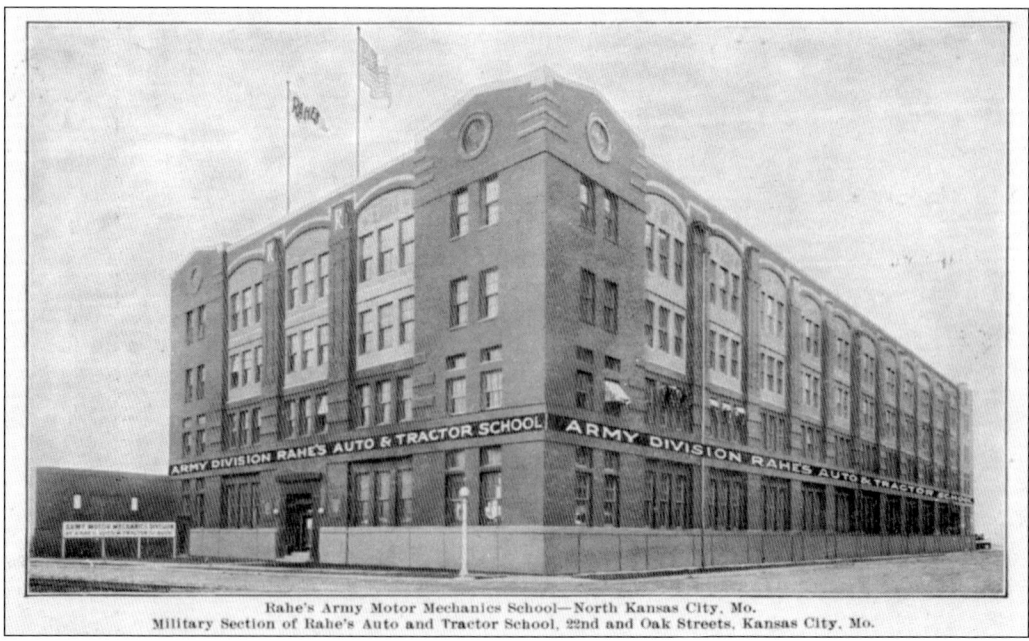

Founded in 1917 by Henry J. Rahe to train mechanics for the burgeoning automotive industry, Rahe's Auto & Tractor School in North Kansas City established an Army Division to train mechanics for World War I. The school closed after the end of the war, and the building was later used for other purposes but was eventually demolished to construct the Crown Center.

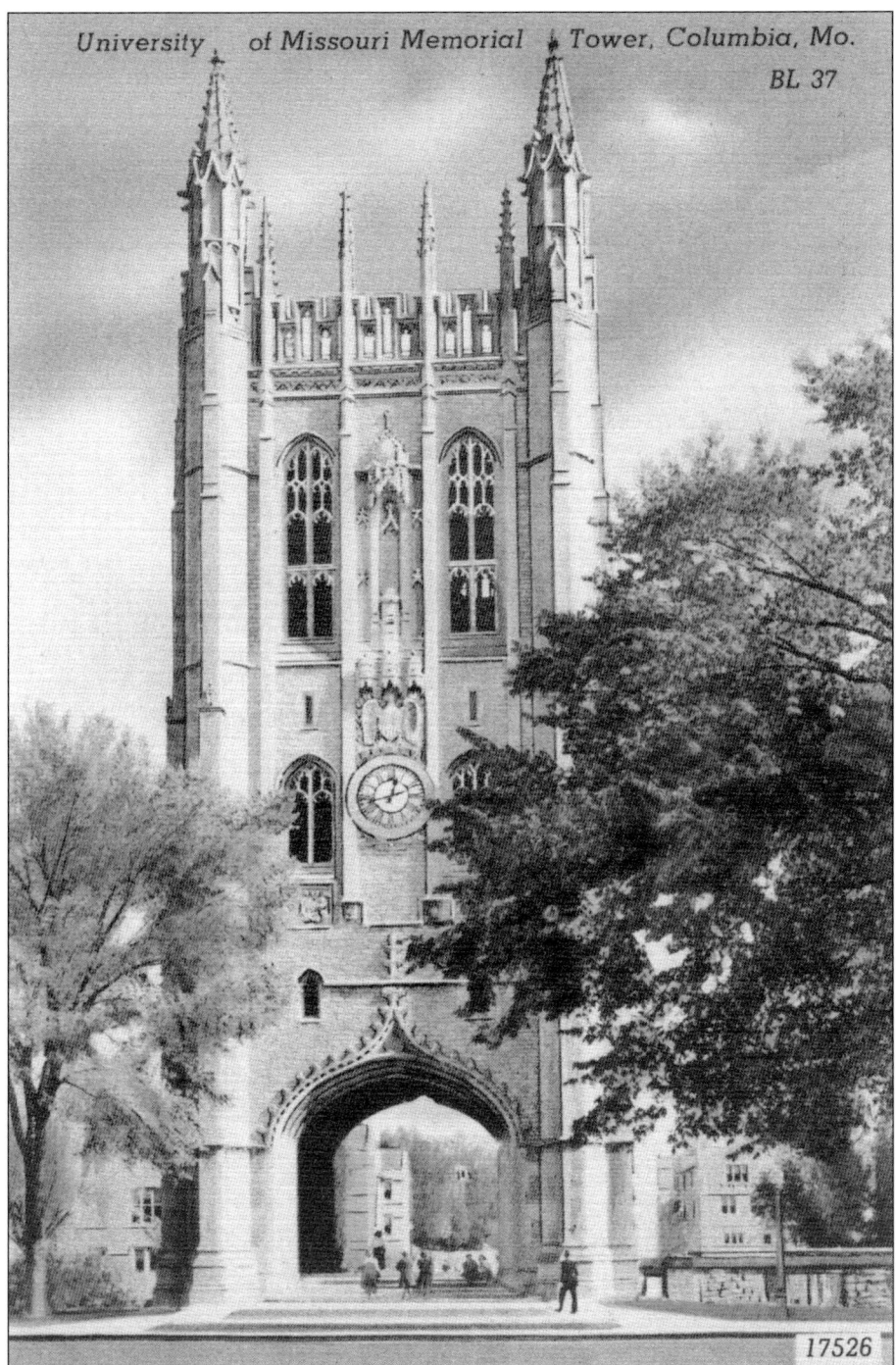

This postcard published by Blair Cedar and Novelty Works in Camdenton, Missouri, shows the Memorial Tower at the University of Missouri that was completed in 1926 and has the names of the 117 university students who lost their lives in World War I carved into the archway. In later years, a north and south wing were added to the tower, and the structure is now known as Memorial Union.

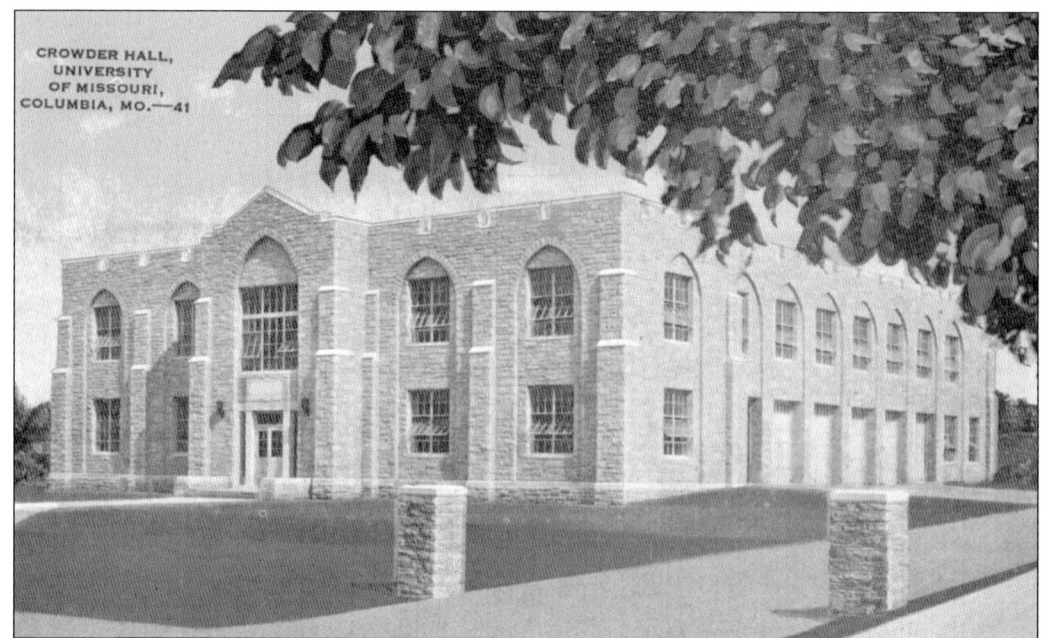

Crowder Hall, as pictured in this postcard by Lawlor Distributing Company of Columbia, was built on the University of Missouri campus in 1938. It is named for Maj. Gen. Enoch Crowder—a Missouri native who is best known for implementing the Selective Service Act during World War I. The hall continues to serve as the military science and leadership department for the school's Reserve Officers' Training Corps (ROTC) program.

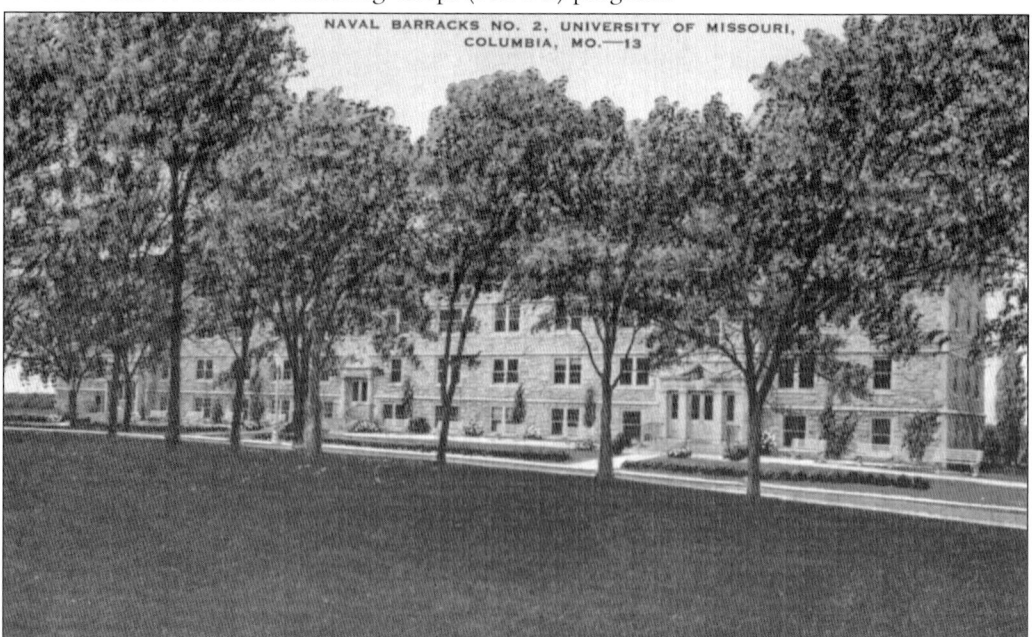

The NROTC program was established at the University of Missouri in Columbia on July 1, 1946. Although the NROTC unit at the university was once located in the building pictured in this linen postcard published by Lawlor Distributing of Columbia, they were relocated to Crowder Hall in early 1972.

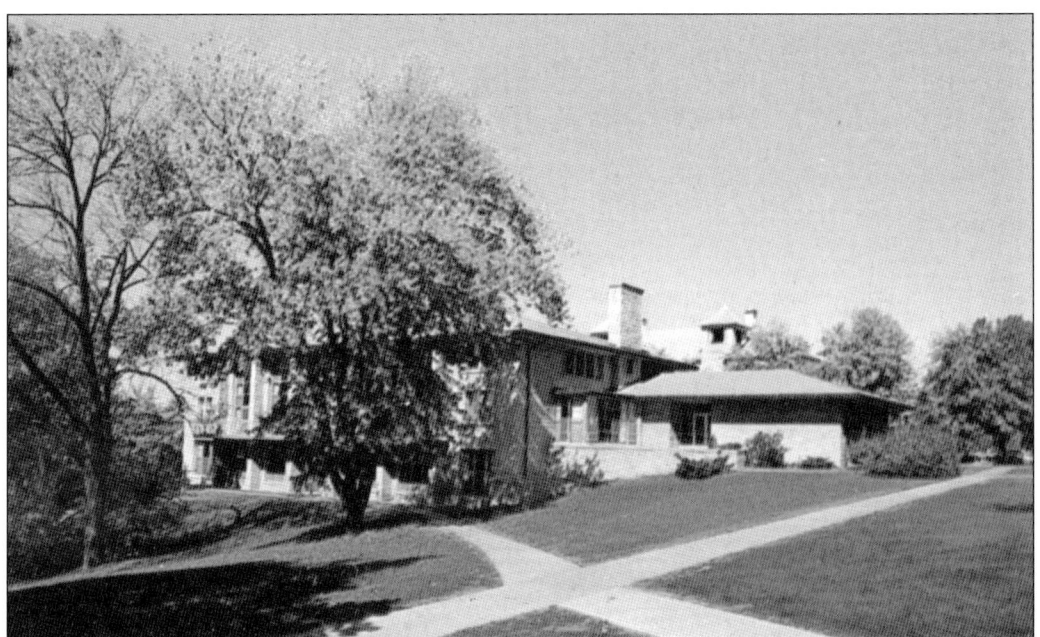

Memorial Hall, on the campus of Southeast Missouri State College (now University) in Cape Girardeau, was constructed in 1950 with limestone from local quarries. The building was named Memorial Hall by the board of regents to pay homage to students and alumni of the school that served in World War II, especially those who lost their lives while in service to the nation.

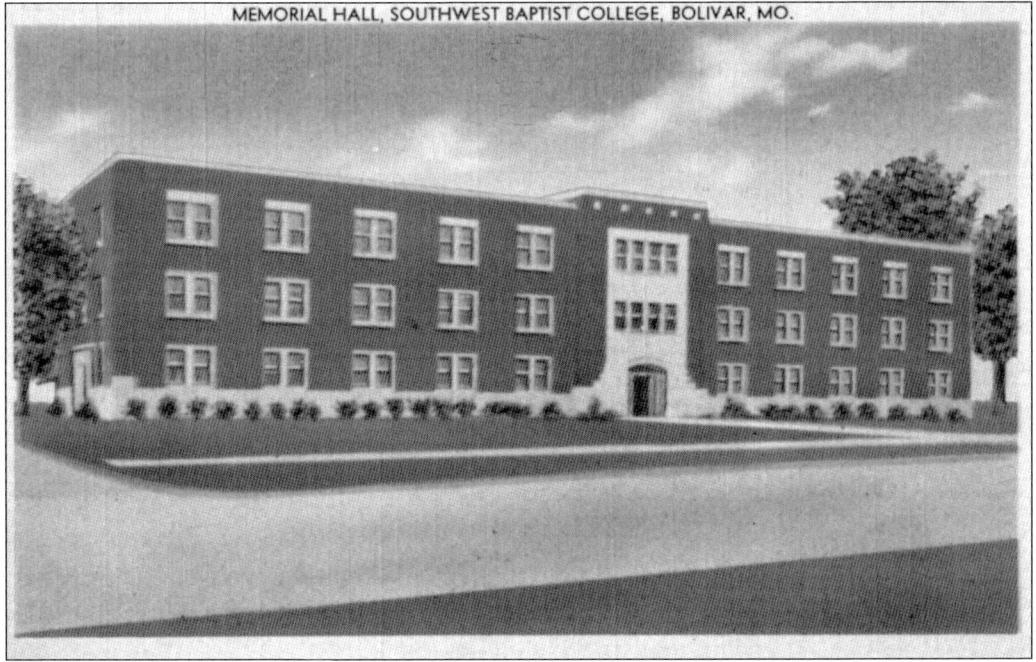

Memorial Hall was constructed on the campus of Southwest Baptist University in Bolivar. Dedicated on May 12, 1949, the hall honors the memory of the school's veterans who served in World War II. The three-story building continues as a men's dormitory and has the capacity to house 82 students.

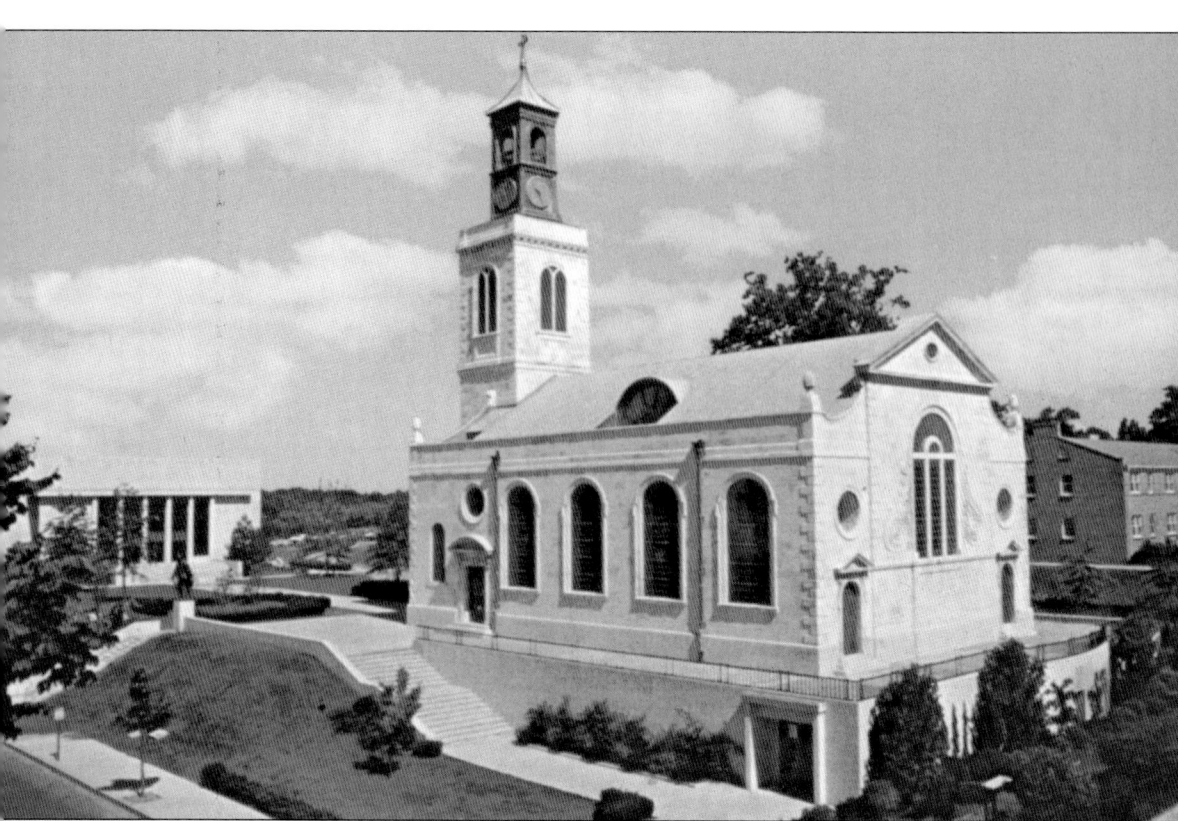

During a visit to Westminster College in Fulton in 1946, Winston Churchill delivered his iconic "Iron Curtain" speech, essentially heralding the beginning of the Cold War. In 1965, St. Mary Aldermanbury, a London church badly damaged during World War II, was moved piece by piece and rebuilt on the Westminster Campus, the basement of which now serves as the National Churchill Museum and Memorial.

Three

MEMORIAL SITES AND TRIBUTES

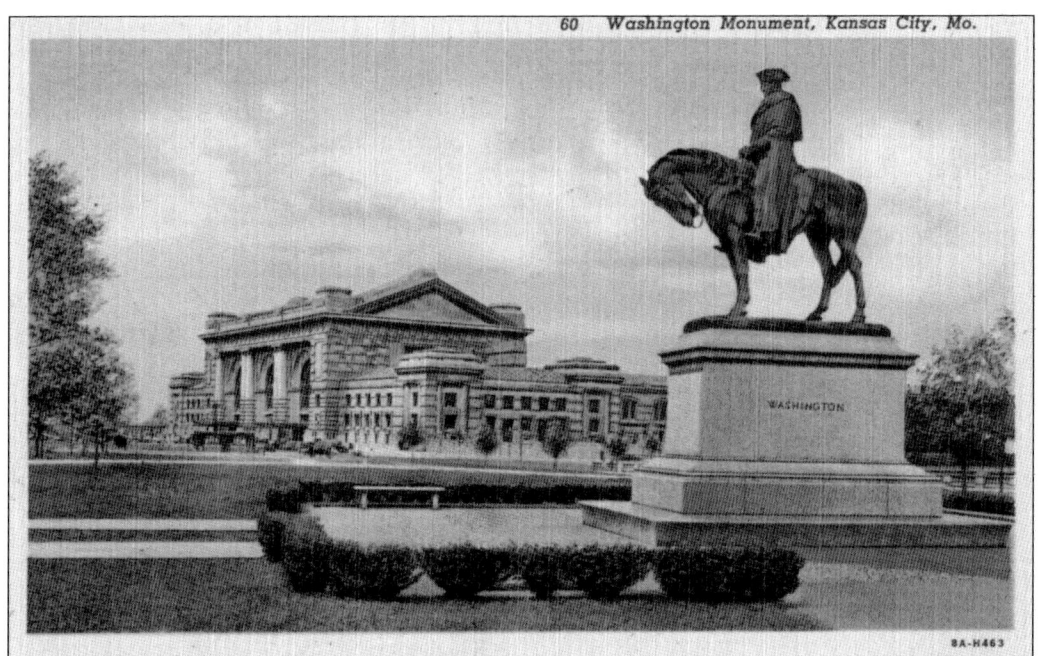

Copied from a statue in Brooklyn, New York, this memorial to Gen. George Washington is in Washington Square Park in Kansas City. The monument was purchased through the donations of local citizens and cost $30,000 when it was dedicated on Armistice Day in 1925. The building pictured in the background is Kansas City's Union Station.

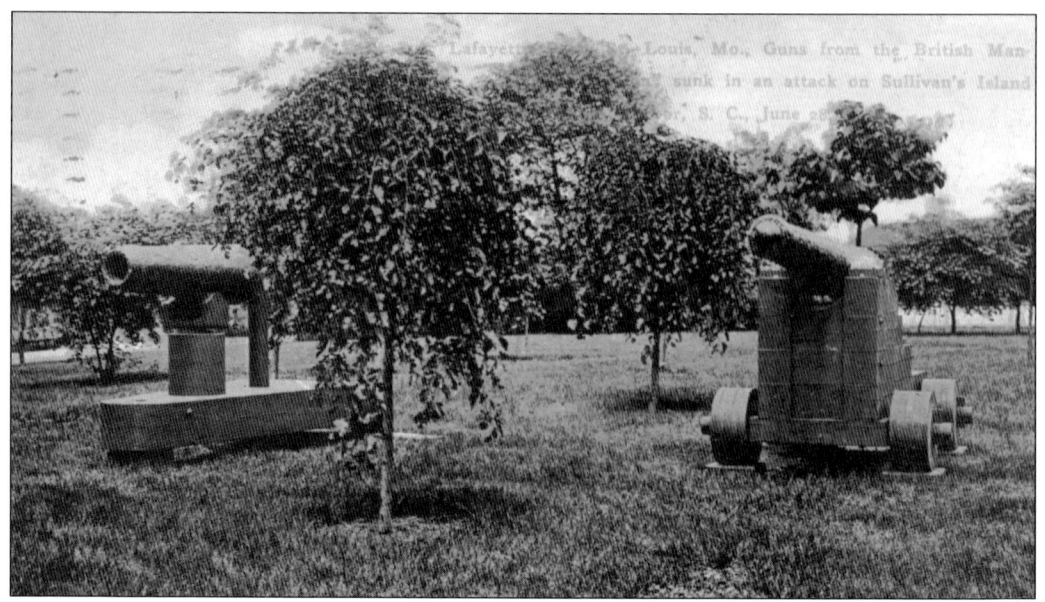

This postcard by the St. Louis News Company features two of three cannons that are on display in Lafayette Park in St. Louis. The cannons came from the British frigate *Actaeon*, which was sunk during the Battle of Charleston during the Revolutionary War. The cannons were later purchased by a group of St. Louis veterans and donated to the park in 1897.

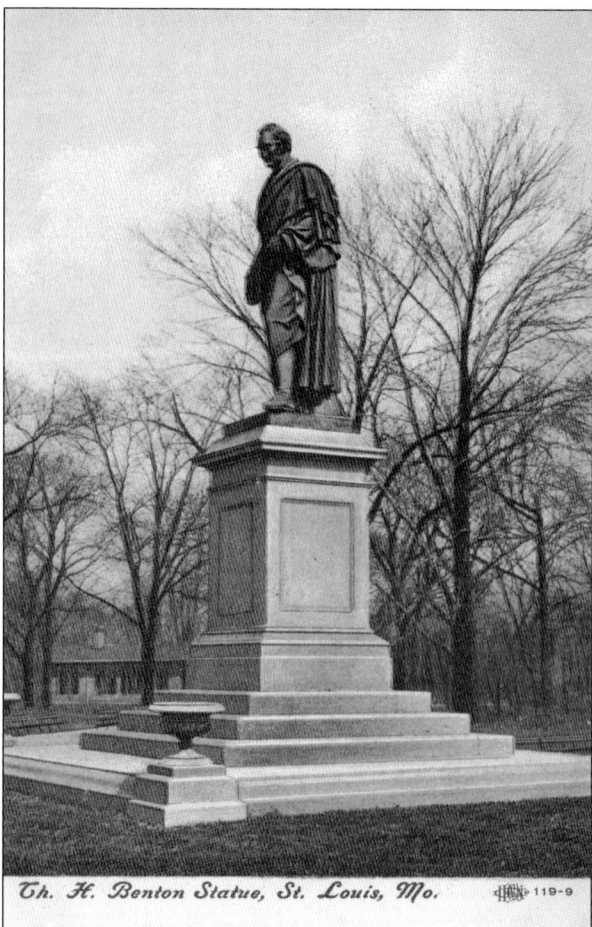

This bronze statue in Lafayette Park in St. Louis is dedicated to the memory of Thomas Hart Benton—a US senator who was commissioned as a lieutenant colonel by Andrew Jackson to serve as his aide-de-camp during the War of 1812. The statue was dedicated in 1868 and is believed to have been the first public monument in the state of Missouri.

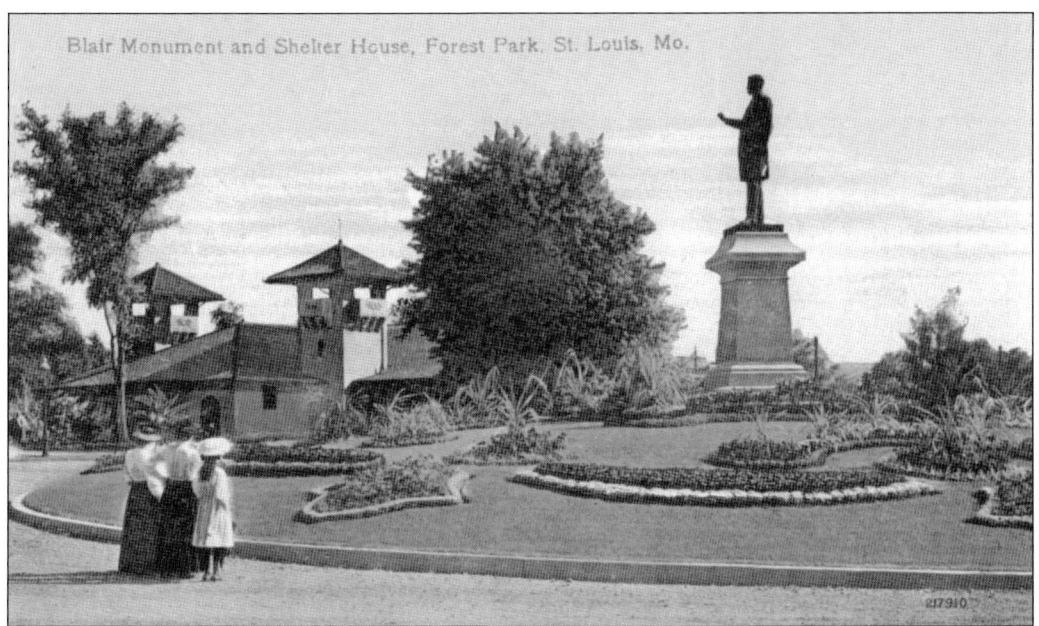

The C.M. Corrington International Novelty and Art Company published this postcard showing the Frank Preston Blair Jr. monument in Forest Park in St. Louis. Though dedicated in commemoration of his service as a US senator, Blair also served as a Union general in the Civil War and became well known for seizing the St. Louis Arsenal.

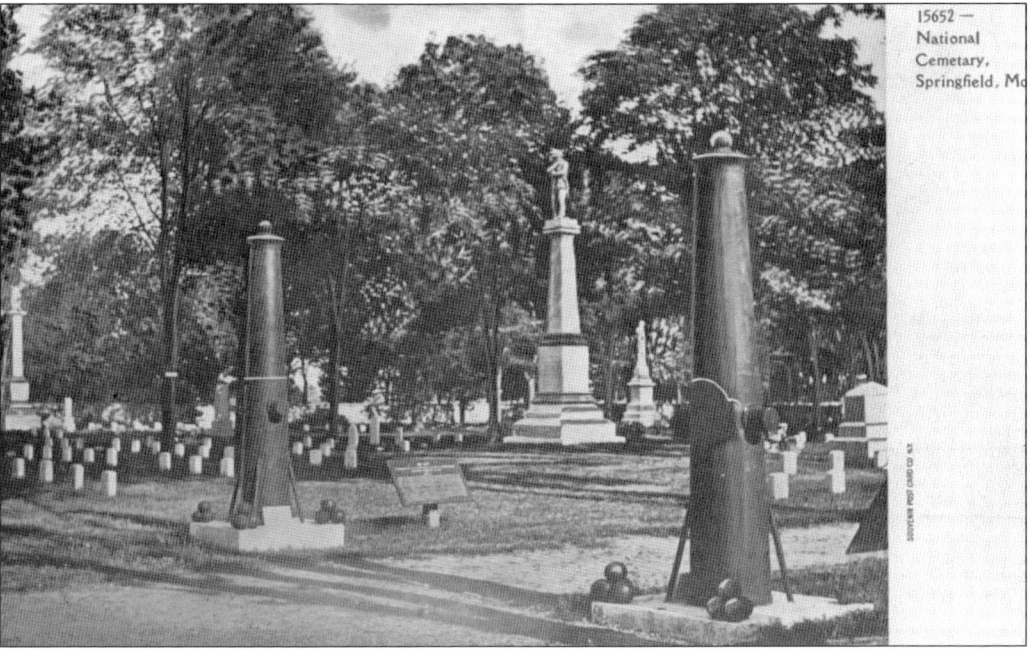

This postcard showing a section of the National Cemetery in Springfield is postmarked 1909. Many of the men who fought in the Battle of Wilson's Creek near Springfield would eventually be interred in the cemetery, established in 1867. Pictured in the background between the two vertical cannons is the T.J. Bailey monument, which was erected in 1907 as a memorial to Union soldiers.

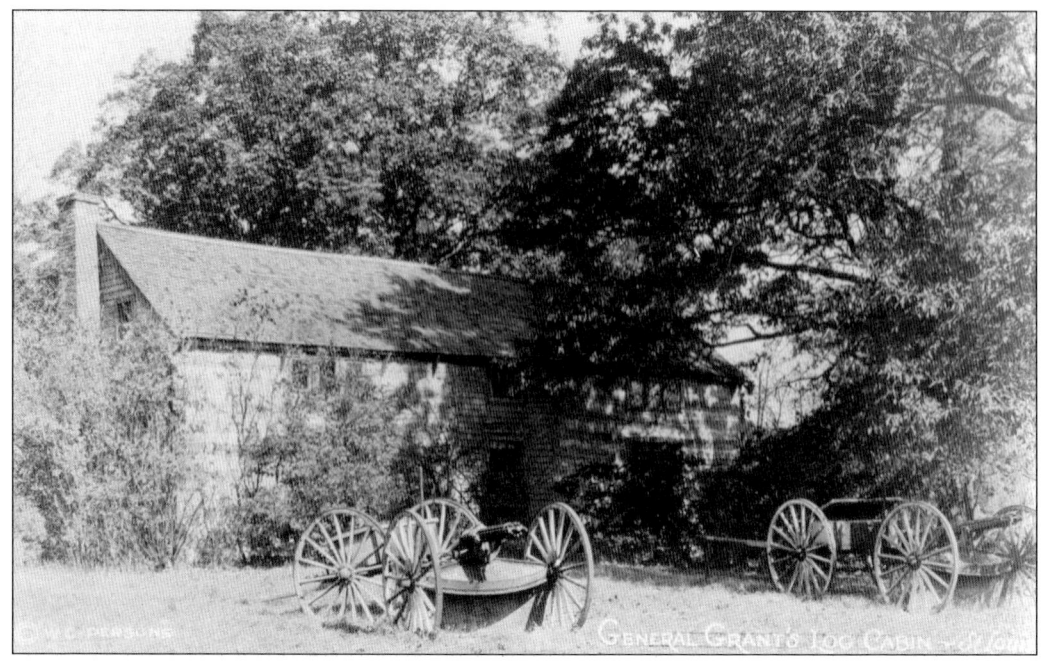

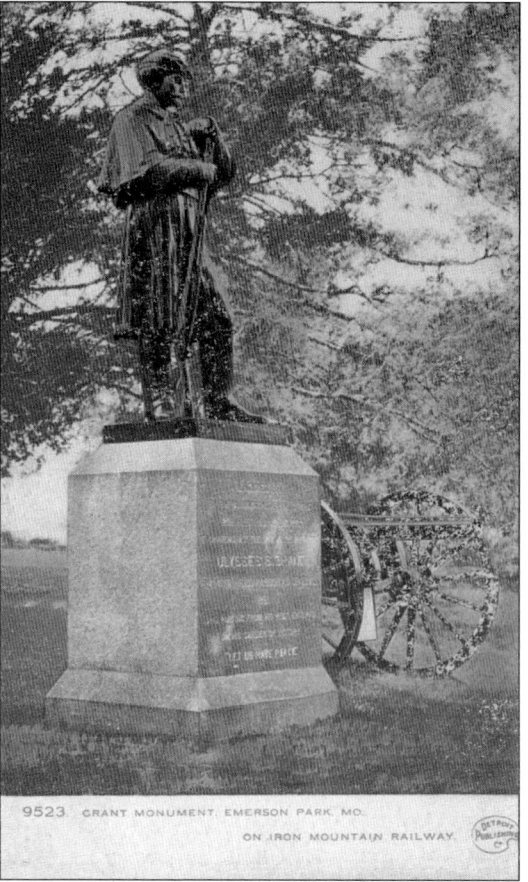

Ulysses S. Grant married Julia Dent in 1848 and was then given 80 acres of property adjacent to the estate of his new father-in law. In 1855, after having resigned from the Army, Grant began building a cabin, which he called Hardscrabble, pictured in this postcard. Located in St. Louis, the cabin was left by the Grants in 1857 following the death of Grant's mother-in-law. Hardscrabble is still standing and can be seen on Grant's Farm in St. Louis.

The Ulysses S. Grant monument is located in Ironton and memorializes the location where he received his commission as brigadier general in 1861. The statue was dedicated in 1886 by members of Grant's 21st Illinois Volunteer Infantry Regiment. A tree limb fell on the statue in 1982, breaking it into two pieces, but in 1989 it was restored to its former glory through the efforts of Ironton's mayor.

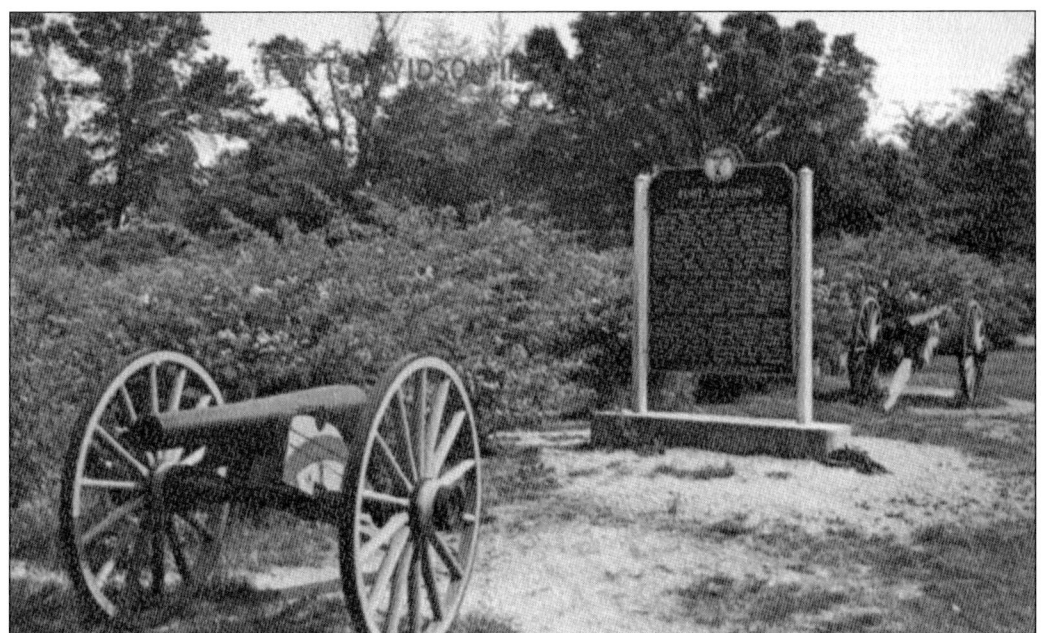

Fort Davidson in Pilot Knob became the site of a major skirmish between Union and Confederate forces in September 1864. During the failed assault against the Union-held fort, the Confederate forces lost a staggering 1,200 soldiers. Known as the Battle of Pilot Knob, the site of this battle is commemorated through the Fort Davidson Historic Site and Museum.

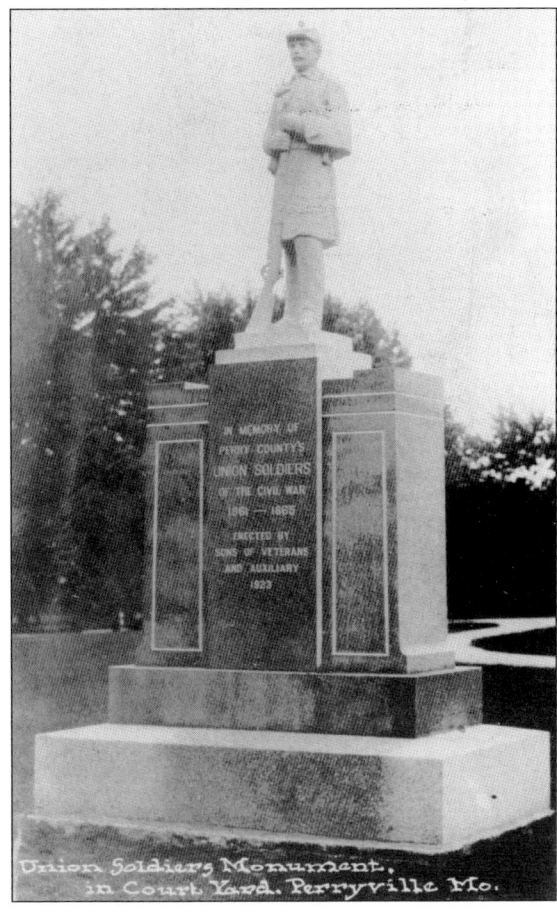

Featured on this real-photo postcard is the Union Soldiers Monument located on the grounds of the Perry County Courthouse in Perryville. The monument features a Union soldier wearing a long overcoat and forage cap while holding a rifle by its barrel as the butt of the weapon rests between his feet. The statue was dedicated on October 7, 1923.

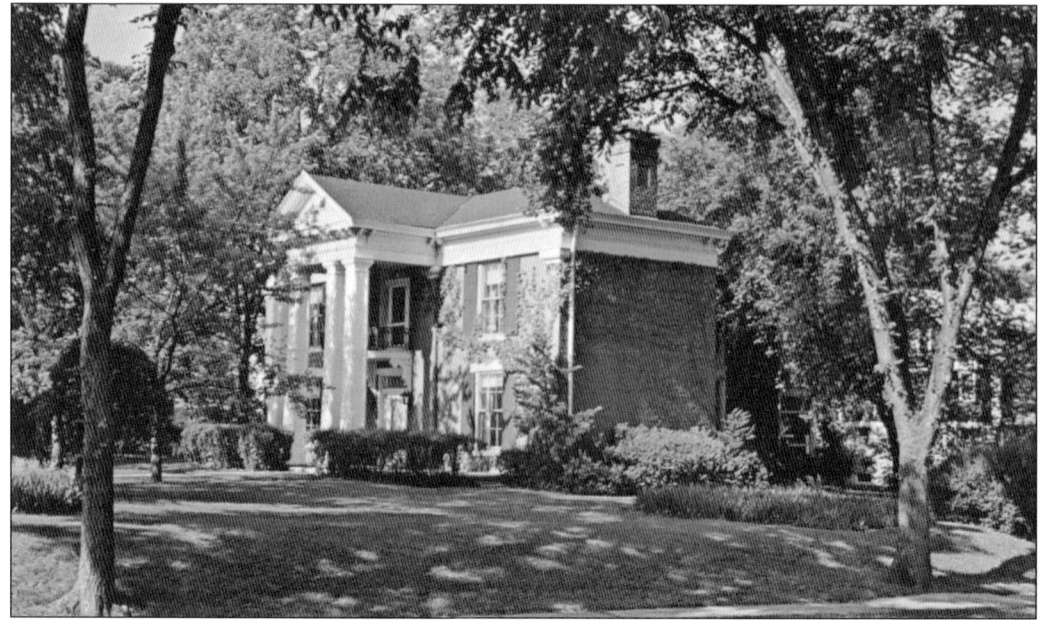

Built in 1858 by John Bristow Wornall, this home in Kansas City served as a battlefield hospital for both Union and Confederate forces during the Civil War skirmish known as the Battle of Westport. The home is listed in the National Register of Historic Places and is now a museum that is open for tours year-round.

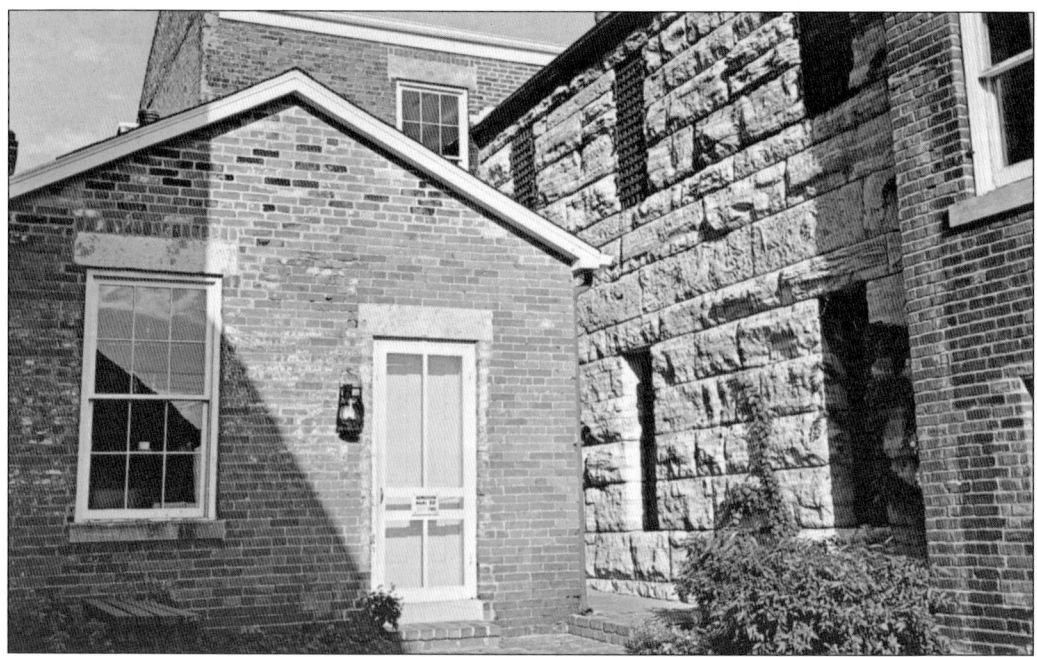

Published by J.E. Tetirick of Kansas City, this postcard shows the old jail and Marshal's Home located in Independence. Built in 1859, the jail held both military and civilian prisoners during the Civil War. The building underwent a major renovation in 1959 and is now a museum operated by the Jackson County Historical Society.

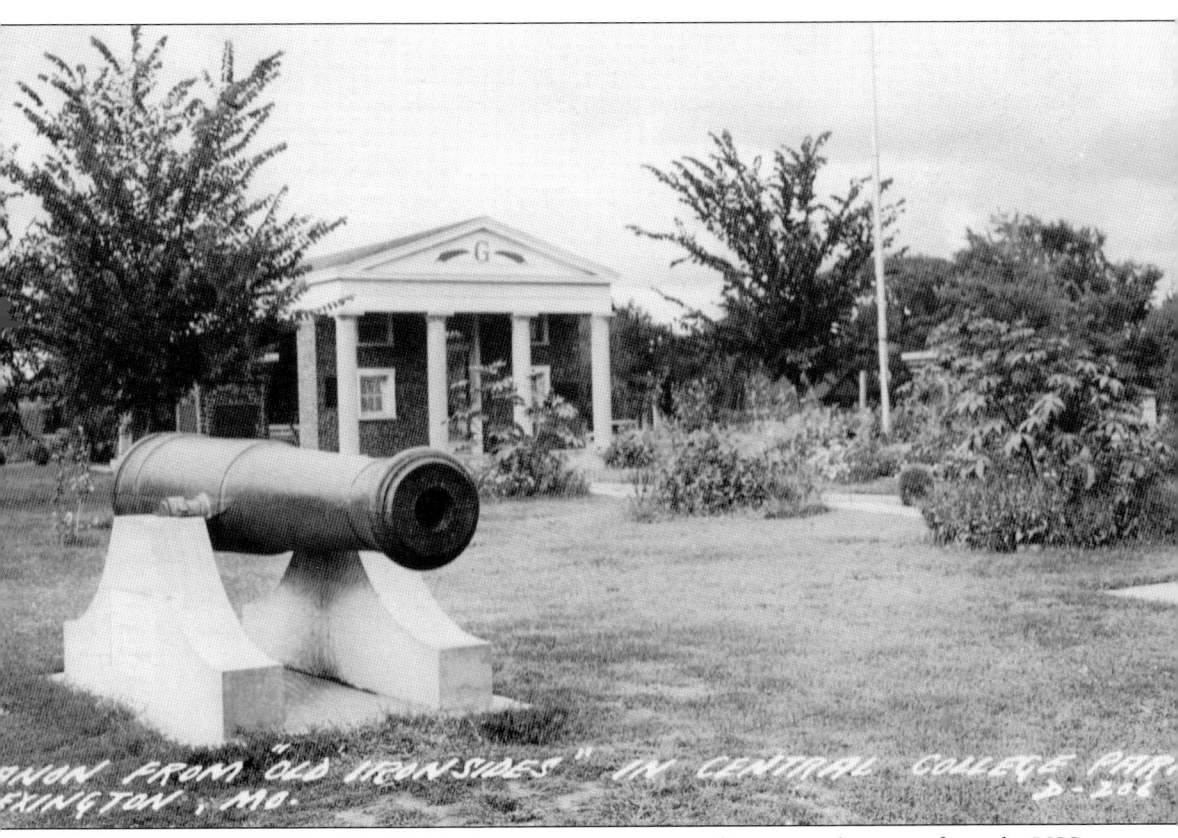

Situated in College Park in the historic town of Lexington is this restored cannon from the USS *Constitution* ("Old Ironsides"). In the background is a one-third-size replica of the Masonic College building that once served as Union headquarters in the Civil War engagement known as the Battle of Lexington.

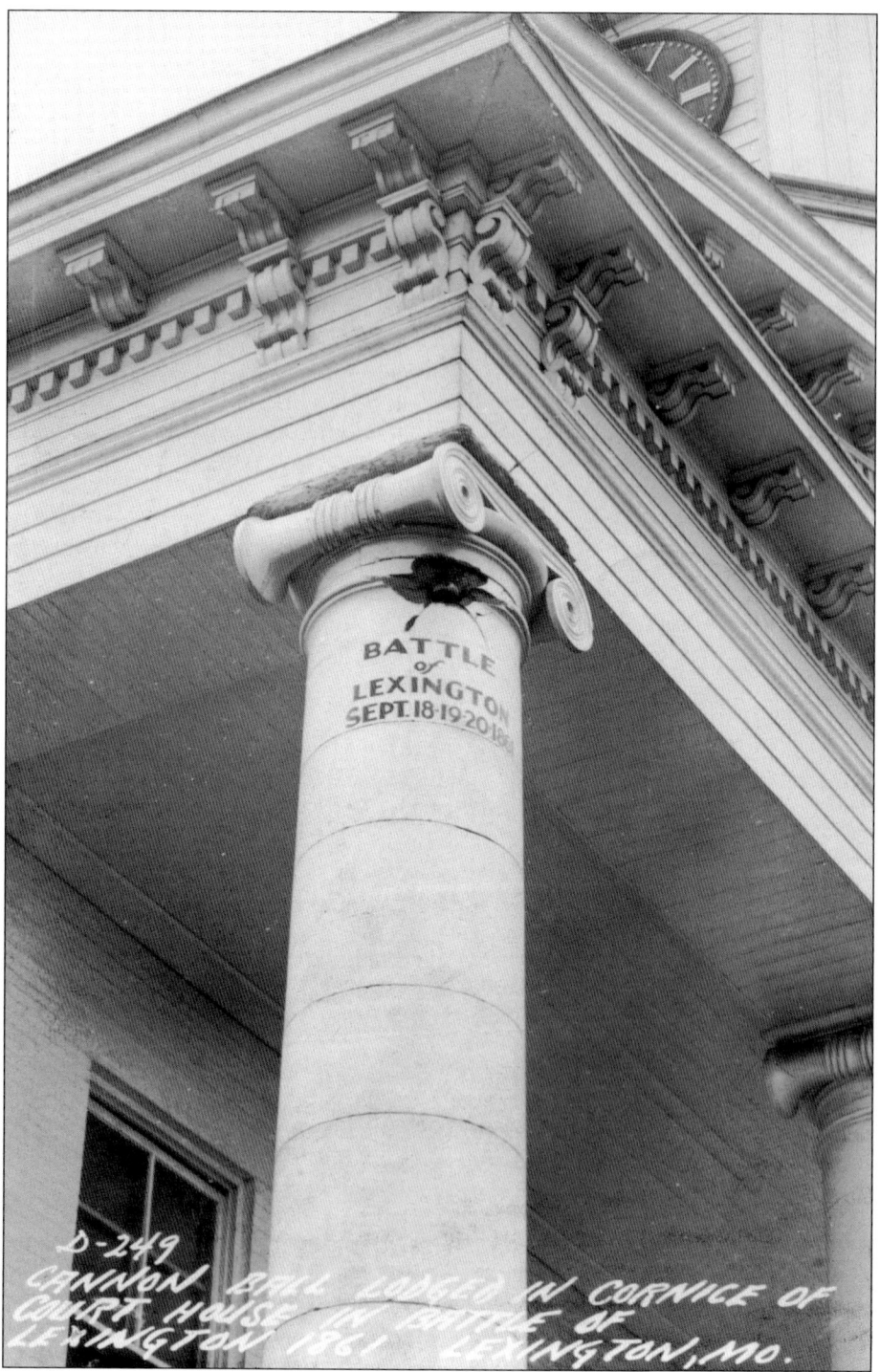

The Lafayette County Courthouse in Lexington was built in 1847 and has become the oldest courthouse still in use in Missouri. A cannonball fired during the Battle of Lexington in 1861 struck the cornice of the far-left column on the facade of the courthouse, evidence of which remains visible to this day.

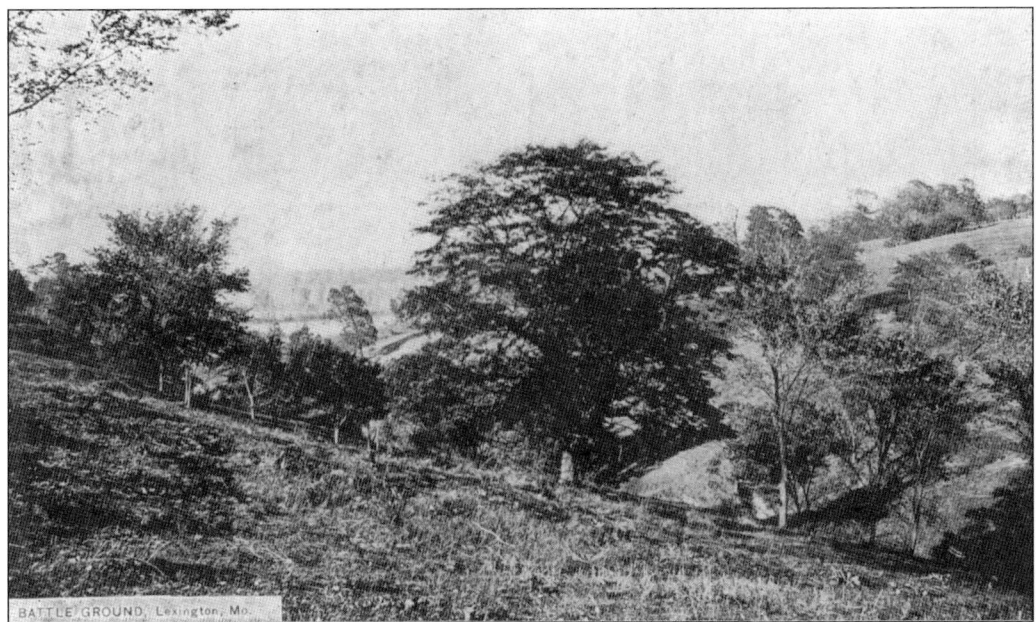
Postmarked 1906, this real-photo postcard shows the simple terrain of a site that was once a Civil War battleground in Lexington. The Battle of Lexington took place September 18–20, 1861, and resulted in the death of 39 Union soldiers and 25 Confederate soldiers. The battlefield is now maintained as a historic site by the Missouri State Parks.

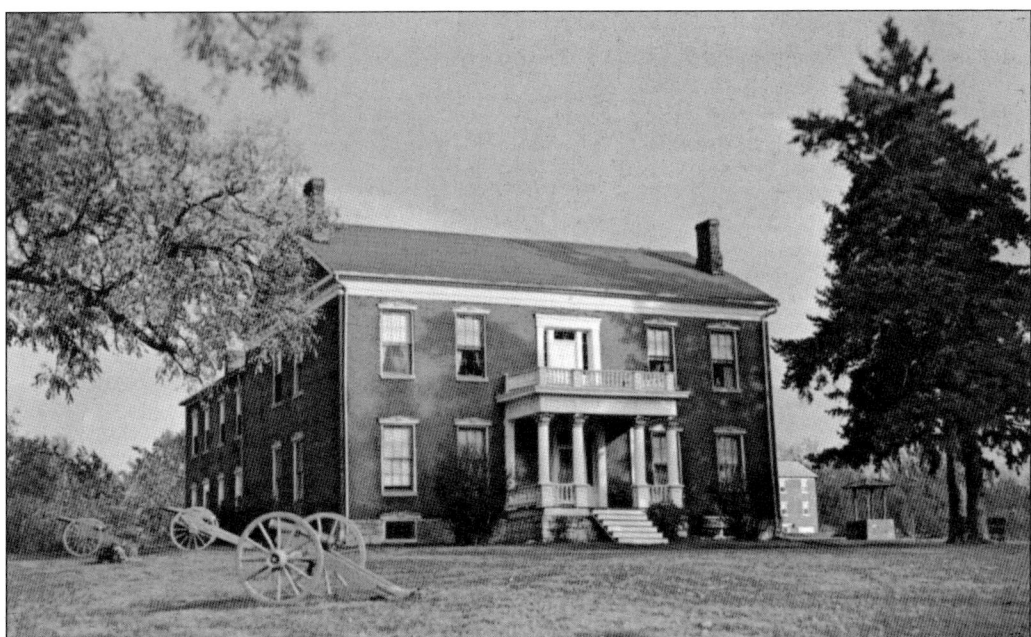
Built in 1853 by Oliver Anderson, this house was seized and used as a hospital by Union forces during the Battle of Lexington. Now part of the Battle of Lexington State Historic Site, the Anderson House, with its evidence of battle scars that include bullet holes in the walls and damage from cannon shot, can be toured by visitors to the park.

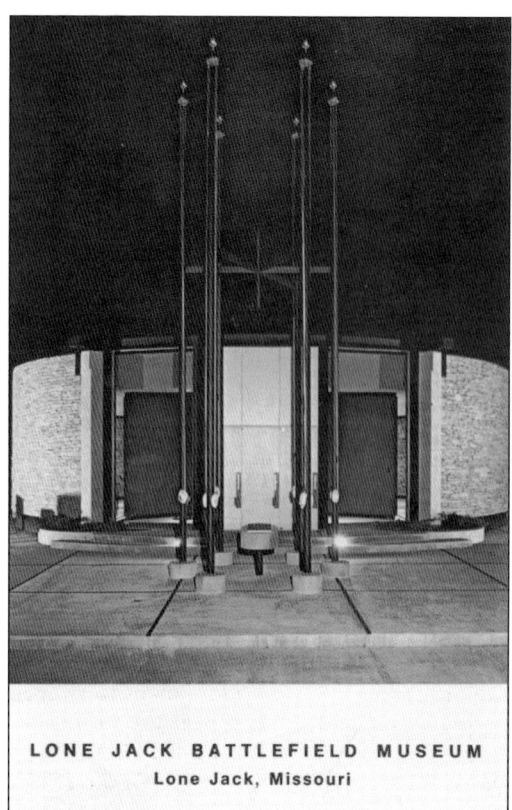

LONE JACK BATTLEFIELD MUSEUM
Lone Jack, Missouri

A circular building constructed in 1963 from native stone, the Lone Jack Battlefield Museum is maintained by the Lone Jack Historical Society. The museum preserves the memory of a local Civil War battle that occurred on August 16, 1862, which resulted in a Confederate victory but left an estimated 270 dead, many of whom were buried in trenches dug along the battlefield.

With a postmark of 1909, this real-photo postcard shows the Grand Army of the Republic monument that was dedicated in 1906 in Park Cemetery in Carthage. Nearly 25 feet in height, the granite column topped with a globe is constructed from marble and features the names of four famous Civil War generals: Grant, Sherman, Meade, and Sheridan.

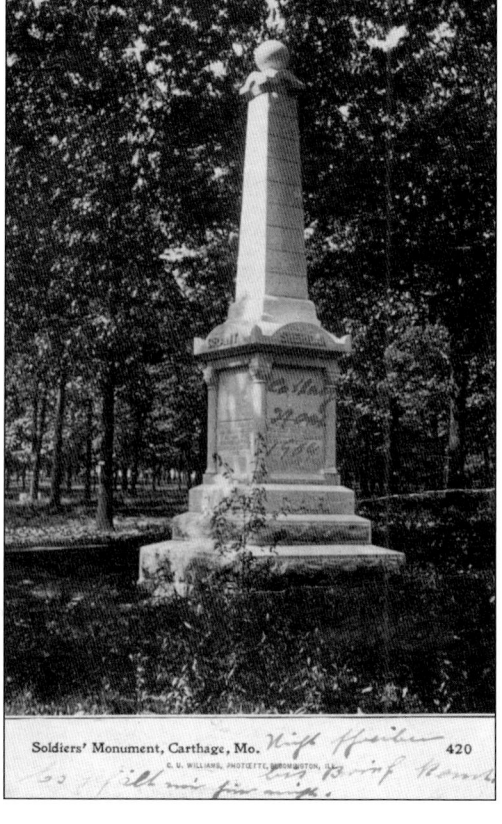

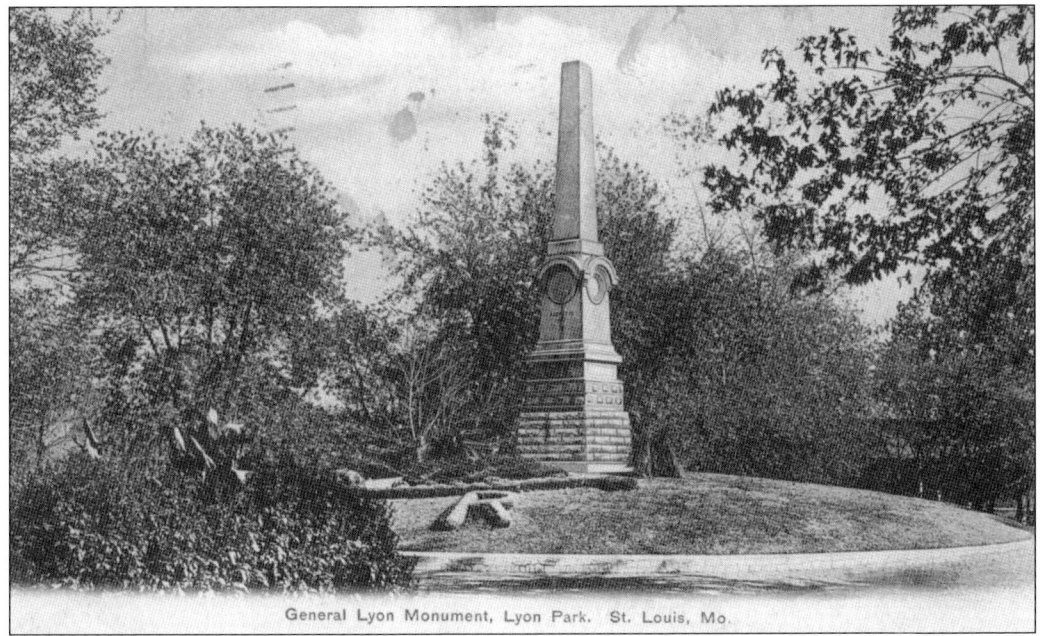

Published by the St. Louis News Company, this postcard features the Gen. Nathaniel Lyon monument. Sculpted by Adolphus Druiding and dedicated in 1874, the monument is in Lyon Park, near the Anheuser-Busch InBev brewery in St. Louis, and situated near the former St. Louis Arsenal that the general helped protect from Confederate forces during the Civil War.

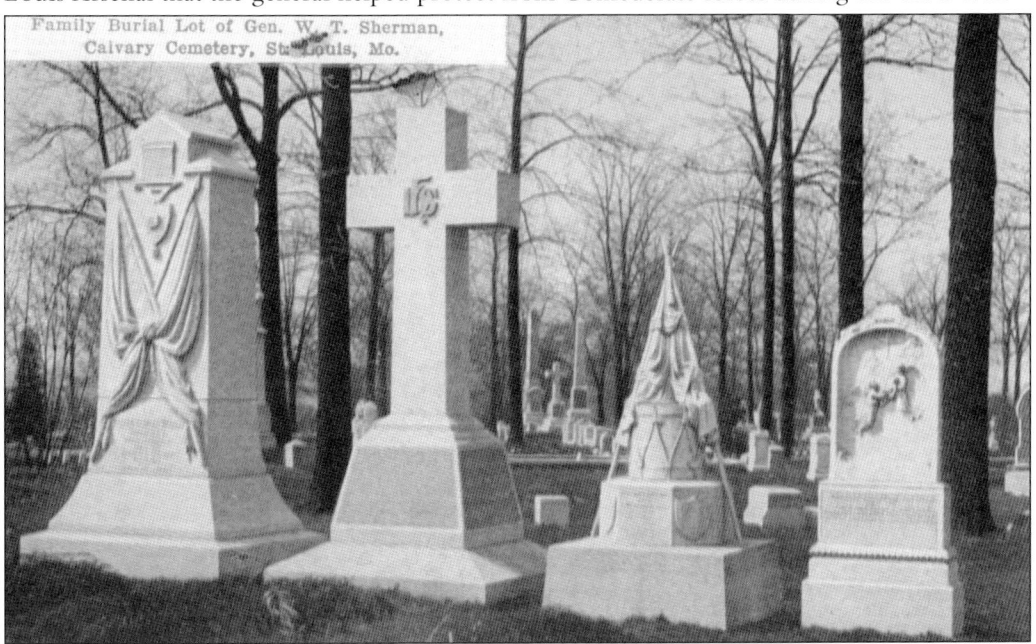

The St. Louis Post Card Company published this postcard of the family burial plot of Gen. William Tecumseh Sherman—a famous general who served in the Union army during the Civil War. On February 21, 1891, an estimated 12,000 soldiers, veterans, and other interested individuals were reported to have participated in a seven-mile funeral procession from downtown St. Louis to Calvary Cemetery, where Sherman was laid to rest.

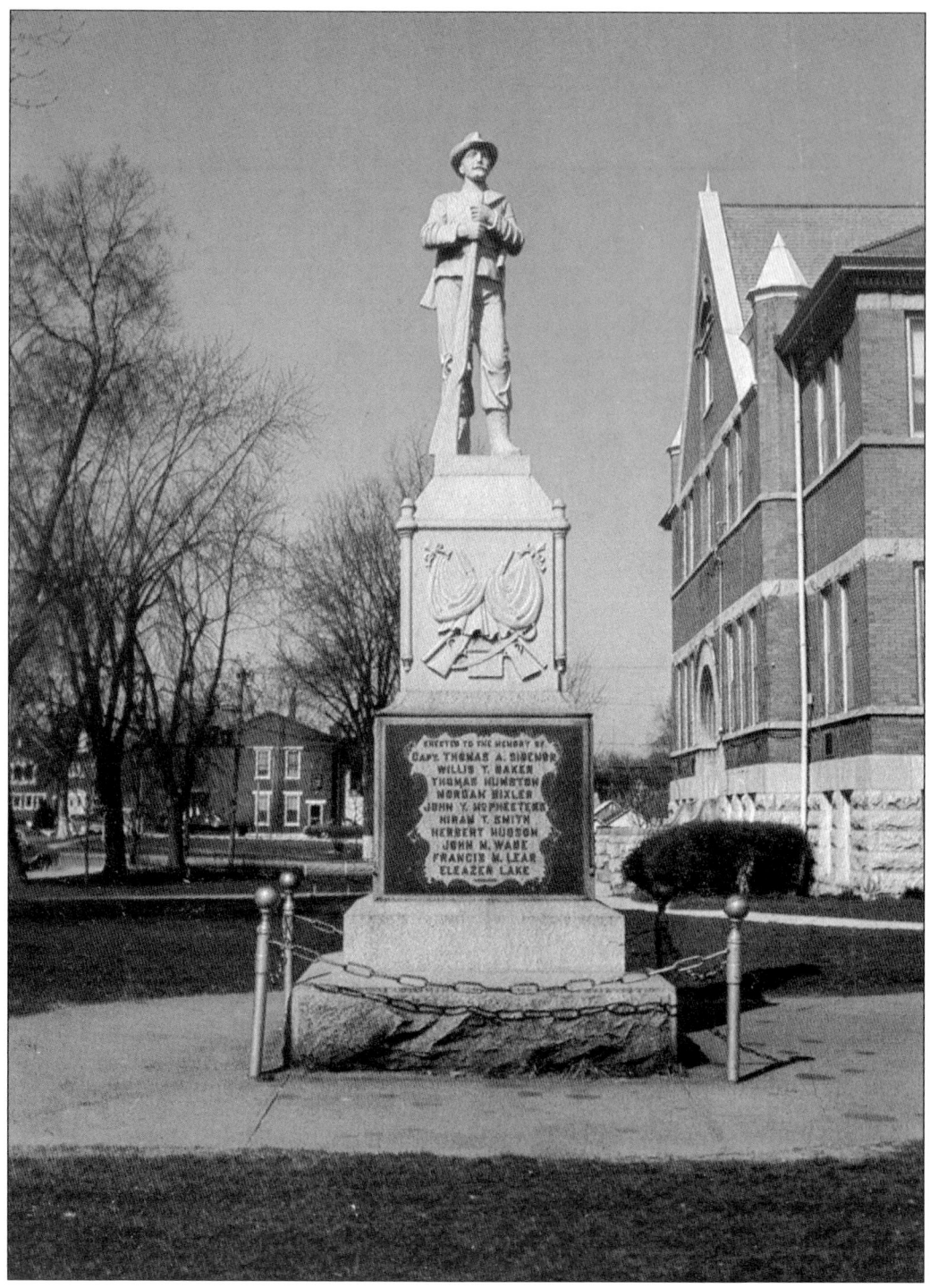

The B.B. Watson Company of Palmyra, Missouri, published this real-photo postcard of the Palmyra Massacre monument. Erected by the Palmyra Confederate Monument Association in 1907 outside the Marion County Courthouse, the monument commemorates the 10 Confederate prisoners who were executed by a Union army firing squad on October 18, 1862.

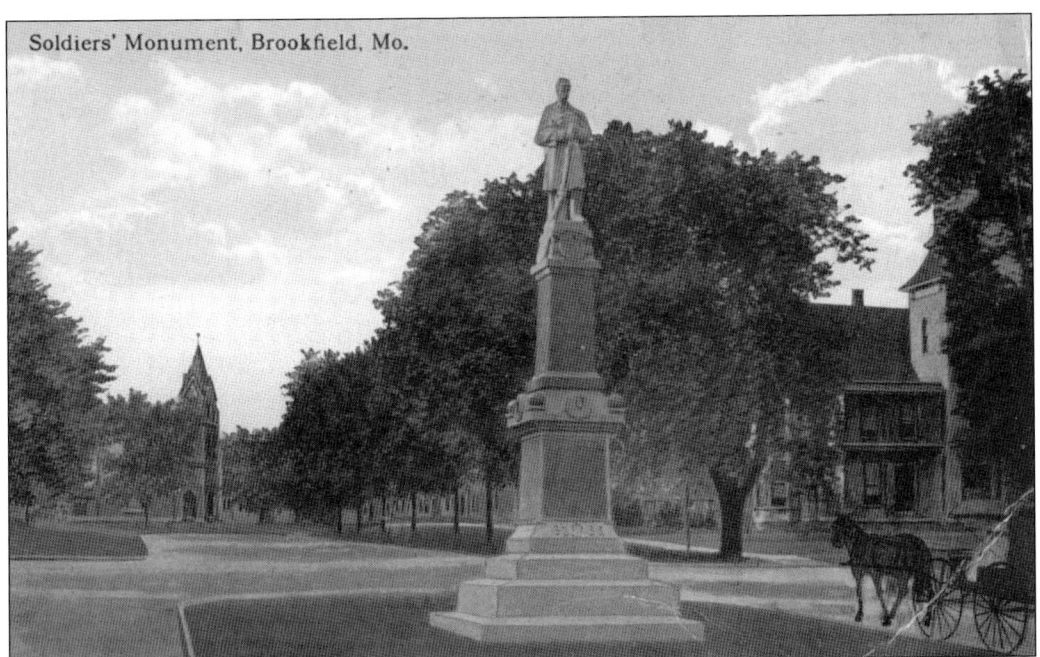

This postcard depicts a Civil War monument erected in the community of Brookfield. The Soldiers' Monument, situated in an area known as Twin Parks, was constructed in 1912 by D.L. Williams at the cost of $1,612. Made of Barre granite, the memorial features a Union soldier holding a rifle, and the statement "61-65 Lest We Forget" inscribed on the base.

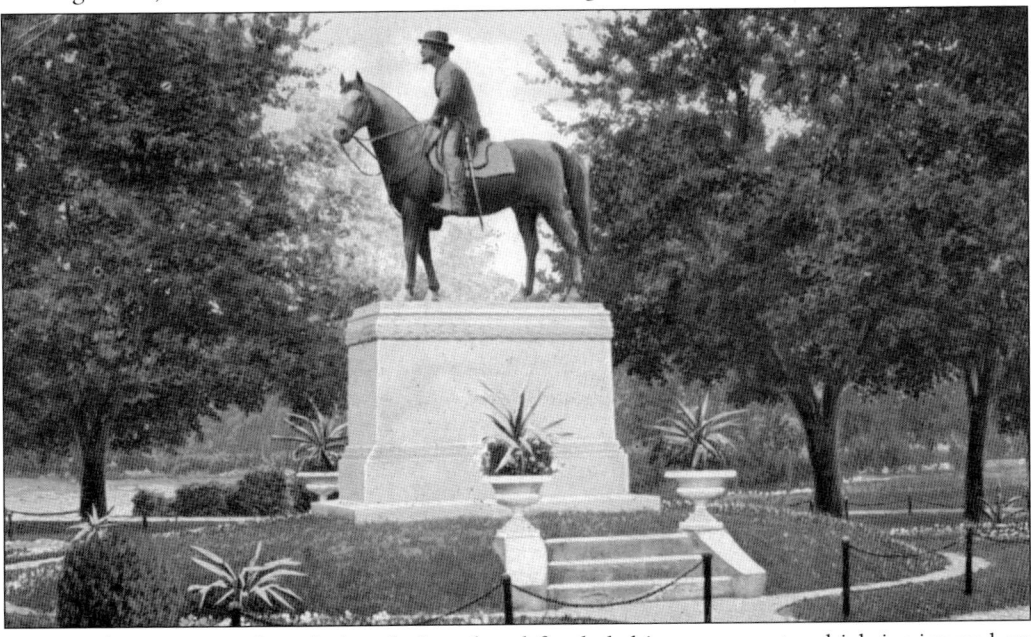

The Sigel Monument Association designed and funded this monument, which is pictured on this postcard printed in Germany for the S.M. Knox and Company, in St. Louis's Forest Park honoring the service of Gen. Franz Sigel. Born in Germany, Sigel later immigrated to the United States and served with the Union army during the Civil War, eventually rising to the rank of major general.

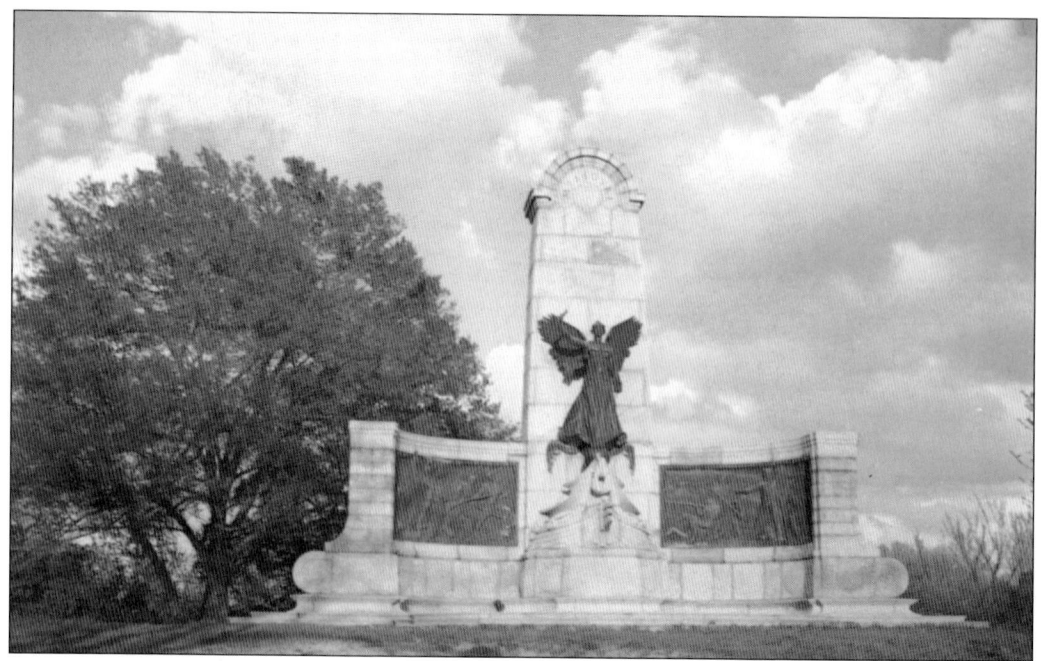

This postcard is of the Missouri Memorial in the Vicksburg National Military Park in Mississippi. Dedicated to the 27 Union units and 15 Confederate units from Missouri that clashed in battle at Vicksburg during the Civil War, the memorial was dedicated on October 17, 1917, and cost $40,000, which was paid for by the State of Missouri.

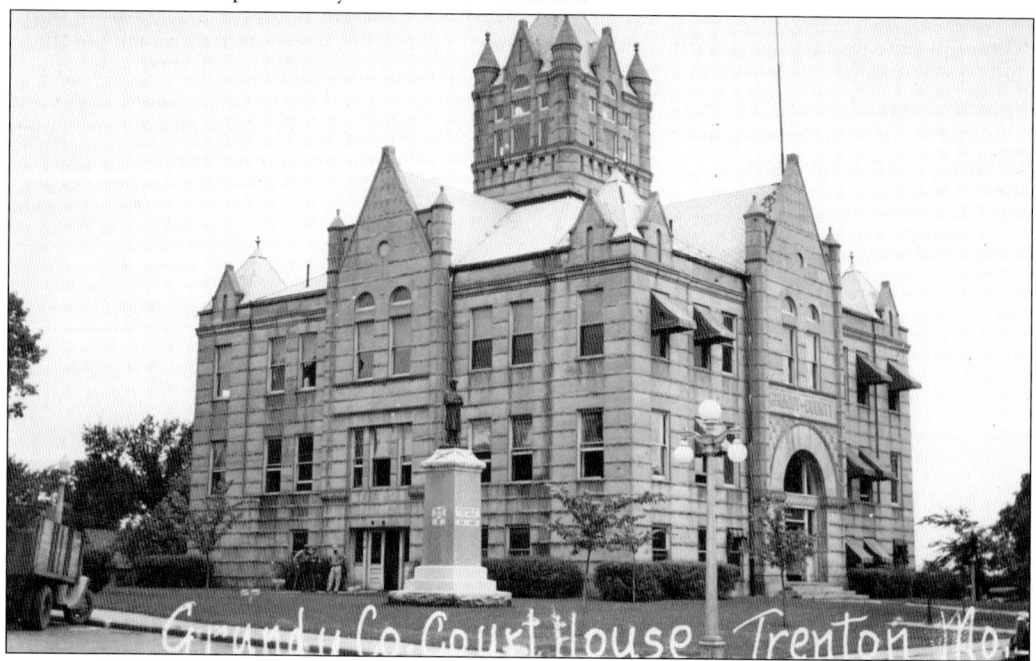

Situated on the grounds of the Grundy County Courthouse in Trenton is a memorial dedicated to the Union soldiers and sailors who served during the Civil War. The memorial was dedicated in 1916 by the citizens of Grundy County under the auspices of the Woman's Relief Corps—an auxiliary of the Grand Army of the Republic organization.

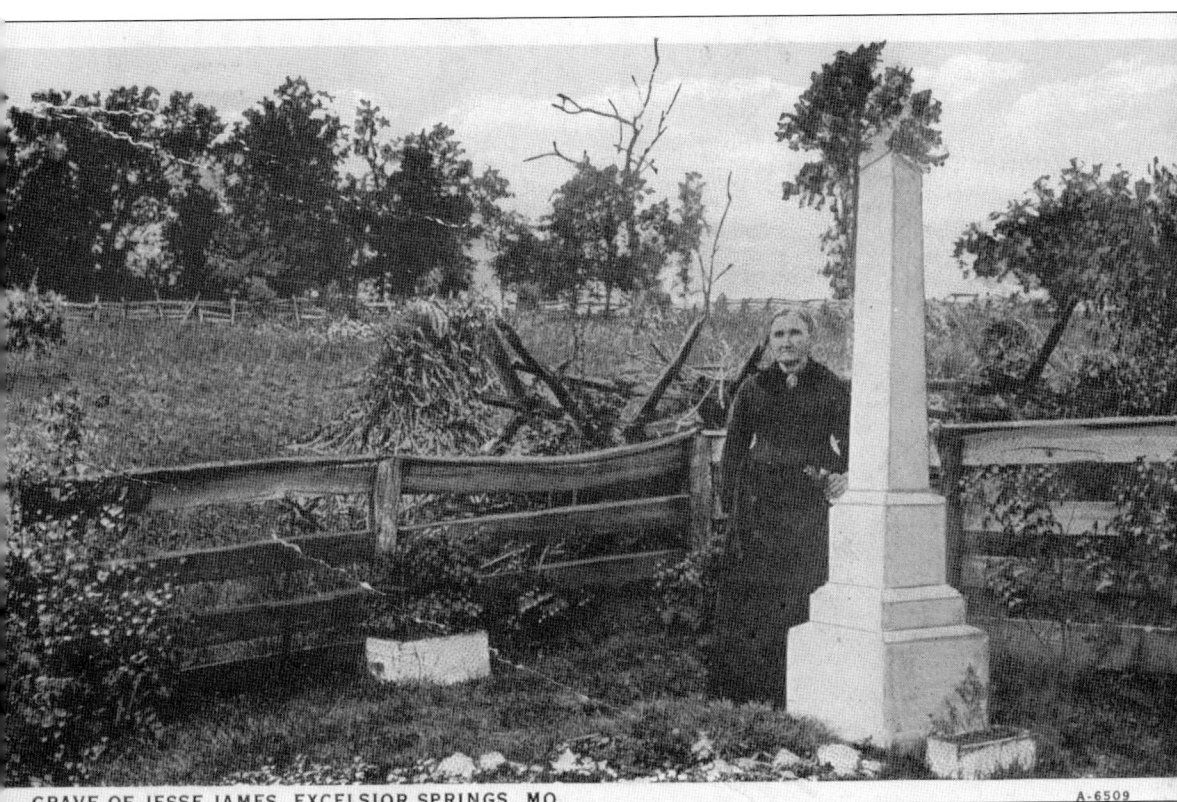

GRAVE OF JESSE JAMES, EXCELSIOR SPRINGS, MO.

Although Jesse James fought with Confederate guerrillas and was associated with such Southern sympathizers as William Quantrill and "Bloody Bill" Anderson during the Civil War, he gained a greater level of notoriety for his activities as an outlaw after the end of the war. This Curt Teich postcard, with a postmark of 1922, shows the original grave site of the famous outlaw on his family's farm; however, his grave was later moved to another site in Kearney.

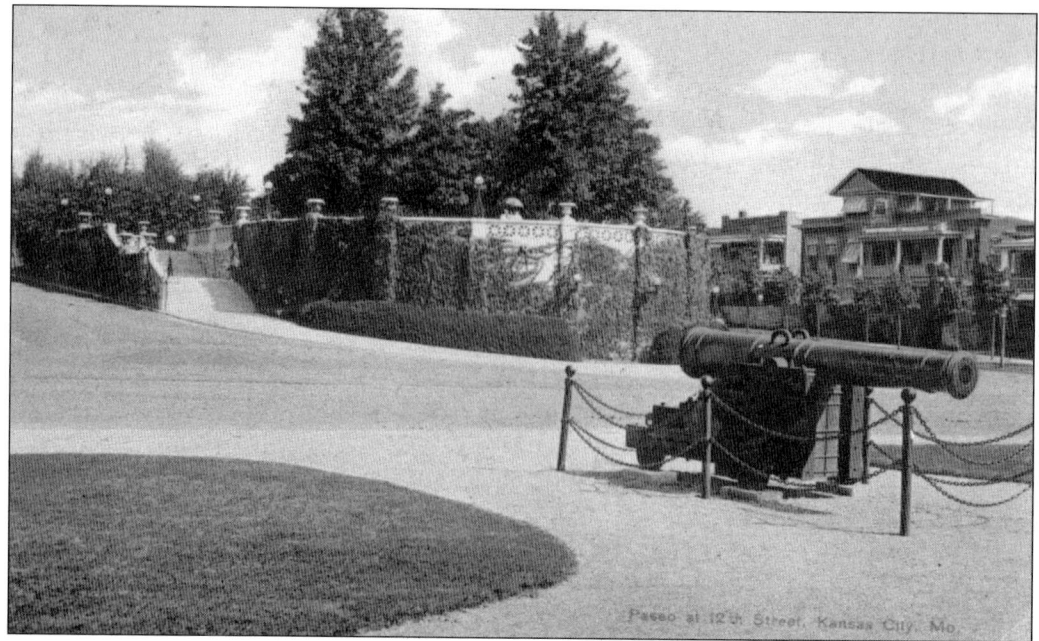

This litho-chrome postcard was made for the South-West News Company and features a Spanish cannon located in a park at Paseo and Twelfth Street in Kansas City. The 11-foot-long cannon was captured by the Navy during the Spanish-American War and was gifted by the United States government to the Kansas City Board of Park Commissioners on August 22, 1899.

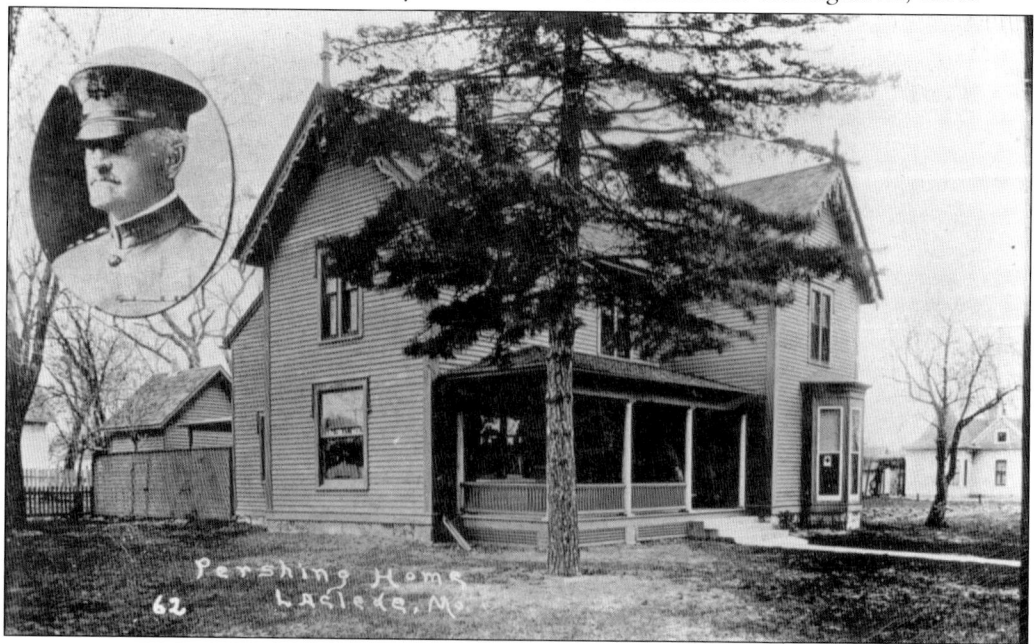

Pictured in this real-photo postcard is the boyhood home of Gen. John J. Pershing in Laclede. After leaving Laclede, Pershing went on to complete a 38-year military career that included command of the American Expeditionary Forces in World War I, eventually receiving promotion to the rank equivalent to a six-star general. His boyhood home is now part of the Gen. John J. Pershing Boyhood Home State Historic Site and is operated by the Missouri State Parks.

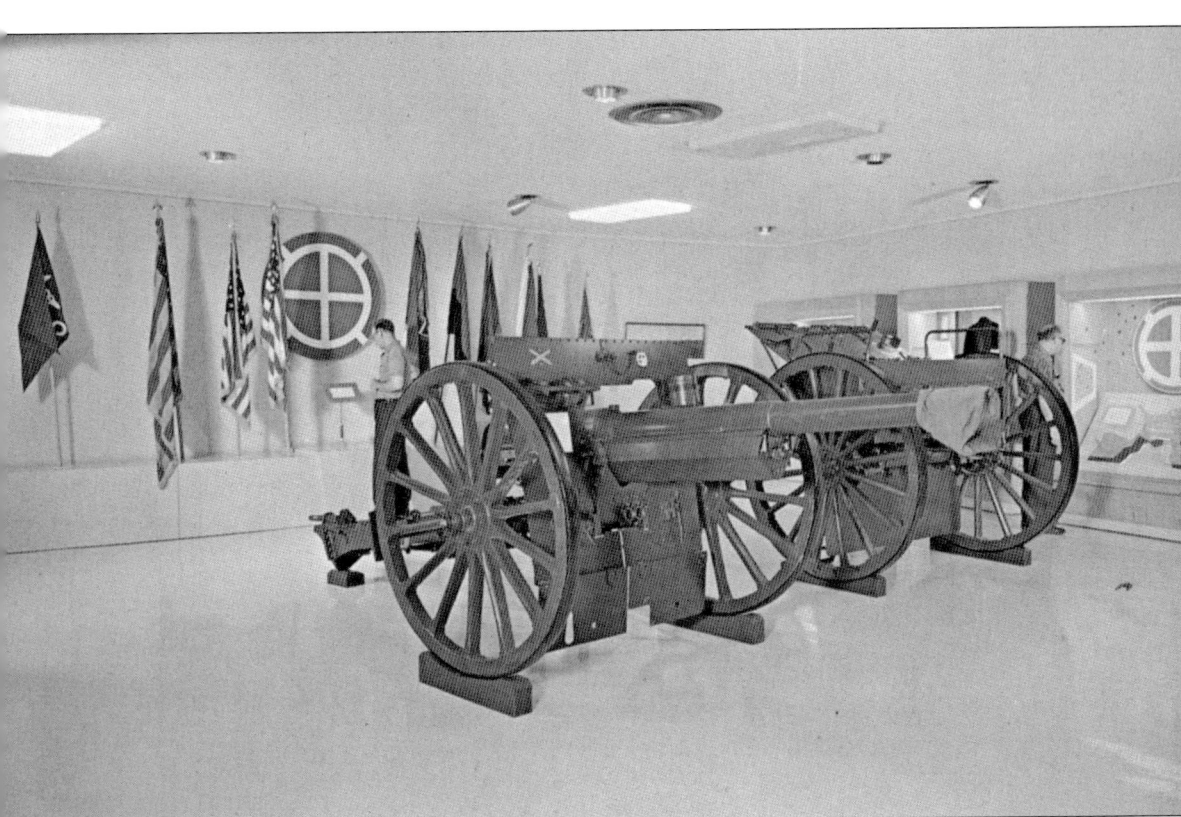

This vintage postcard shows one of the exhibits at the Harry S. Truman Library in Independence, which featured a French 75-mm artillery piece similar to type that Captain Truman would have fired while serving in World War I. During the war, the man who would become president served as commander of the Missouri National Guard's Battery D, 129th Field Artillery under the 35th Infantry Division.

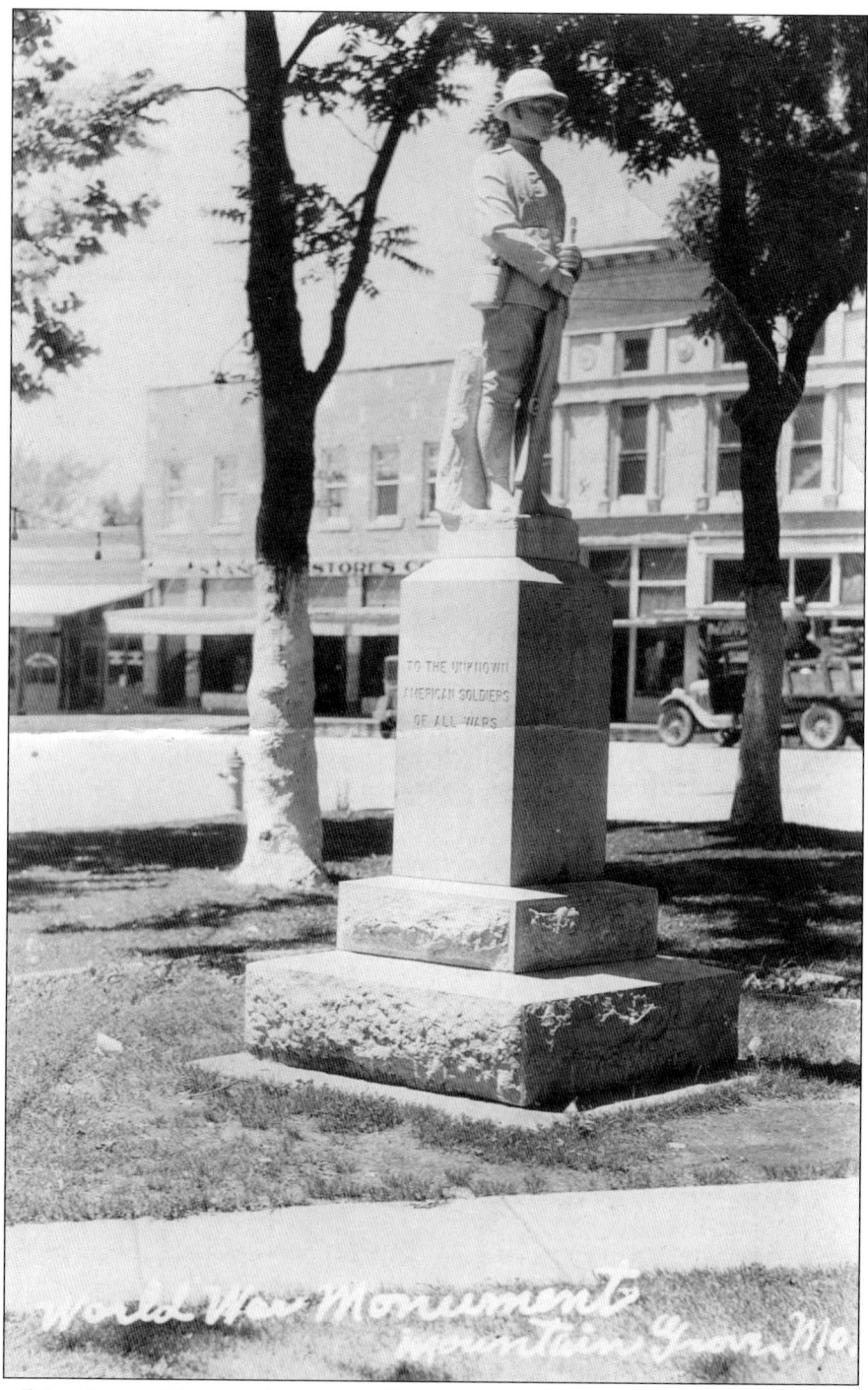

As part of the County Memorial Act passed by the state legislature in 1919, many communities throughout Missouri erected monuments to honor their local citizens who served in World War I. One such memorial exists in Mountain Grove, as is pictured on this real-photo postcard. The monument features a doughboy with the inscription "To the unknown American soldiers of all wars" and lists the names of local residents killed during the war.

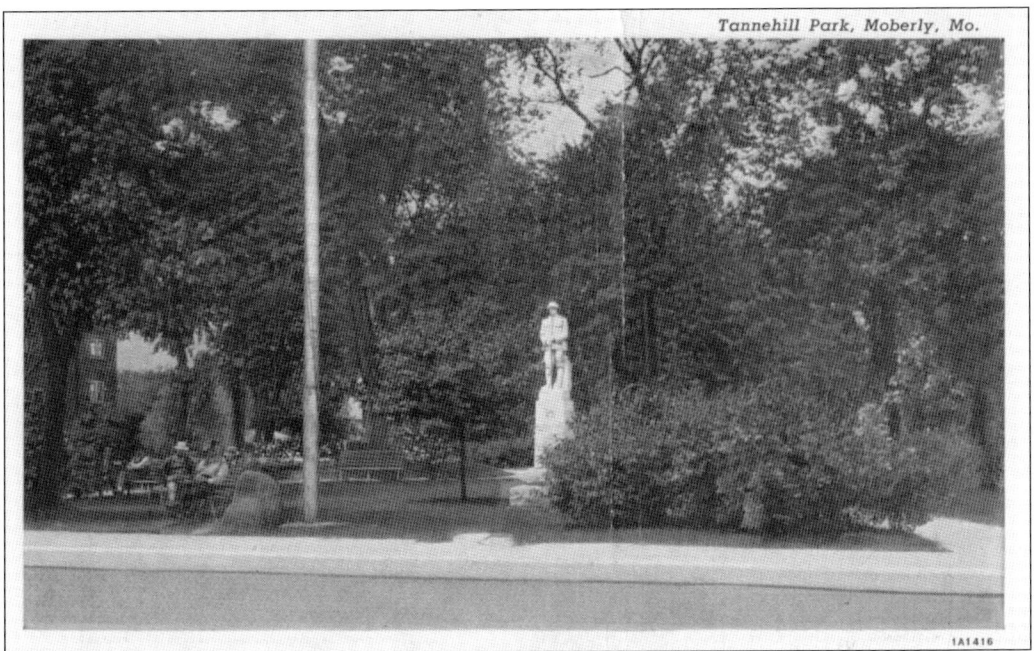

On November 11, 1927, in Moberly, the Tabitha Walton Chapter of the Daughters of the American Revolution dedicated a white marble statue of a World War I doughboy in Tannehill Park. Honoring the World War I dead of Randolph County, the statue was relocated to Rothwell Park in 1966 to make room for construction of a post office and is now situated in proximity to other memorials, including one dedicated to the memory of a Moberly-area native, Gen. Omar Bradley.

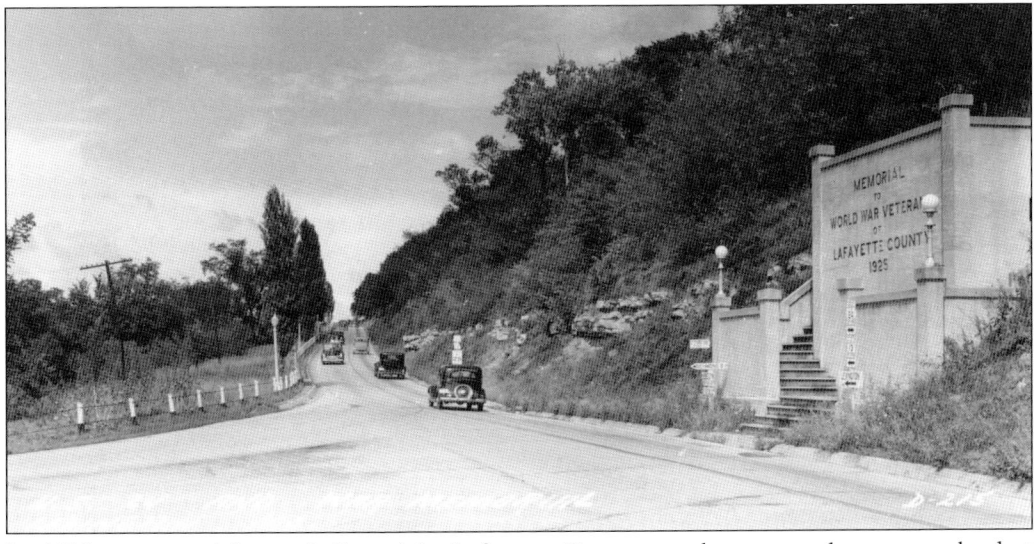

In 1925, a memorial was dedicated in Lafayette County to the men and women who lost their lives in World War I. The memorial, which is along Highway 224, appears to have been constructed in an odd location but is situated at a spot where it once greeted visitors as they crossed the former Lexington Bridge. The bridge was removed and replaced by the Ike Skelton Bridge in 2005, which is two miles east of this location. Behind the memorial is a span of stairs leading to Highland Avenue.

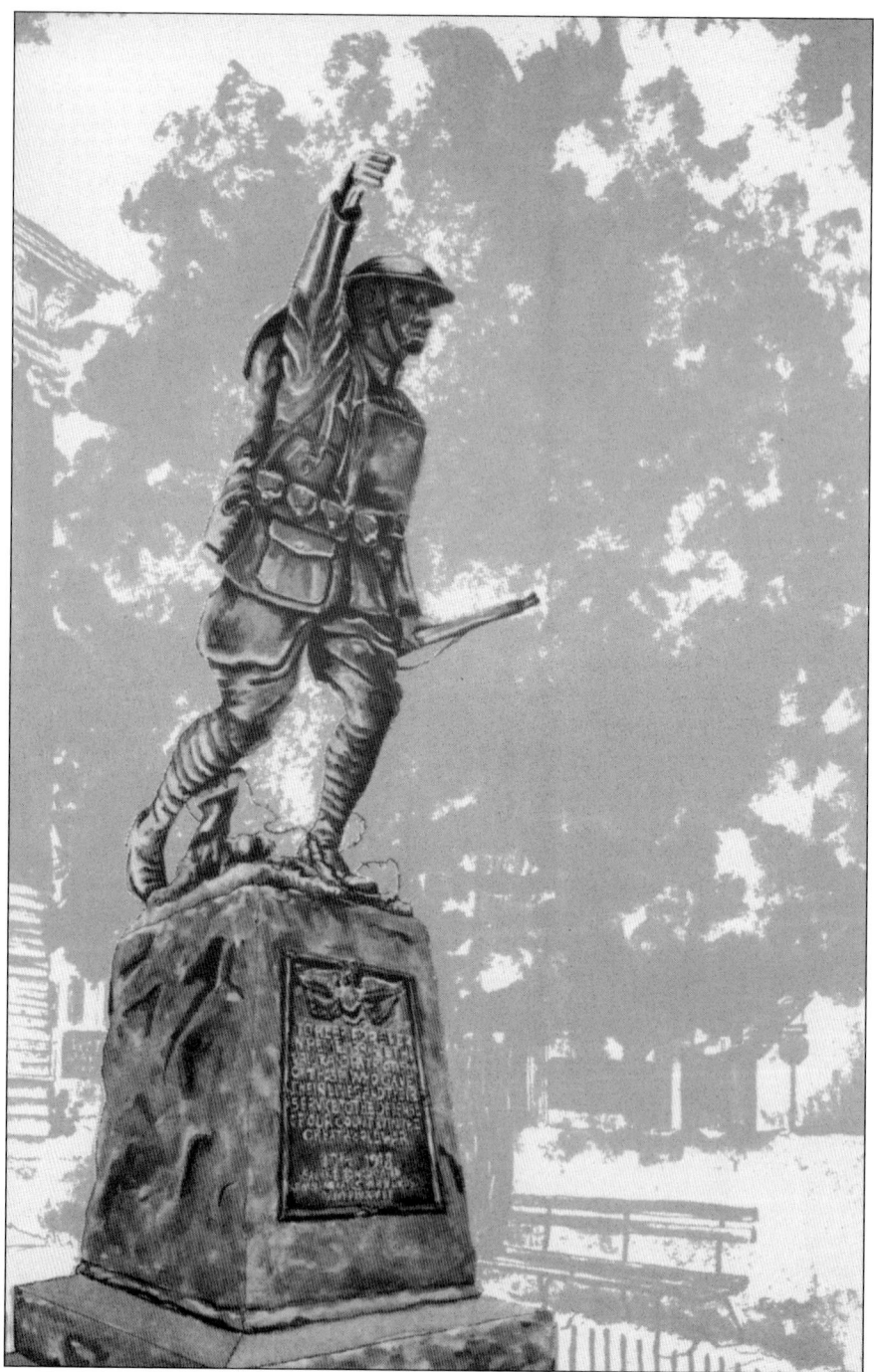
The Saline County World War I Doughboy Memorial, located on the grounds of the Saline County Courthouse in Marshall, was unveiled on October 12, 1927. The bronze memorial depicts an American soldier, with barbed wire tangled around his left foot and ankle, holding a rifle in his left hand and raising his right hand in the form of a clenched fist. The soldier is also carrying a bedroll and day pack and is wearing a cartridge belt with a canteen and bayonet scabbard attached.

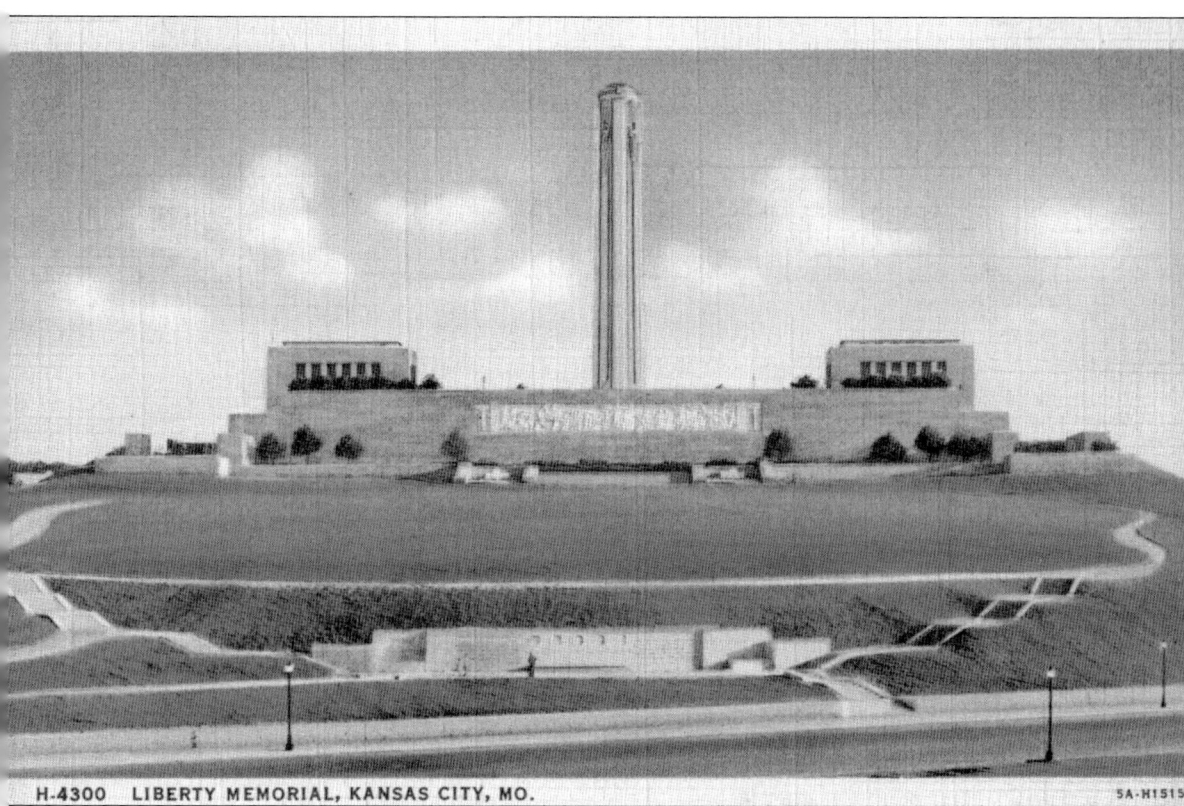

H-4300 LIBERTY MEMORIAL, KANSAS CITY, MO.

Designed by Harold Van Buren Magonigle—an American architect best known for his work on memorials—the Liberty Memorial sits on a hill overlooking Union Station in Kansas City. In 1919, the Liberty Memorial Association and citizens of Kansas City raised, in just 10 days, more than $2.5 million to build the memorial, the site of which was dedicated in 1921. In 1926, the completed memorial was dedicated by Pres. Calvin Coolidge with an estimated 150,000 people in attendance.

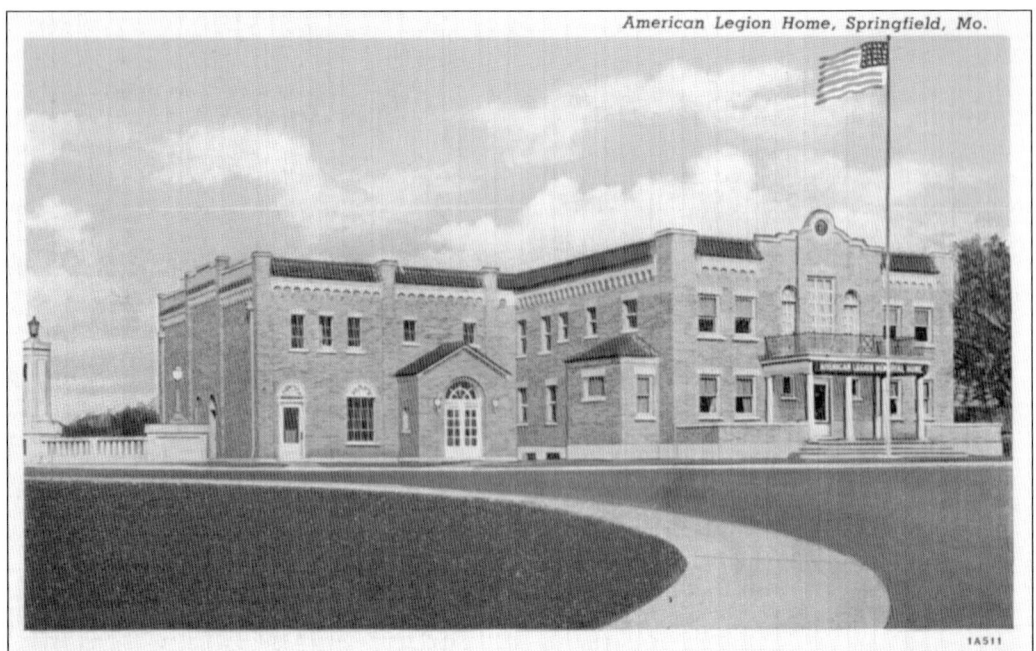

This Curt Teich postcard features the American Legion Memorial Home in Springfield, which was dedicated in 1930 with World War I hero Sgt. Alvin C. York in attendance. In later years, the home was divided into two separate American Legion Posts and is now known as the American Legion Goad-Ballinger Post 69. This American Legion home is one of the oldest in the state, and the building was designated as a historical landmark in 1987.

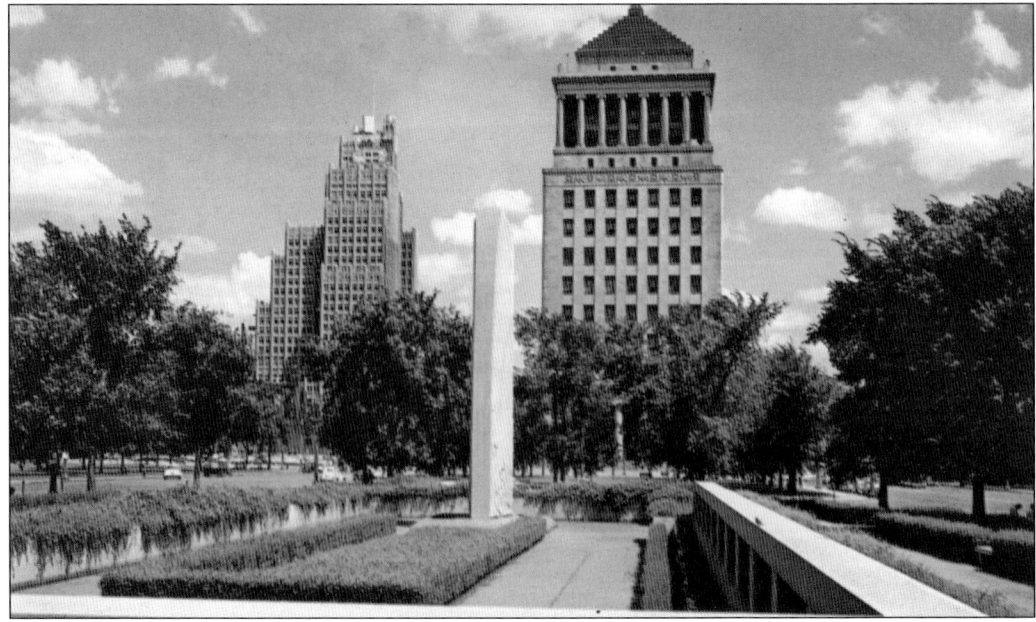

The World War II Court of Honor located in front of the Soldiers Memorial in downtown St. Louis features a 40-foot limestone pillar designed in the shape of a broken blade with low-relief figures of soldiers in battle. Dedicated in 1948 and sculpted by artist Hillis Arnold, the memorial was a gift to the City of St. Louis by the St. Louis War Memorial Committee.

A tetricolor postcard published by James Tetirick features a memorial by the Campo-Manfre-Barbieri American Legion Post 151 in Kansas City to Pres. John F. Kennedy—a fellow American Legion member, as is noted on the memorial. Dedicated on May 29, 1965, the memorial consists of a vertical sandstone slab on a limestone base with a bronze profile of the late president and is located in the Concourse on Benton Boulevard.

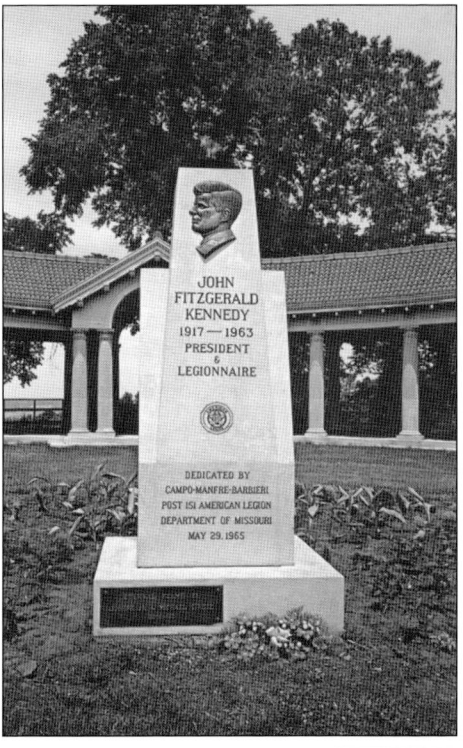

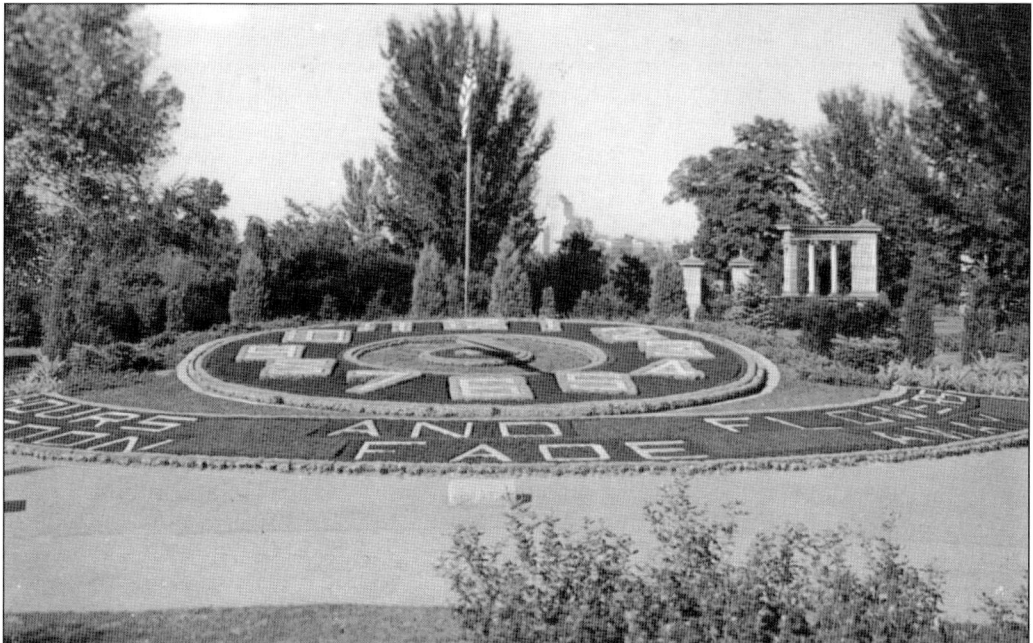

This lusterchrome postcard by Tichnor Brothers, Inc., shows the Korean War Memorial in Forest Park in St. Louis as it appeared shortly after its dedication on July 2, 1951. The memorial consisted of a large floral clock that was more than 35 feet in diameter and contained 25,000 flowers. In 1989, a 10-foot-tall working sundial was installed as a tribute to the Americans who never returned home from the war.

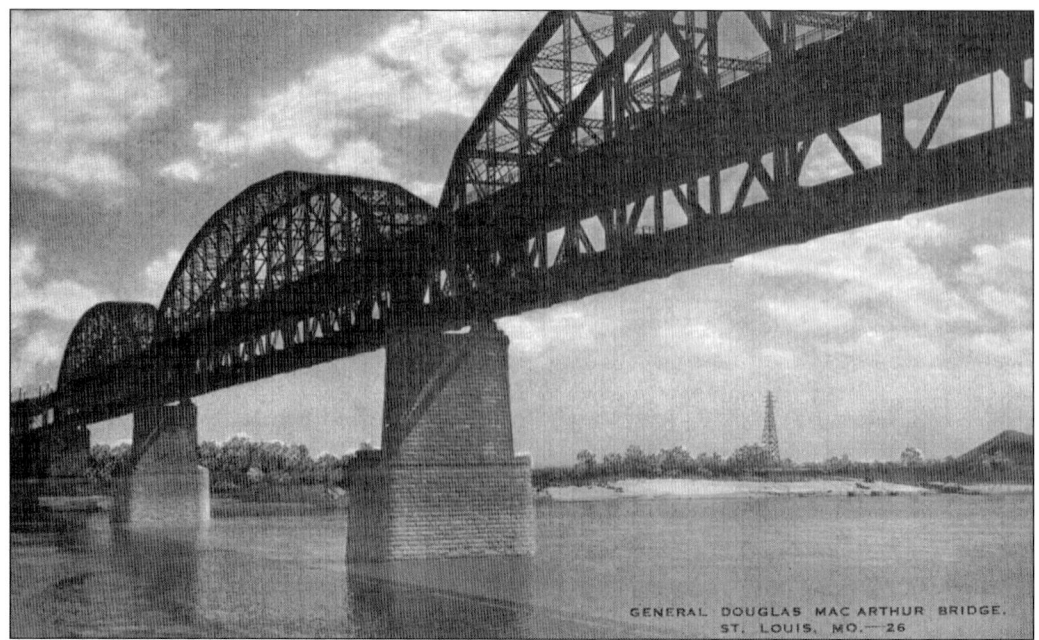

The General Douglas MacArthur Bridge, pictured in this linen postcard, crosses the Mississippi River between St. Louis, Missouri, and East St. Louis, Illinois. The bridge opened in 1917 as the St. Louis Municipal Bridge but was renamed in honor of Douglas MacArthur—a five-star general of World War II—in 1942. The bridge is no longer open to automobile traffic and is used exclusively by the railroad system.

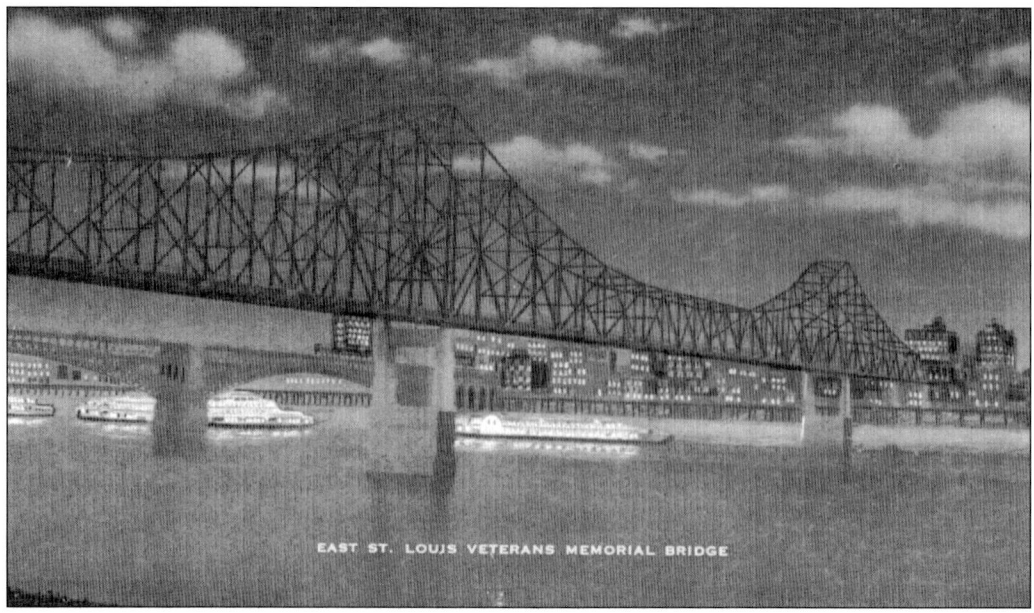

The St. Louis Greeting Card Company published this linen postcard of the Veterans Memorial Bridge. Built in 1951 at a cost of $11 million, it spanned the Mississippi River between St. Louis, Missouri, and East St. Louis, Illinois. The bridge was renamed the Martin Luther King Bridge in 1968 following the assassination of the civil rights leader. Pictured in the background is the historic Eads Bridge.

Four

ARMORIES, BUILDINGS, AND SERVICE ORGANIZATIONS

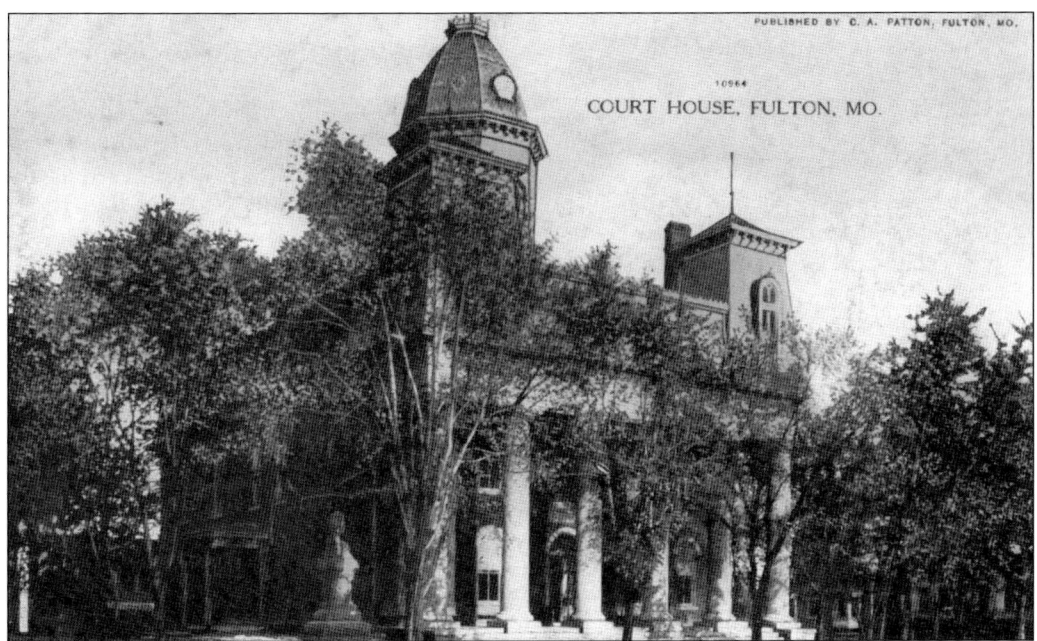

The third Callaway County Courthouse is featured in this postcard published by C.A. Patton; this courthouse has since been demolished and replaced. Once located on the town square in Fulton, the courthouse was built by Alfred Moore in 1856 for $20,000. In April 1861, the courthouse became the site of a local rally after war was declared and Missouri governor Claiborne Fox Jackson announced he would not provide troops to the federal government. During the Civil War, Callaway County remained essentially pro-Southern and raised a company of troops known as the Callaway Guards.

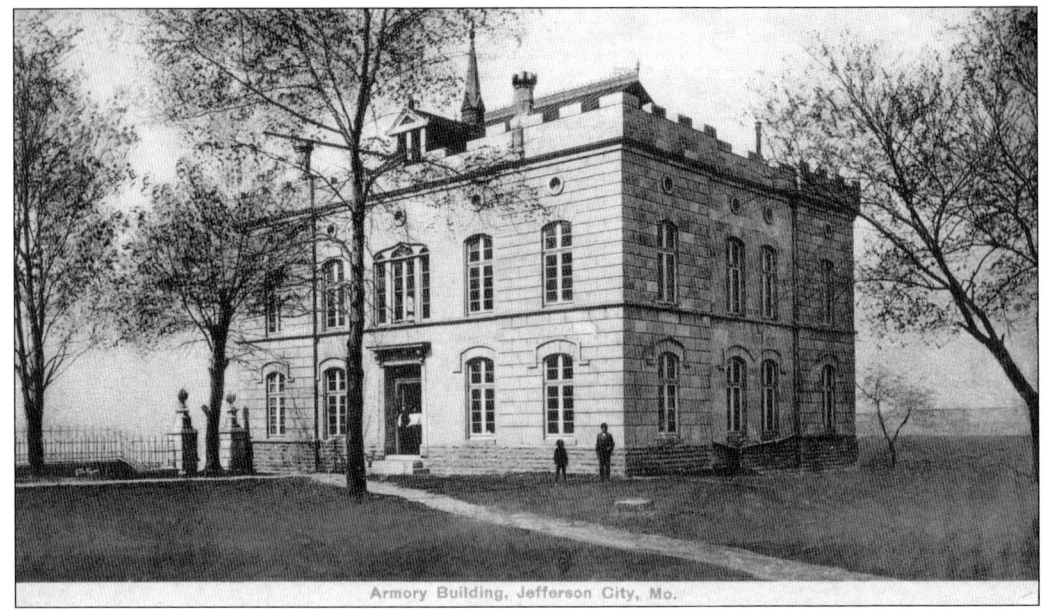

Published by Samuel H. Smith & Company, this postcard highlights the state armory that once stood on the grounds of the state capitol. Built as an arsenal in 1863, the armory became the headquarters for the state militia (later known as the National Guard). After the state capitol burned down in 1911, the armory was used to store construction supplies for the rebuilding. In 1919, the building was sold to the Pope Construction Company for $225 and demolished.

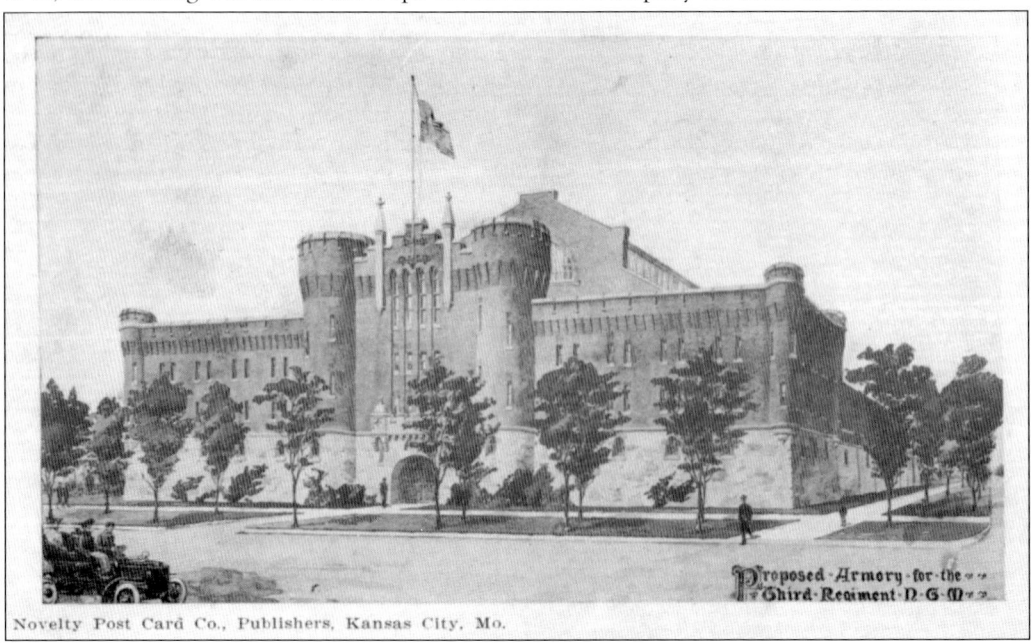

This postcard shows the proposed armory for Third Regiment of the Missouri National Guard, although this armory was never constructed. The regiment's commander, Col. Cusil Lechtman, began stumping for a new armory in 1909 since the current armory was perceived as inadequate and outdated. A special municipal bond election was held in early 1910 but failed to garner the necessary votes to authorize the construction.

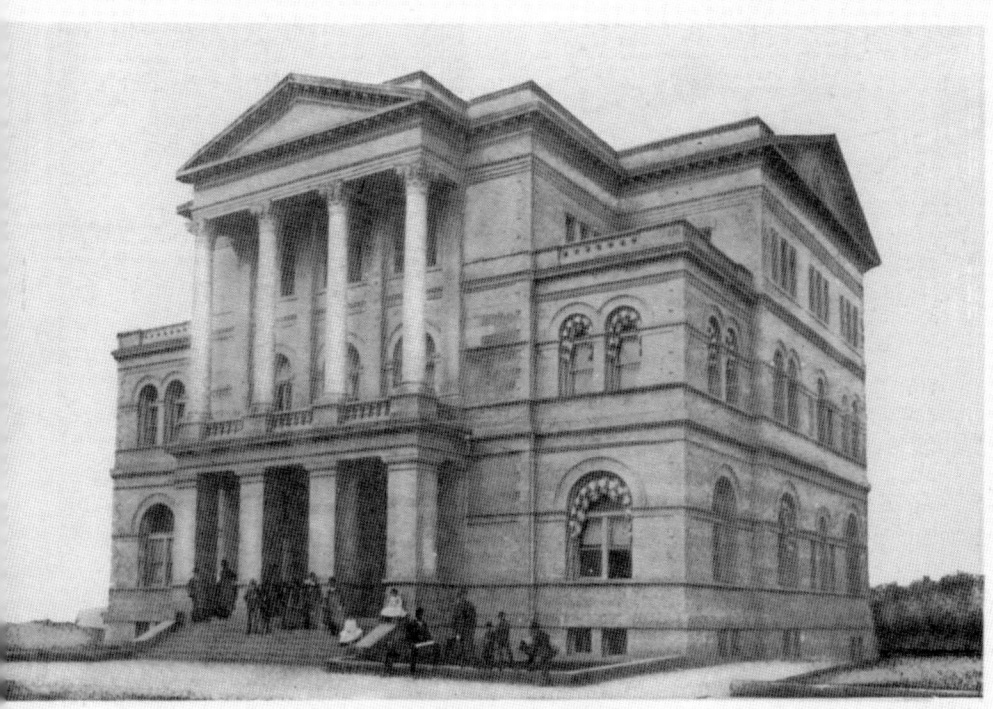

FEDERAL COURT AND POST OFFICE.

The Federal Court and Post Office featured in this postcard once stood on the south side of the state capitol grounds in Jefferson City. Built in 1884, the building was purchased by the state in 1930 for the sum of $1 and acquired its military connection in the 1950s when it served as the headquarters of the Missouri National Guard. The building was torn down in 1972 because of advanced deterioration of plumbing, wiring, and the roof's steel beams.

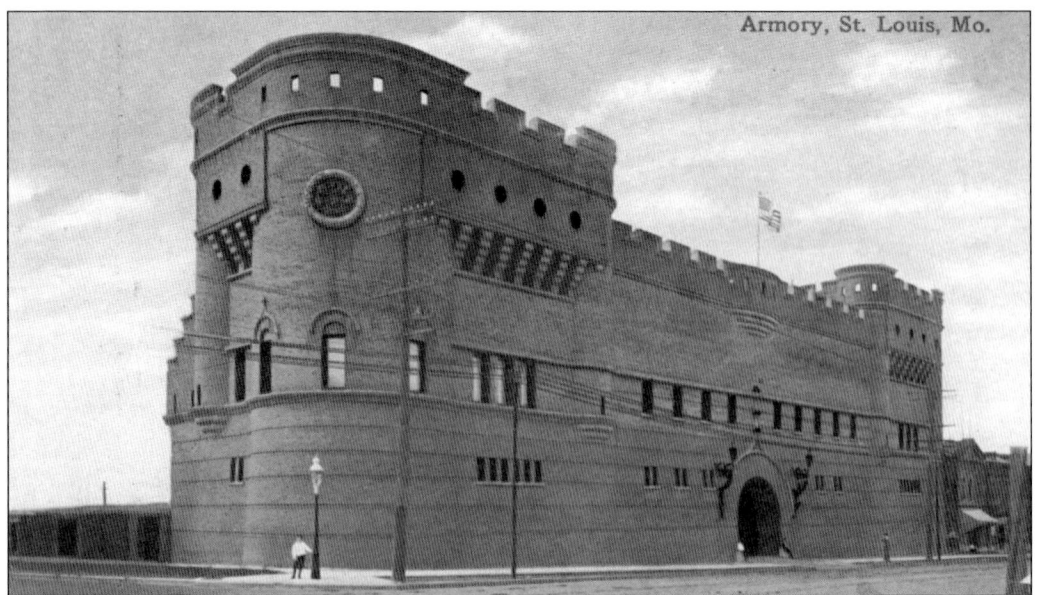

In this divided back postcard published by the Majestic Publishing Company is the armory of the St. Louis Light Artillery Armory Association, which was financed through funds donated by citizens in St. Louis. Dedicated in December 1908, the armory was situated on a lot on 1221 South Grand Avenue. The armory cost an estimated $100,000 to construct and was used by Battery A of the Missouri National Guard. The armory passed from existence when it was demolished in 1960.

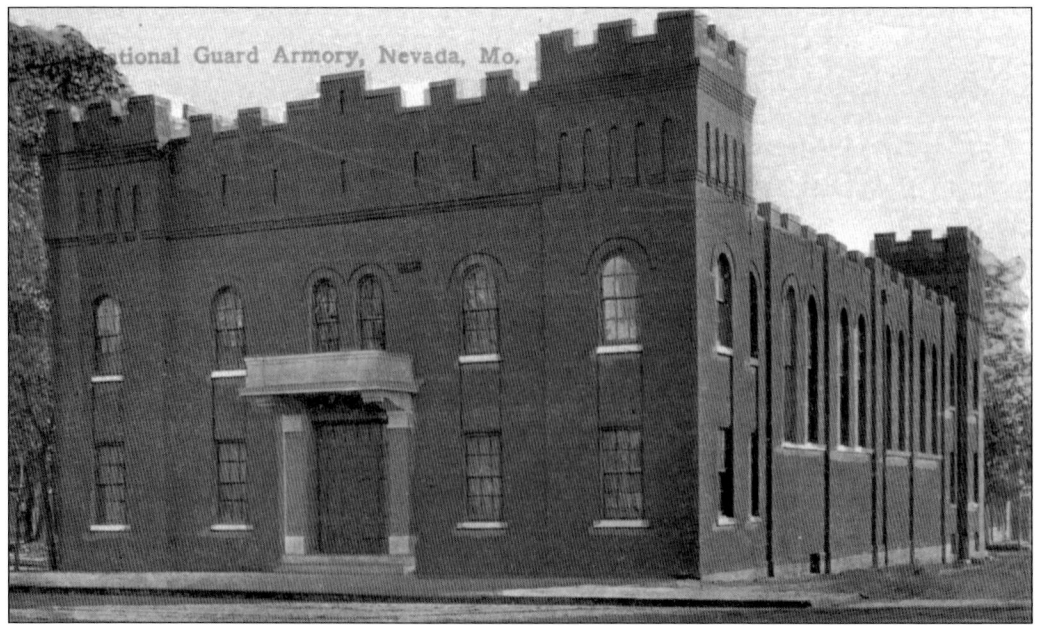

The S&W Company of Nevada, Missouri, published this divided back postcard of the castellated armory built in 1909. As was the situation with the Battery A armory in St. Louis, the Nevada armory was built from a subscription of funds from private donors. After the National Guard moved to nearby Camp Clark, the vacated building became home to American Legion Post 2.

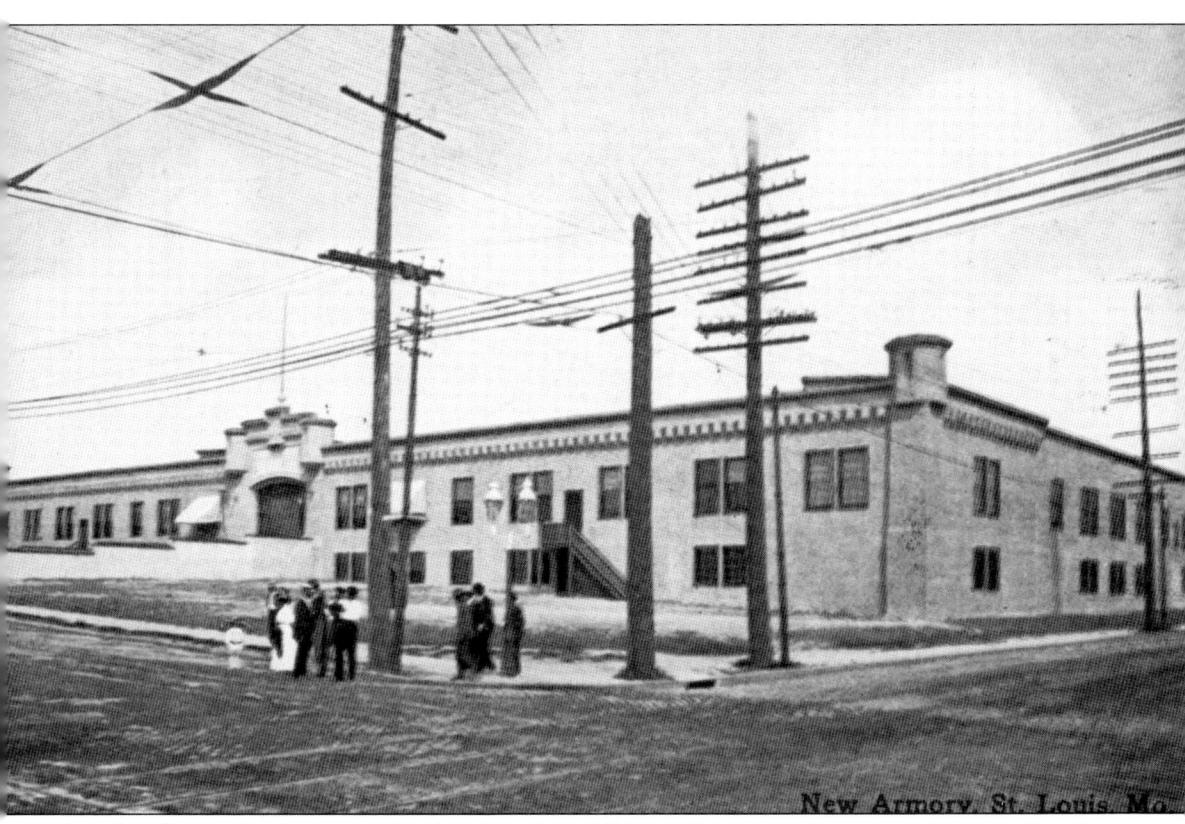

Another divided back postcard by the Majestic Publishing Company pictures another castellated armory in St. Louis that was built from private funds—this one was completed and occupied in 1908 and belonged to the First Regiment of the Missouri National Guard. The armory was constructed at a cost of $100,000 along Grand, Manchester, and Clark Avenues but was demolished in 1939 after the National Guard took possession of a new armory built at Spring Avenue and Market Street.

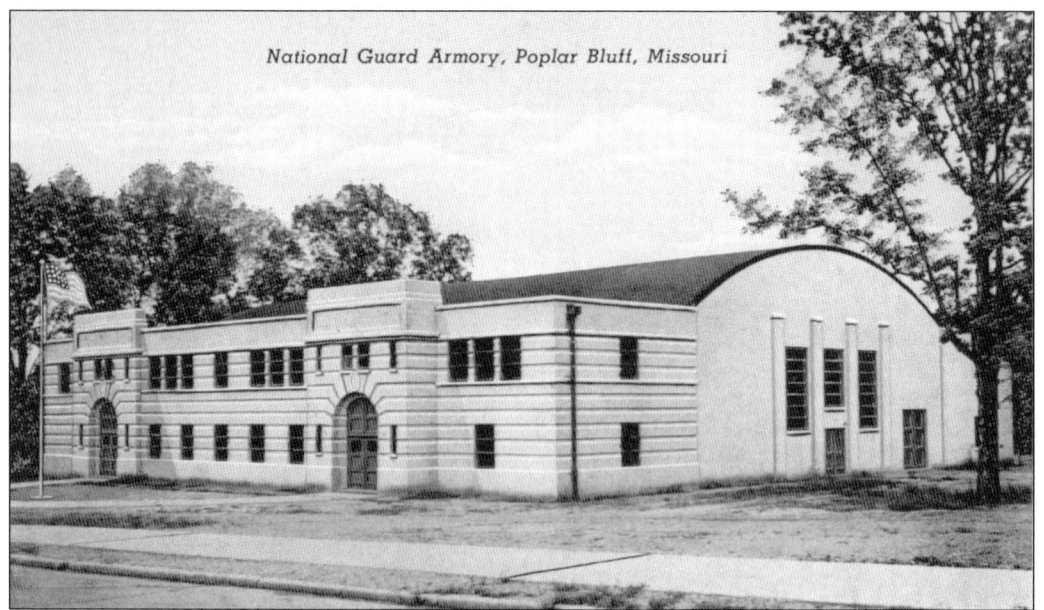

The original National Guard Armory in Poplar Bluff, as featured on this postcard by E.F. Nelson Novelty Company, was completed in 1942 as a project under the work-relief program known as the Works Progress Administration. The armory served the Missouri National Guard until the late 1990s, at which time a new armory was constructed. The building is currently being used by the Poplar Bluff R-1 School District.

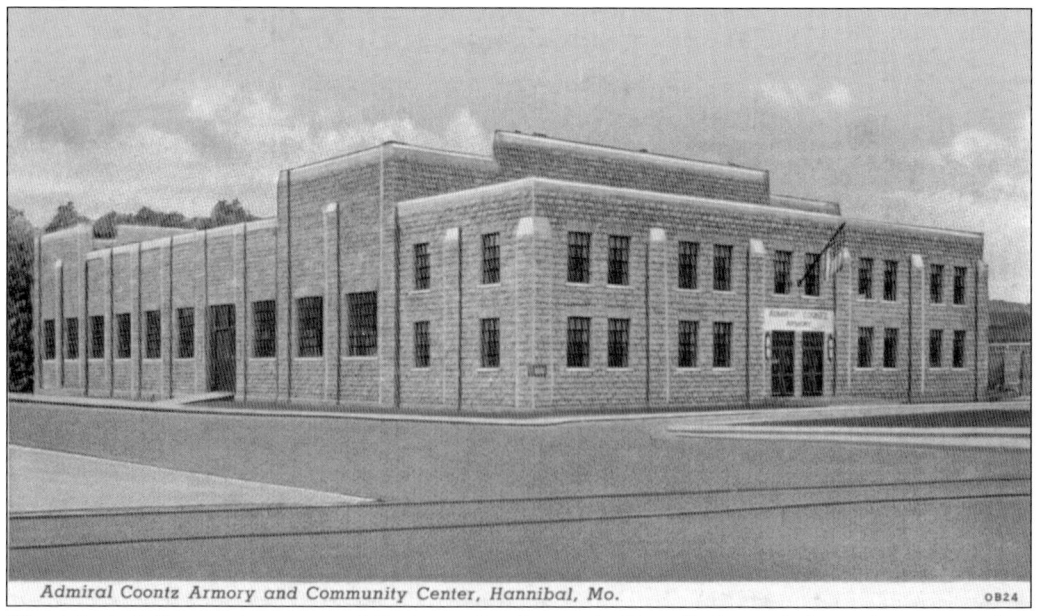

The Admiral Coontz Armory and Community Center in Hannibal was dedicated on November 4, 1939, during a ceremony at which Missouri governor Lloyd C. Stark was the main speaker. Built at the approximate cost of $170,000, the armory was one of several Works Progress Administration projects in the state and served as home to the Missouri National Guard's Company L, 138th Infantry. The armory now serves the community as the Admiral Coontz Recreation Center.

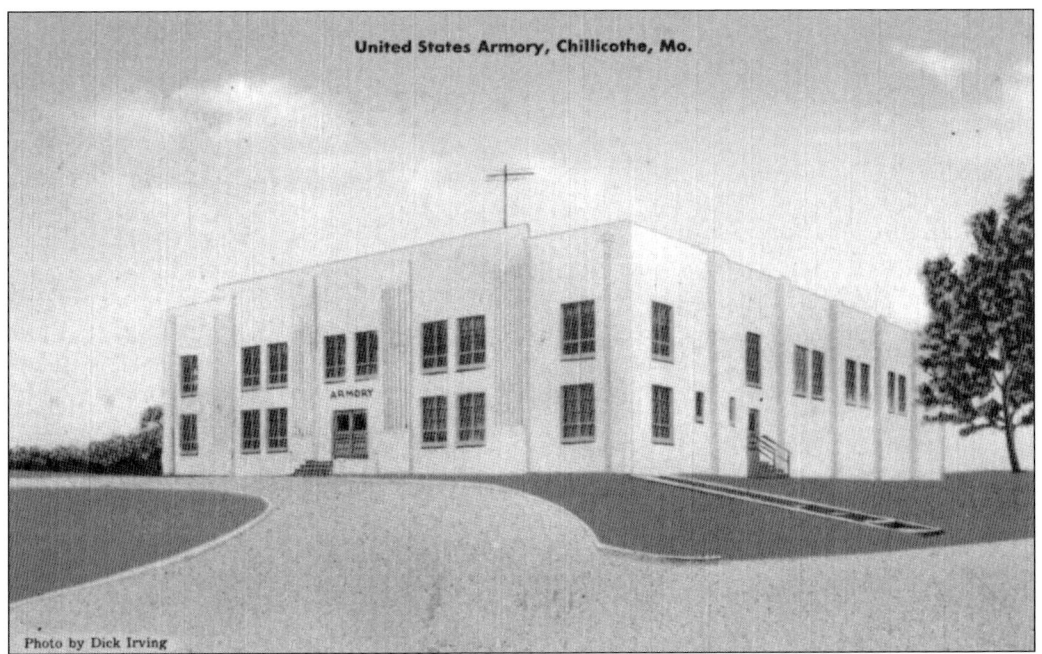

This linen postcard features the National Guard armory in Chillicothe, which was dedicated during a ceremony held on November 7, 1940. The armory became the ninth to be built in the state in the 3.5 years preceding its dedication. It once housed a detachment of the 35th Signal Company of the 35th Infantry Division.

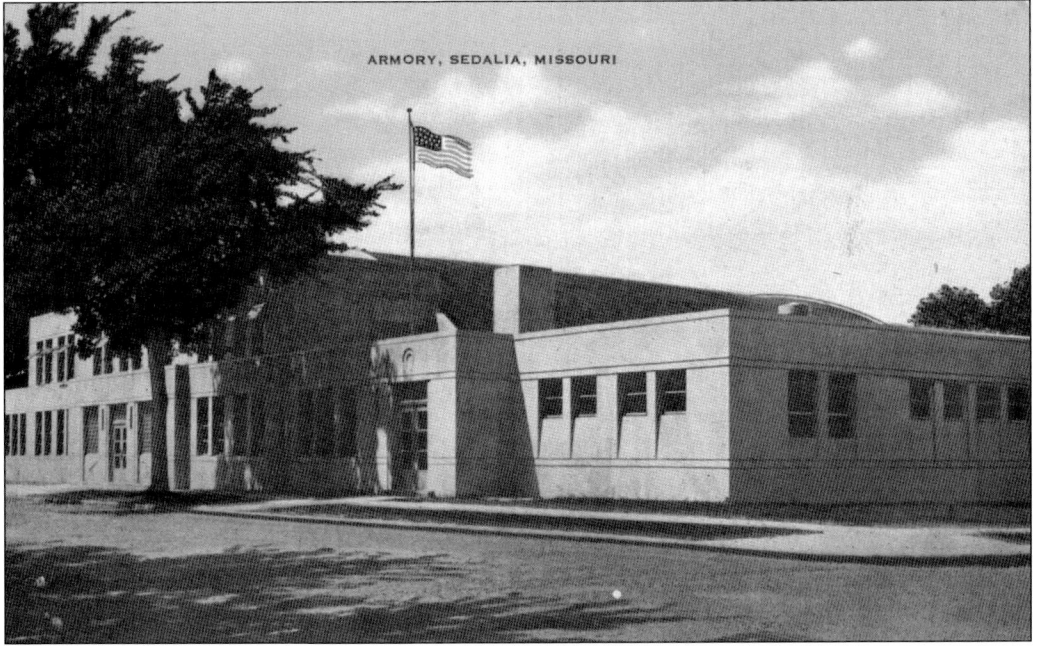

The Central News Agency published this postcard of the Missouri National Guard armory in Sedalia, which underwent construction in 1940 as a Works Progress Administration project. The armory remained in use for several decades but was sold after the Missouri National Guard moved to their new armory location at the Missouri State Fairgrounds in 2003.

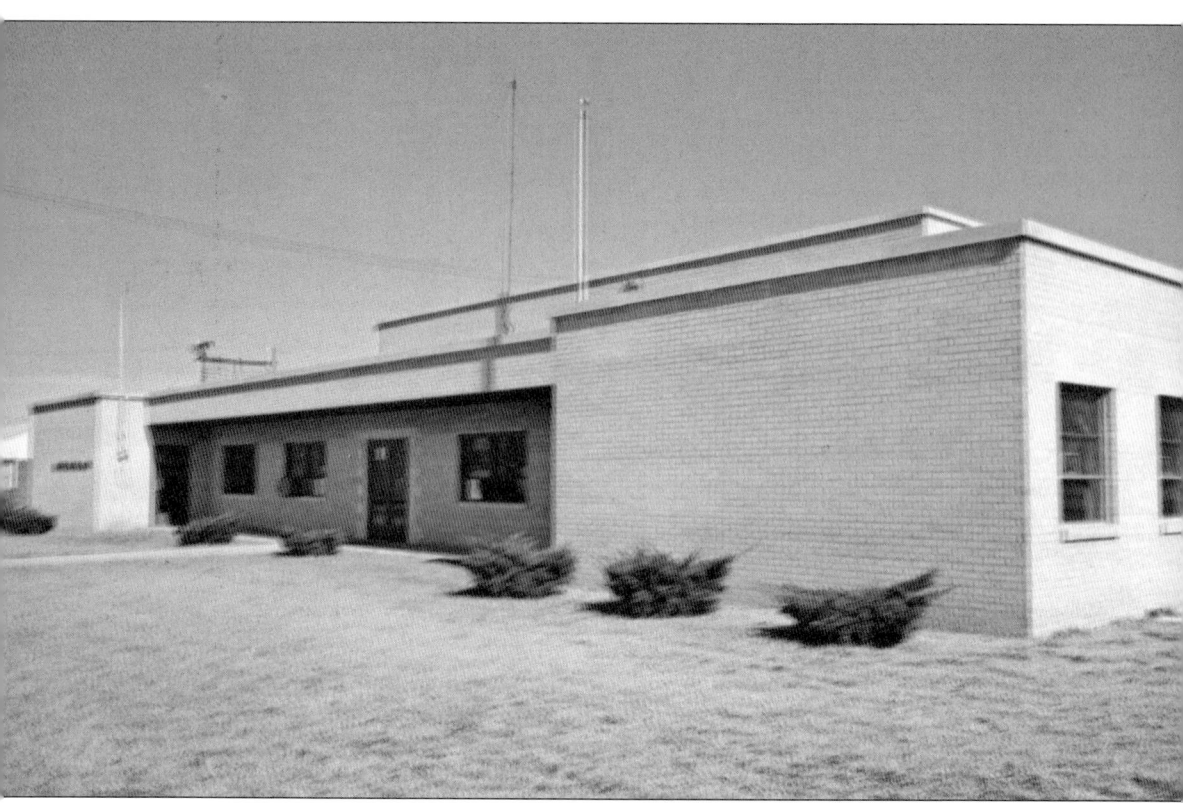

The National Guard armory in the southwest Missouri community of Lamar, pictured in this postcard by the W.C. Pine Company of Raytown, was built in 1958 at 106 Broadway Street as part of a program that authorized federal assistance for new armory construction. The Cold War–era armory continues to be used by the Missouri National Guard.

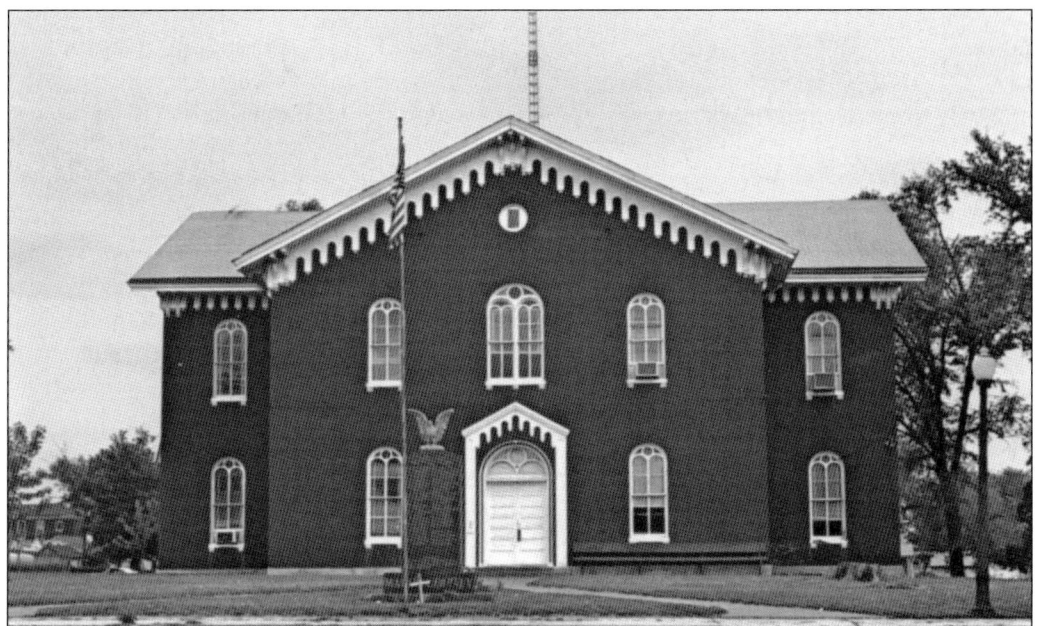

Prior to the outbreak of the Civil War, the courthouse for Macon County was located in Bloomington. During the Civil War, Union general Lewis Merrill ordered the community of Bloomington to be burned because of their Southern sympathies. Instead, Maj. Thomas Moody lobbied to have the county seat moved to Macon, which occurred through an act of the legislature in 1863. The Macon County Courthouse was erected in 1864–1865 for approximately $30,000. As can be seen in this postcard, in front of the courthouse is a memorial dedicated to county residents who lost their lives in World War I.

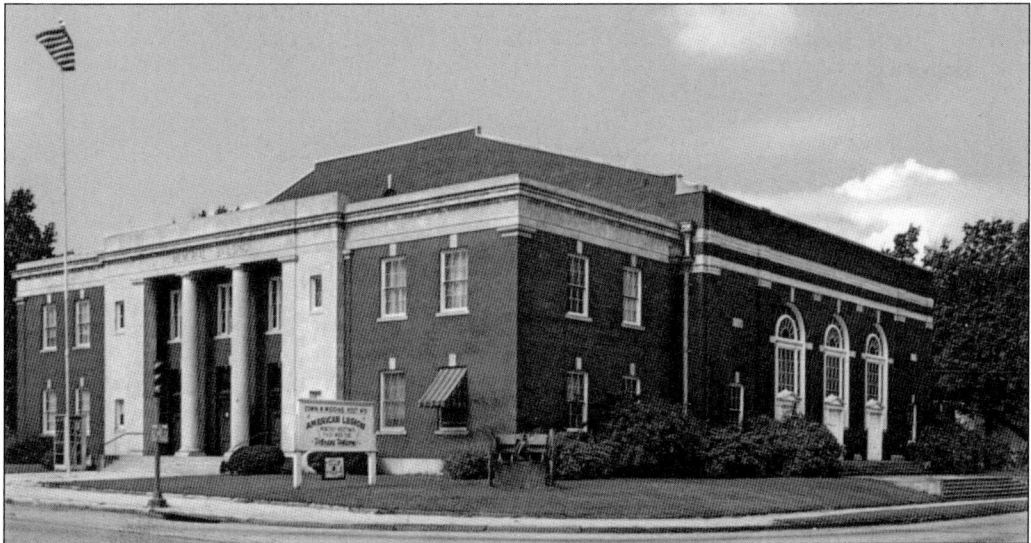

In a ceremony on September 12, 1924, during which Missouri governor Arthur Hyde was the featured speaker, the Carthage Memorial Hall was dedicated to the soldiers who made the ultimate sacrifice in World War I. The building's auditorium and meeting rooms are now used for local events, such as auctions and concerts, while the second floor is used by the American Legion Edwin Wiggins Post 9.

Memorial Hall, Joplin, Mo.

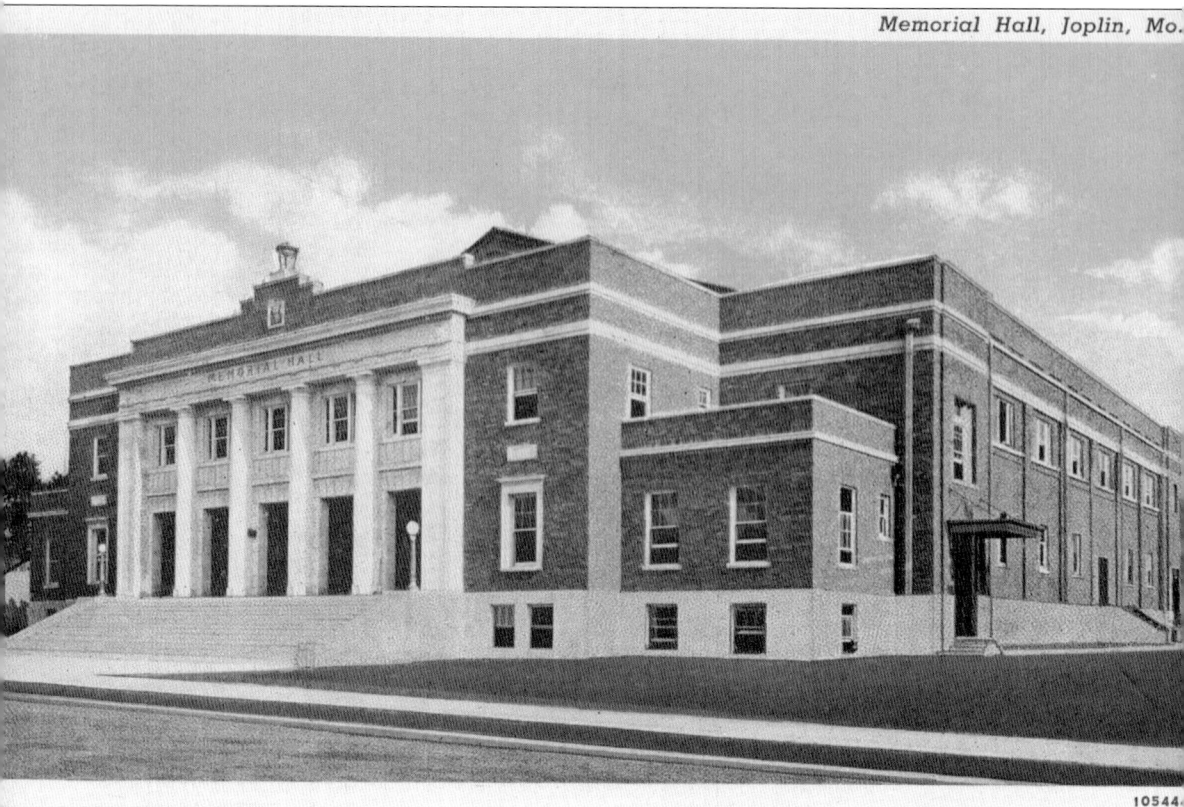

The Joplin Memorial Hall featured in this postcard by the Adams News Company of Joplin was dedicated before a crowd of 2,000 people on October 18, 1925, in memory of those killed in various wars. On November 14, 1925, ceremonies were held to dedicate rooms in the Joplin Memorial Hall to veterans of the Civil War and Spanish-American War. The hall is now operated by Joplin's Parks and Recreation Department and is used for indoor sporting and recreational activities in addition to being rented for a variety of entertainment events.

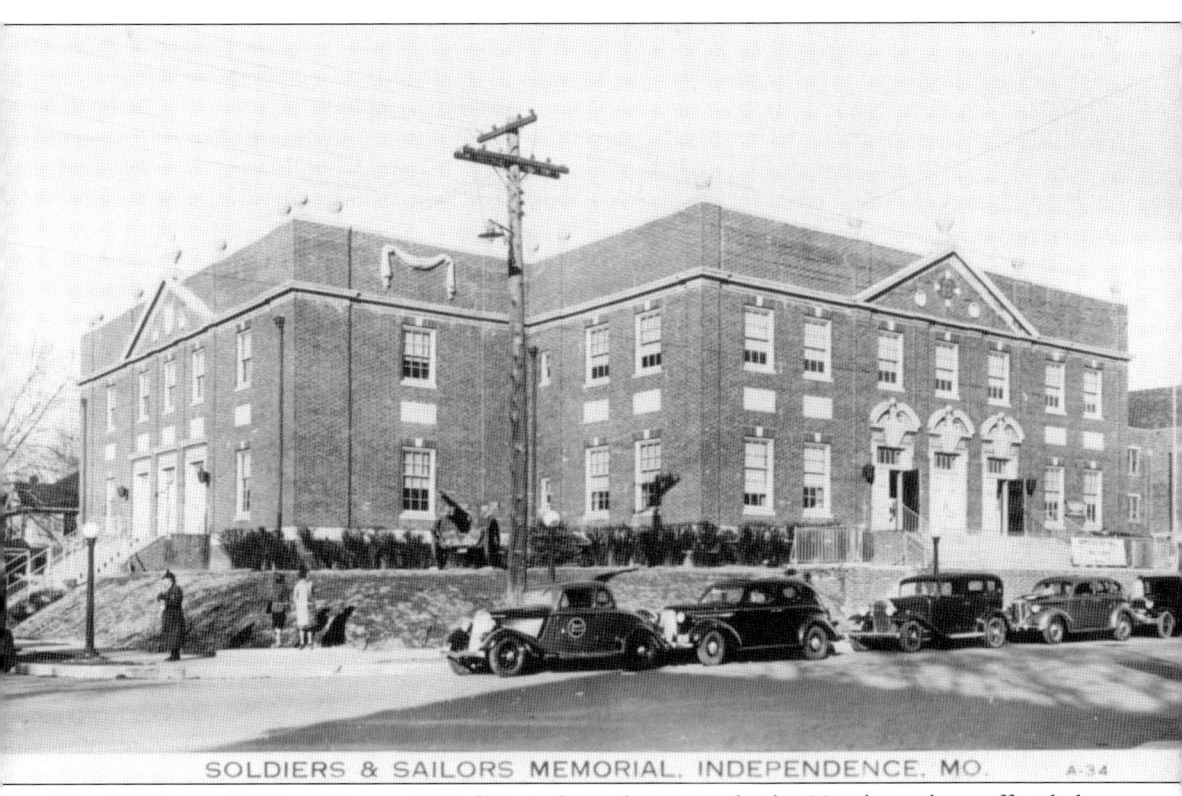

SOLDIERS & SAILORS MEMORIAL, INDEPENDENCE, MO.

The Soldiers and Sailors Memorial Hall in Independence was built 1926 through an effort led by Harry S. Truman. The hall was dedicated as a tribute to those who lost their lives in World War II and has since been renamed Truman Memorial Hall. The building continues in its service to the community as a meeting space and recreational center.

79—Soldiers' and Sailors' Memorial, Kansas City, Kansas

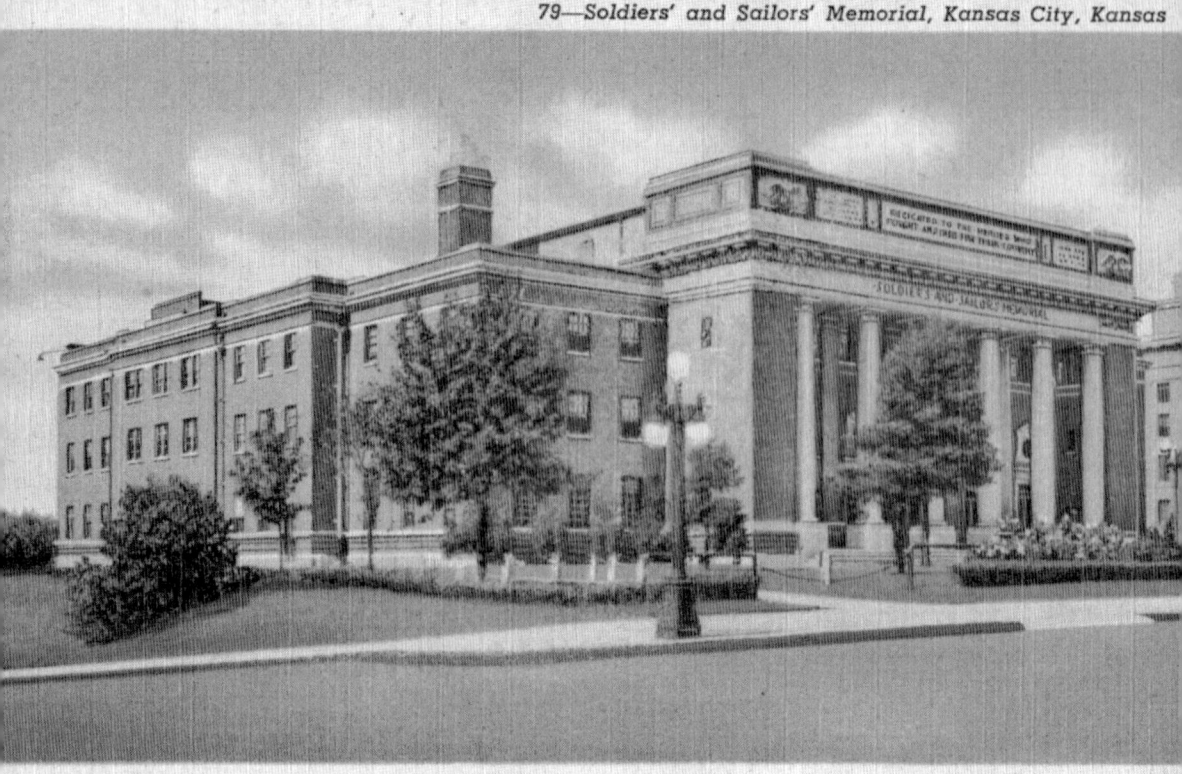

Located just across the state lines in Kansas City, Kansas, the Soldiers and Sailors Memorial Hall was completed in 1925. The building served briefly as home to the National Headquarters of the Veterans of Foreign Wars (VFW); however, because of a lawsuit regarding the details of the lease given the veterans organization, the VFW moved their national headquarters across the state line to Kansas City, Missouri, in 1930.

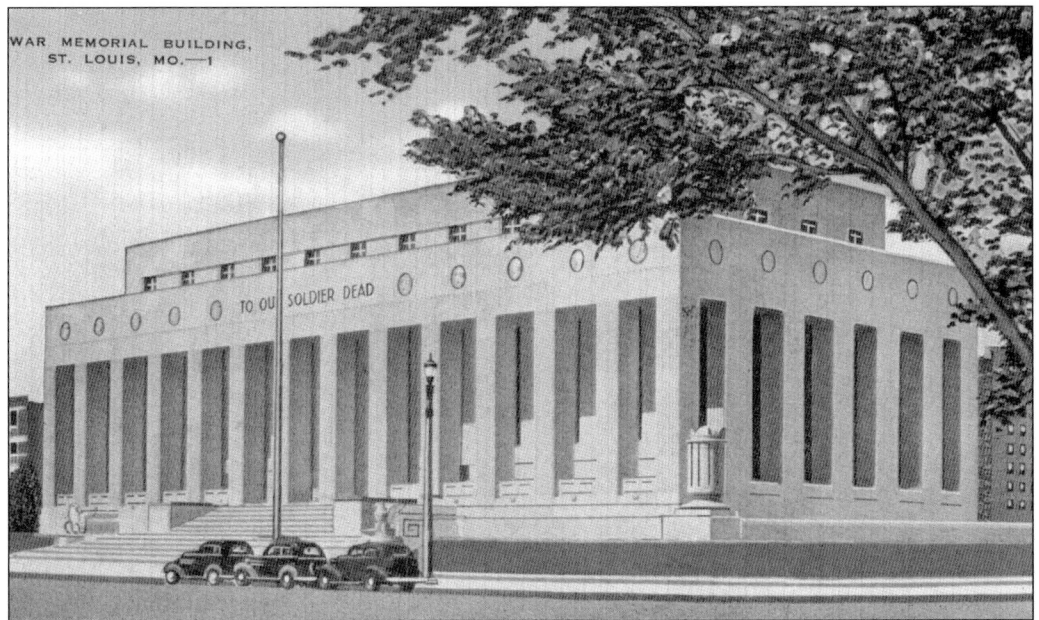

The War Memorial Building, featured in this postcard by the St. Louis Greeting Card Company, was constructed from funds raised by the citizens of St. Louis over a period of several years. The memorial and museum opened in 1938 and is dedicated to the service and sacrifice of military members, veterans, and their families. The building is now named the Soldiers Memorial Military Museum and located in an area known as Memorial Plaza.

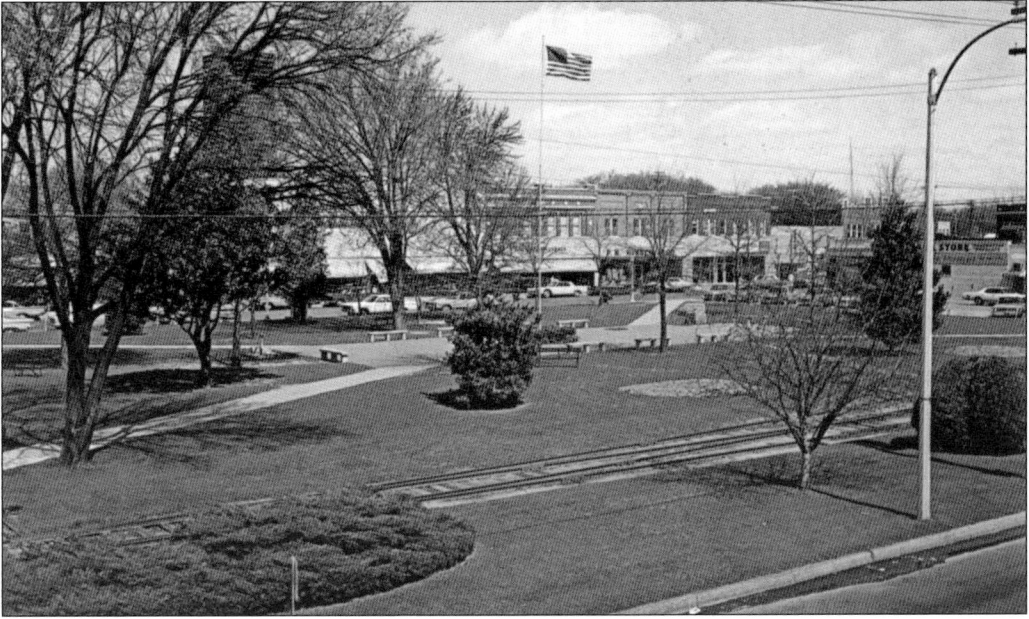

The American Legion Park (also known as Legion Square) in Sikeston was established by the Missouri Pacific Railroad as East Railroad Park, but it was turned over to the City of Sikeston in 1928. Located at 115 Front Street, the local American Legion post has supported improvements in the park throughout the years, and it now features benches, a veteran's monument, and a drinking fountain and frequently plays host to various entertainment events.

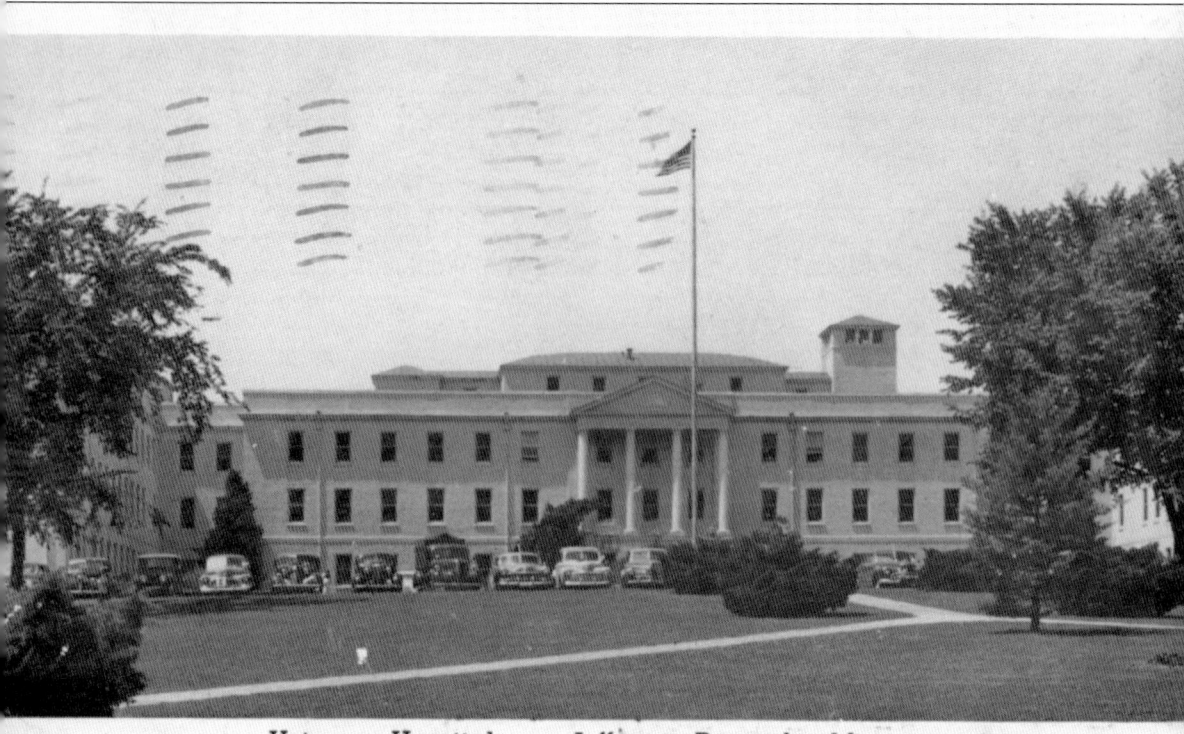

Veterans Hospital . . . Jefferson Barracks, Missouri

Missouri's American Legion Auxiliary printed this postcard featuring the Veterans Hospital at Jefferson Barracks in the early 1950s. The main hospital and administration buildings were constructed between 1922 and 1923; several additions have been added in the ensuring decades. This hospital is now part of the VA St. Louis Health Care System, which includes not only the Jefferson Barracks site, but the John Cochran VA Medical Center in downtown St. Louis.

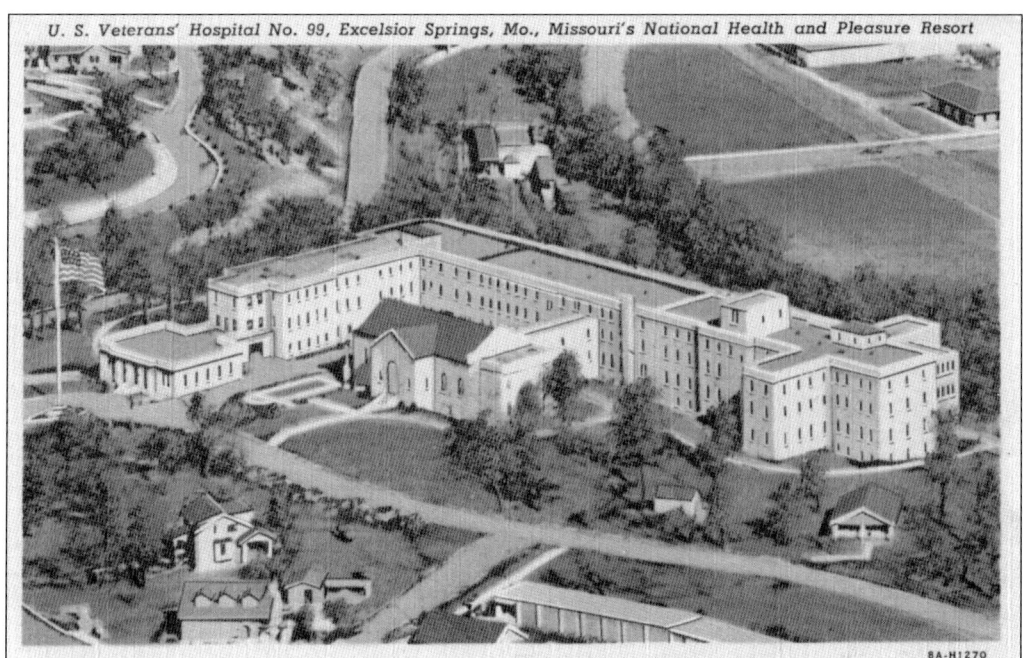

Pictured in this postcard from the late 1930s, the Veterans' Hospital in Excelsior Springs—a community that became known as Missouri's National Health and Pleasure Resort after the discovery of its mineral waters—was established on November 11, 1924. The hospital underwent later expansions and remained in operation until July 31, 1963, at which time it was closed. A portion of the facility has been demolished, while remaining sections are being used as a Job Corps Center.

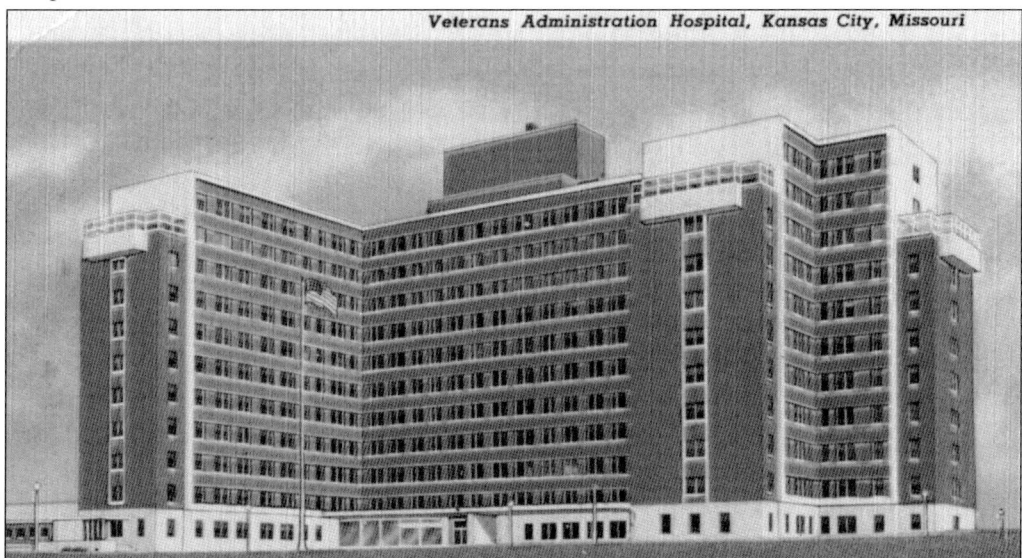

The ground was broken for the construction of the Kansas City VA Medical Center on September 27, 1949, on a section of land located at Linwood and Van Brunt Boulevards. It took approximately three years to complete the $10 million facility, which was dedicated on October 5, 1952. Having undergone several upgrades and expansions, the hospital continues to serve veterans in the Kansas City area.

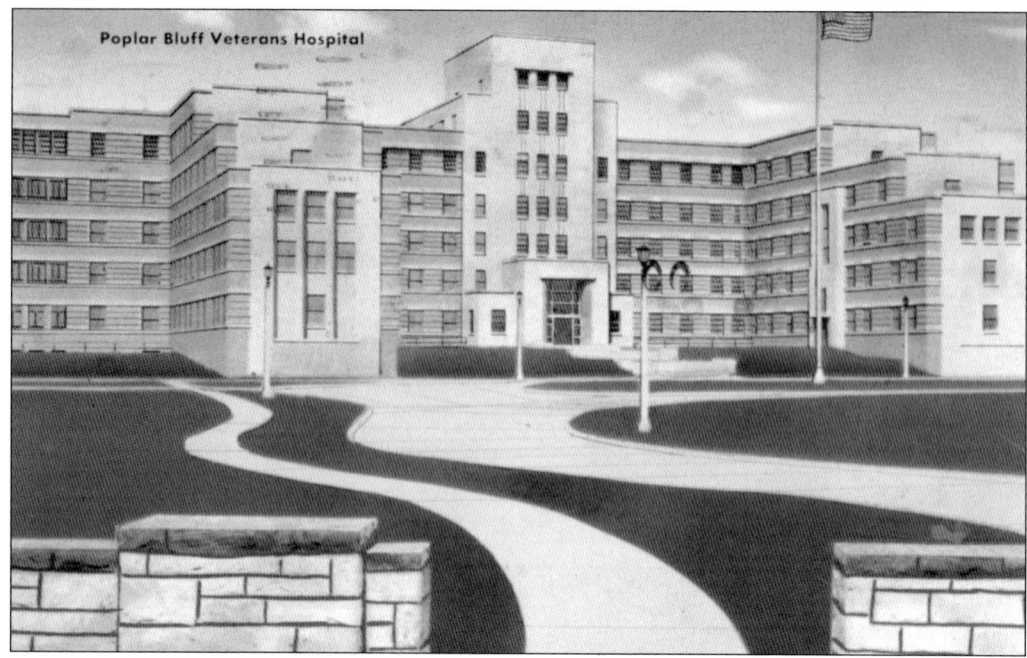

The $5 million Veterans' Hospital in Poplar Bluff formally opened in November 1950 and was—at the time—believed to have been one of the biggest building projects launched in southeast Missouri. It opened its doors as a six-story, 200-bed facility and, in 1985, was renamed the John J. Pershing VA Medical Center.

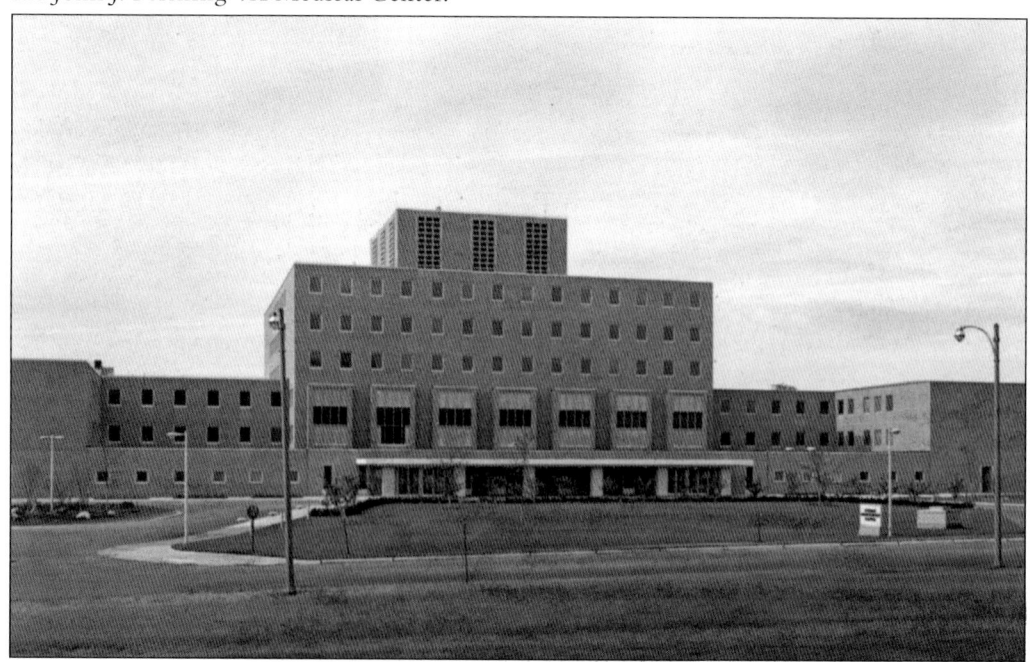

Construction of the $15 million Veterans Hospital in Columbia began in 1968, but the facility was not dedicated until June 17, 1972, because of delays caused by bad weather and labor disputes. The six-story building with an initial 460-bed capacity was renamed the Harry S. Truman Memorial Veterans' Hospital in 1975.

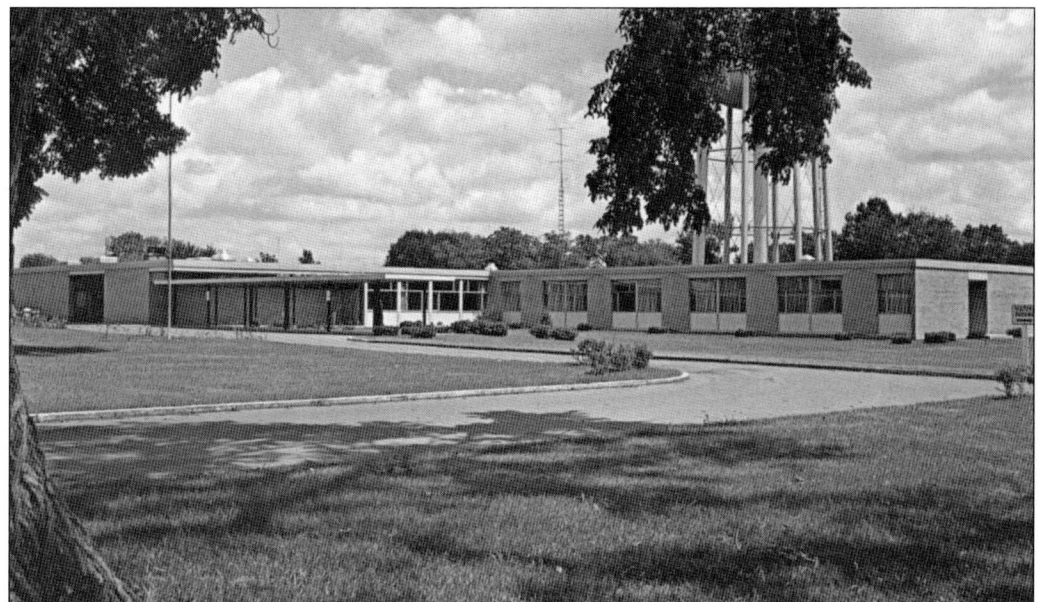

Though not a Department of Veterans Affairs facility, featured in this postcard is a hospital with a strong military tie—the nonsectarian, not-for-profit General John J. Pershing Memorial Hospital in Brookfield. Named for the Missouri native who served as General of the Armies in World War I, the hospital opened in Brookfield on January 11, 1960, and continues to serve Brookfield and the surrounding area to this day.

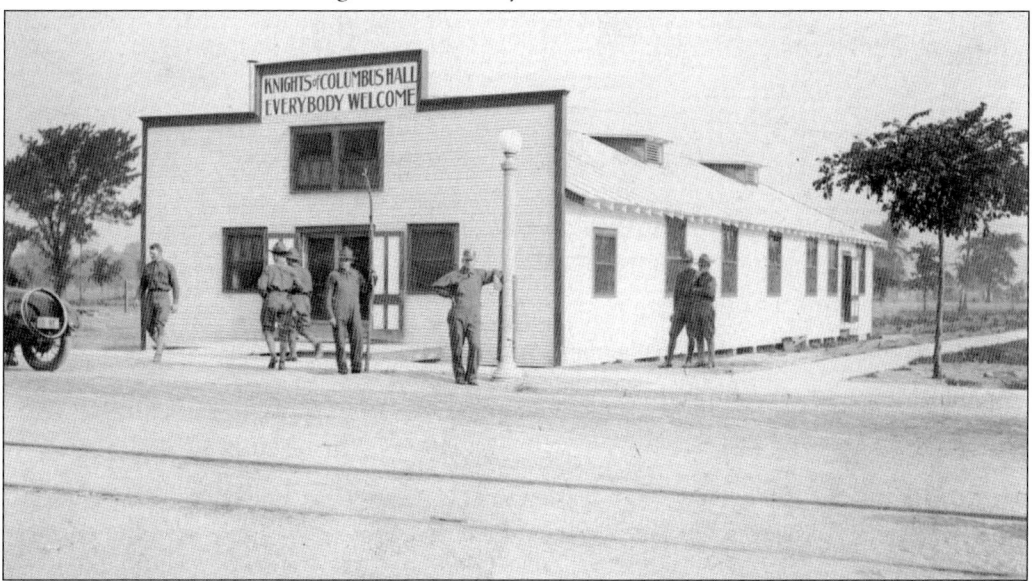

The field headquarters of the Knights of Columbus (K of C) at Jefferson Barracks is pictured in this real-photo postcard from 1917. During World War I, the K of C joined several organizations such as the YMCA and USO in establishing sites called "huts" at home and abroad (250 of which were located in Europe during World War I) that provided recreational amenities to service members regardless of race or religion. The types of events hosted at the K of C in Jefferson Barracks ranged from vaudeville shows and dinners to ice cream socials for soldiers and their guests.

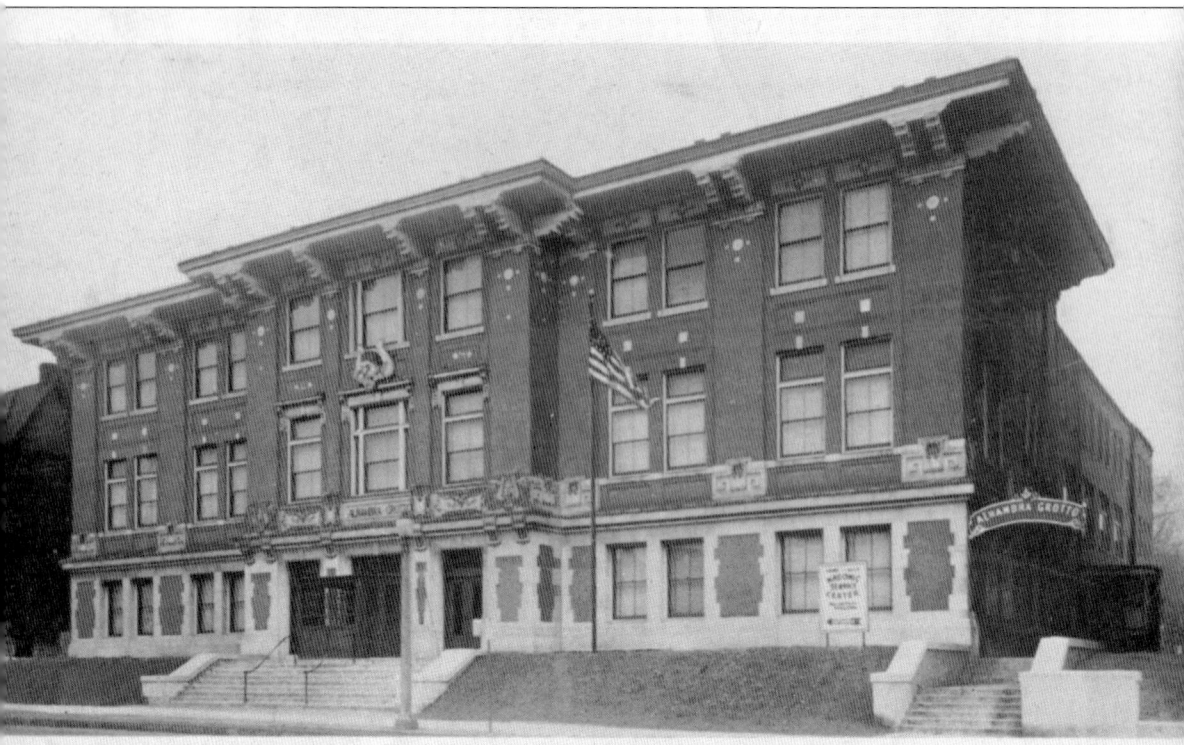

Army and Navy Masonic Service Center—Alhambra Grotto Temple, 2626 S. Grand Blvd., St. Louis, Missouri

The Freemasons became actively involved in supporting the nation's service members in World War II by establishing service centers, which were very much like USO canteens. By the end of World War II, the Masonic Service Association had raised enough funds to support approximately 40 service centers abroad and in the United States, including one in St. Louis, featured on this real-photo postcard.

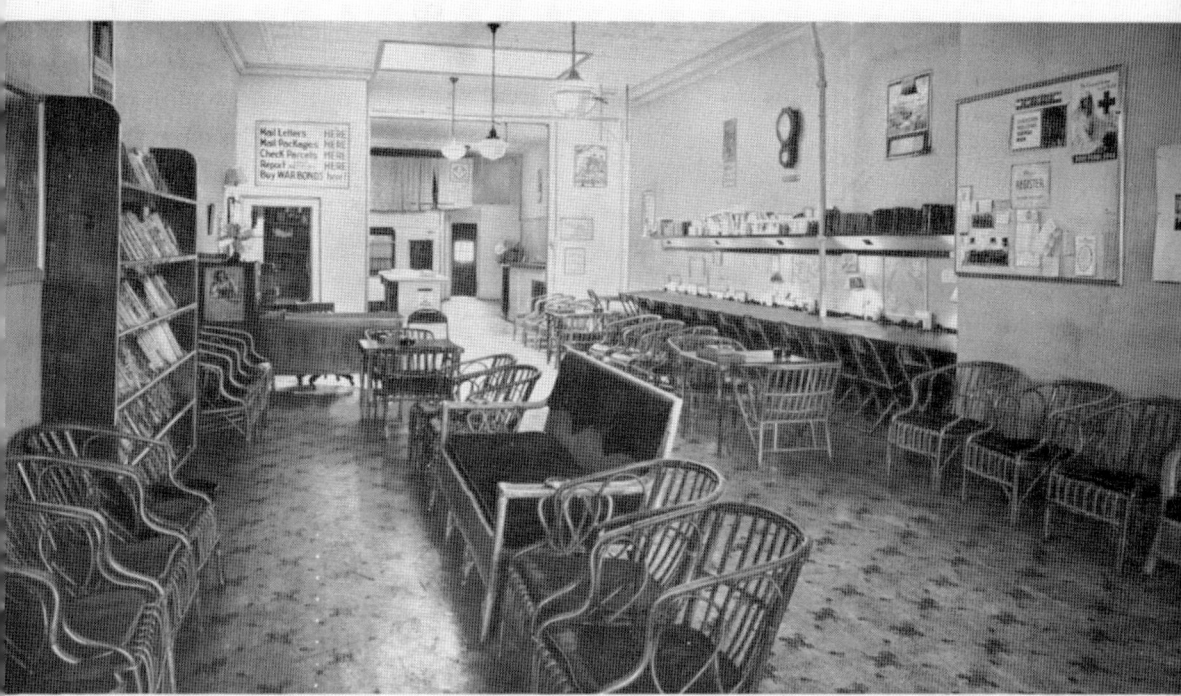

Army and Navy Masonic Service Center—105 South Washington Street, Neosho, Missouri

The Army and Navy Service Centers were often established in areas of the country that had a strong military presence and were laid out in a manner similar to the one pictured on this postcard, postmarked 1944. Located in the community of Neosho, this club would have played host to the thousands of soldiers serving at nearby Camp Crowder during World War II.

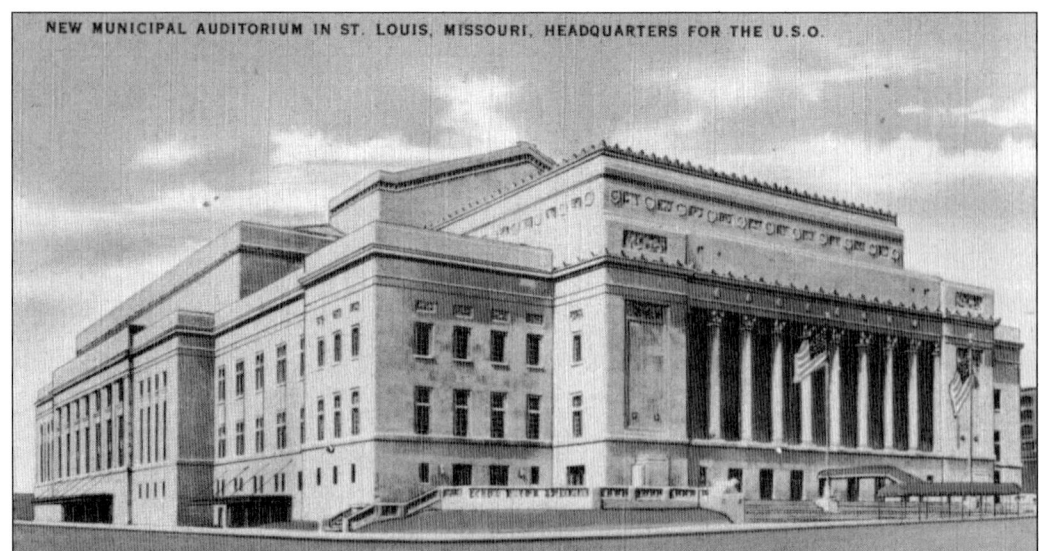

During World War II, the USO—an organization that provides morale and recreational services to US military members—established their headquarters in the new Municipal Auditorium in St. Louis. Dedicated on April 14, 1934, the building was renamed Kiel Opera House in 1943. The auditorium section of the complex was demolished the early 1990s and replaced by the Scottrade Center, while the opera house has undergone renovation and is now the Peabody Opera House.

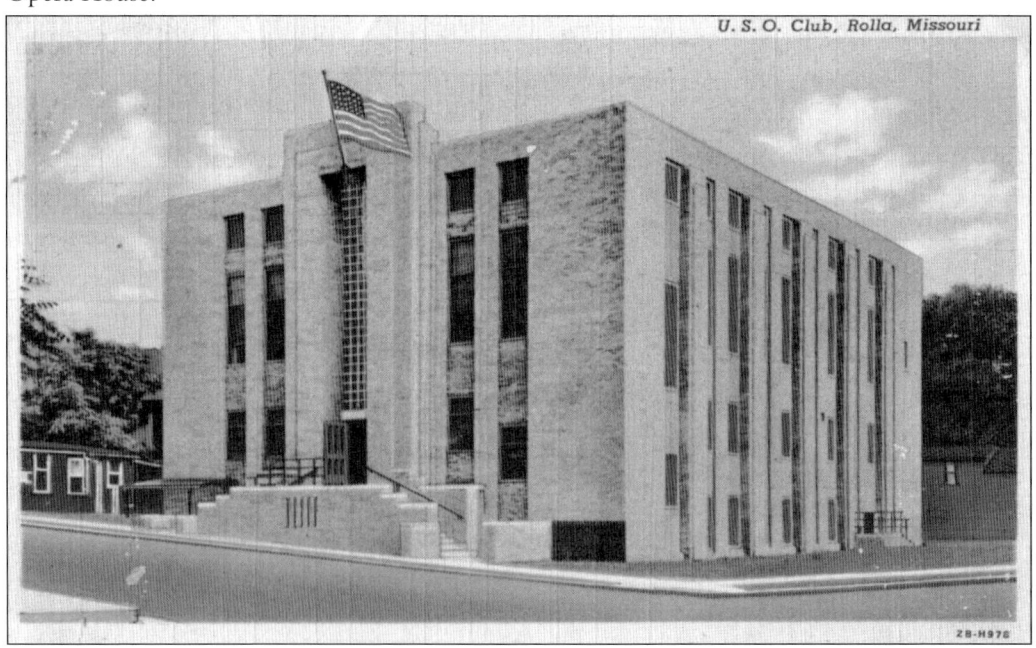

The Corwin News Agency of Jefferson City produced this linen postcard depicting the USO club in Rolla. Established in early 1942 in a rented building on the corner of Eighth and Rolla Streets, the club soon began hosting dances, dinners, and other activities for the white soldiers stationed at nearby Fort Leonard Wood; a USO club for black soldiers was also established in Rolla. Now known as the Buehler Hall, the former USO club provides living facilities for local college students.

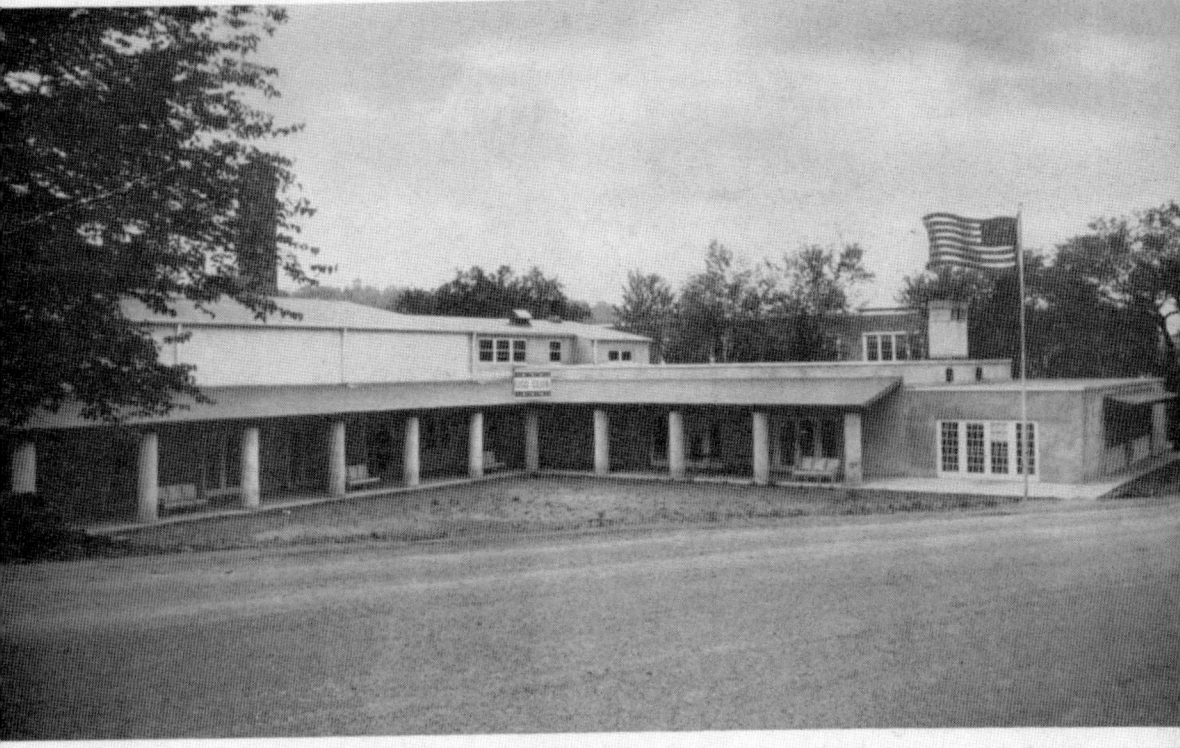

U. S. O. Club, Waynesville, Missouri

The Graycraft Card Company of Danville, Virginia, produced this real-photo postcard in the mid-1940s showing the exterior view of the USO club that was established in Waynesville during the Second World War. Dedicated on March 7, 1942, this USO occupied rented space and, during the days of segregation in the military, served only white soldiers from nearby Fort Leonard Wood.

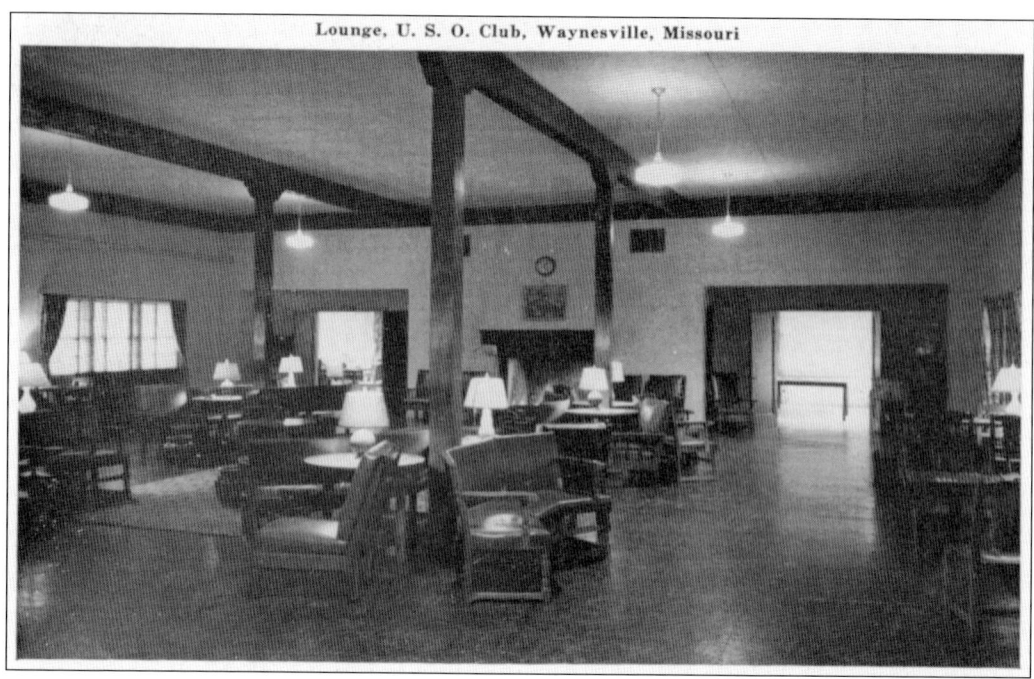

The interior of the Waynesville USO Club is featured in this real-photo postcard. The building that housed the club was constructed in an L-shape with a main lobby that was two stories high and located at the corner of Highway 17 and School Street. The left wing of this building is all that remains and has since been converted into apartments.

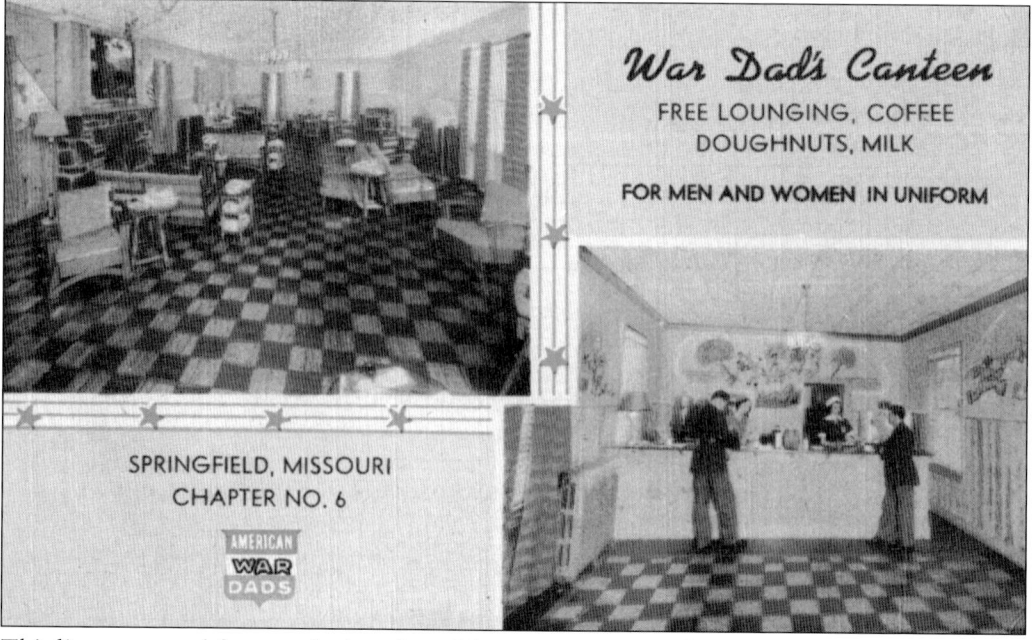

This linen postcard features the interior of the canteen operated by Chapter 6 of the American War Dads in Springfield. These canteens were similar to those operated by organizations such as the Freemasons and USO and offered a variety of services for men and women in uniform. The American War Dads grew to 500 chapters in 42 states and had a membership of 70,000.

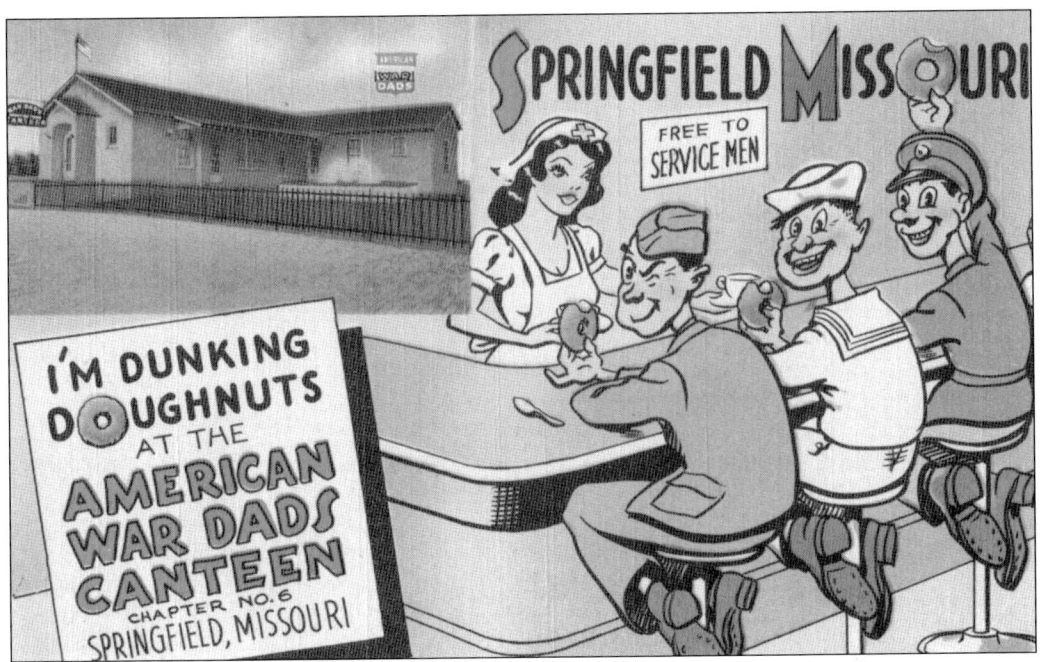

American War Dads Chapter 6 was located at the former Frisco Railroad Passenger Station since it became an important hub for military members coming to or leaving the area. This canteen was very involved in providing support to the wounded soldiers recovering at the nearby O'Reilly General Hospital and even paid the expenses for 65 mothers to visit their sons recovering there.

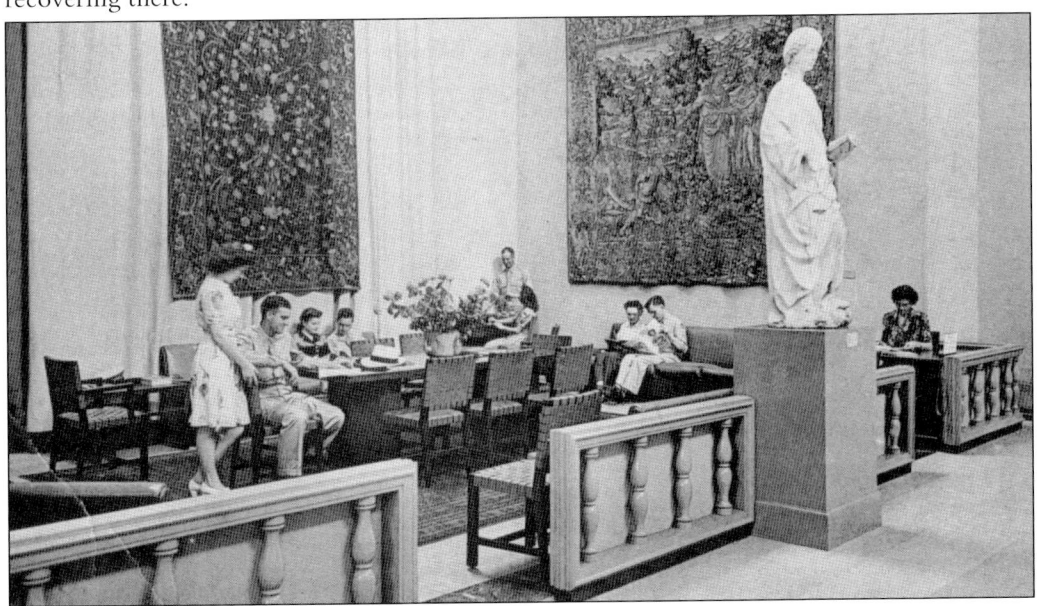

Featured on this real-photo postcard by the Meriden Gravure Company is the US Service Lounge that was established inside the City Art Museum in St. Louis during World War II, which provided a relaxing atmosphere for men and women of the armed forces visiting the various exhibits and displays. Located inside Forest Park, the museum has since been renamed the St. Louis Art Museum.

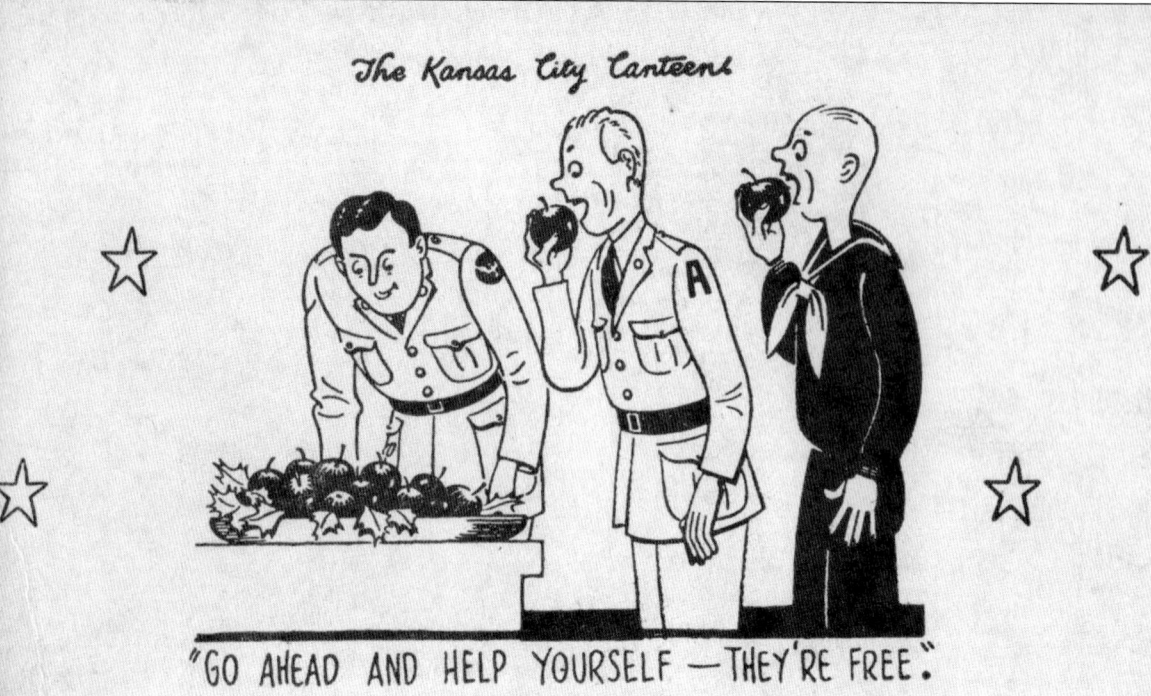

In addition to the many canteens operated by organizations such as the USO and the Freemasons during World War II, many local groups did their part in providing morale and welfare support to the troops. This postcard highlights the Kansas City Canteen, which was sponsored by the Kansas City Servicemen's Recreational Association and officially opened on October 21, 1942, at 1021 McGee Street.

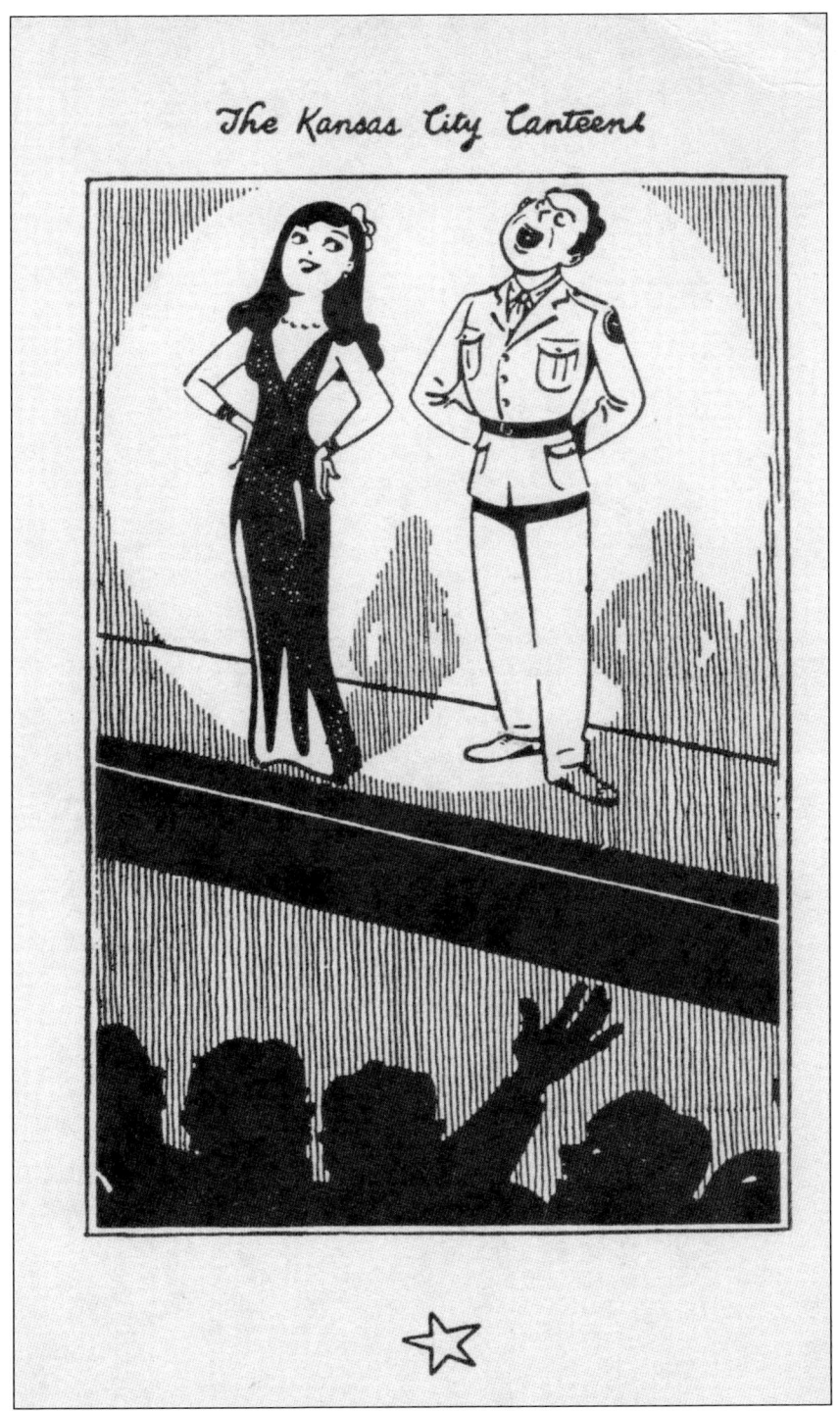

The Kansas City Canteen featured a snack bar, provided aid to military travelers, and hosted Sunday suppers, evening dances, and other entertainment events. However, one the most notable moments in the venue's history occurred in November 1942 when a soldier serving at Camp Crowder married his sweetheart at the canteen.

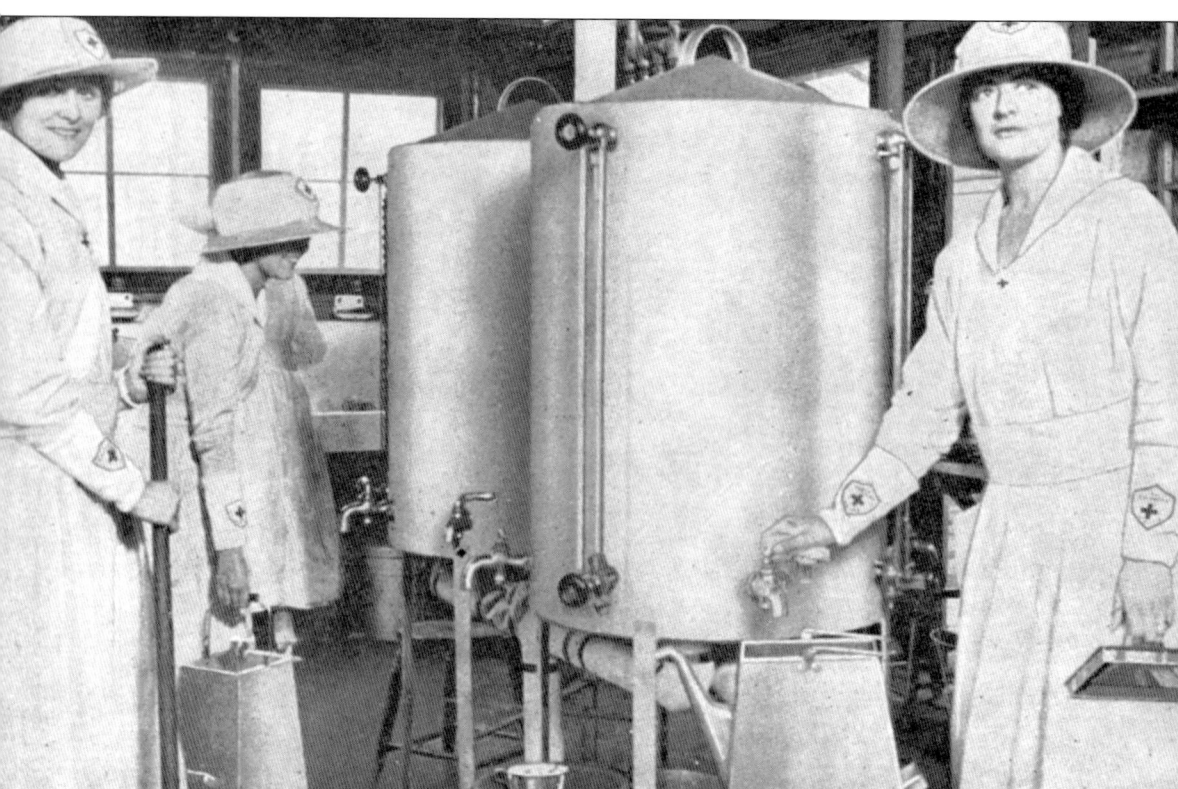
The St. Louis Chapter of the American Red Cross was officially chartered at the beginning of America's involvement in World War I. This postcard shows Red Cross canteen workers in St. Louis during the World War I era. As part the Red Cross Canteen Corps, the canteen workers served snacks and meals at locations where there was concentration of soldiers, such as airports, railroad depots, and military posts.

Five

PEOPLE, EVENTS, AND NAVAL HISTORY

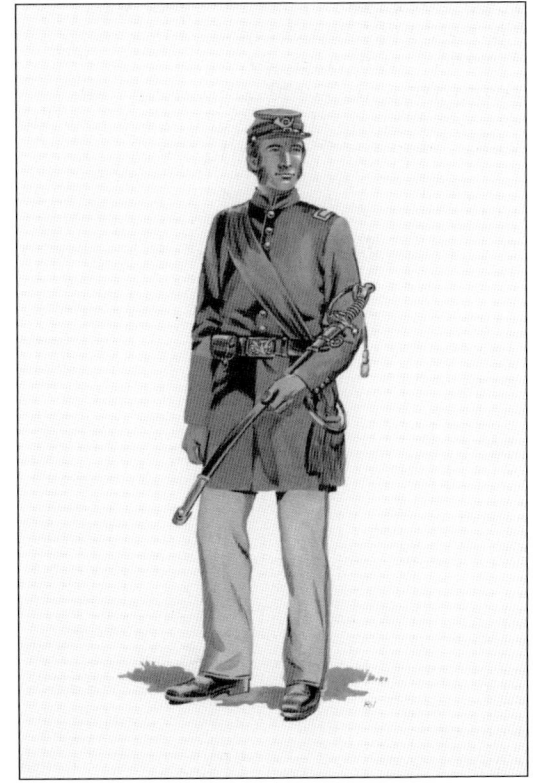

Featured on this postcard is an officer of the 17th Missouri Infantry during the period of the Civil War. The Seventeenth was organized as a Union army infantry regiment in St. Louis in August 1861 and participated in many important battles of the war, including Maj. Gen. John Fremont's campaigns in Missouri, the Battle of Pea Ridge, the Vicksburg campaign, and was later part of Gen. William T. Sherman's "March to the Sea."

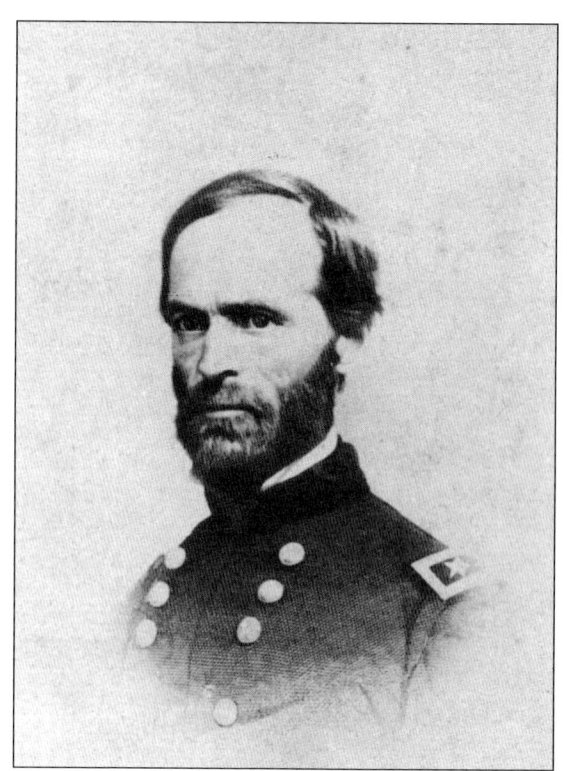

William Tecumseh Sherman was born in Ohio in 1820 and went on to graduate from the US Military Academy at West Point in 1840. Sherman later moved to St. Louis and after the Civil War broke out, fought in many major battles, including Bull Run, Shiloh, Vicksburg, and Chattanooga. In late 1864, he led 62,000 Union soldiers from Atlanta to Savannah, Georgia, in what became known as his "March to the Sea"—total warfare intended to end the Southerners' will to fight. Sherman died in 1891 and is buried in Calvary Cemetery in St. Louis.

Born in Virginia in 1809, Sterling Price's family later moved to Missouri where he went on to serve in the state legislature and later as an officer in the Mexican-American War. Price became Missouri's governor from 1853 to 1857 and, during the Civil War, commanded the Confederate Missouri State Guard at Wilson's Creek and Pea Ridge. He is best known for his raid into Missouri during the fall of 1864 in a failed attempt to seize control of the state for the Confederacy. Price died in St. Louis in 1867 and is buried in the city's Bellefontaine Cemetery.

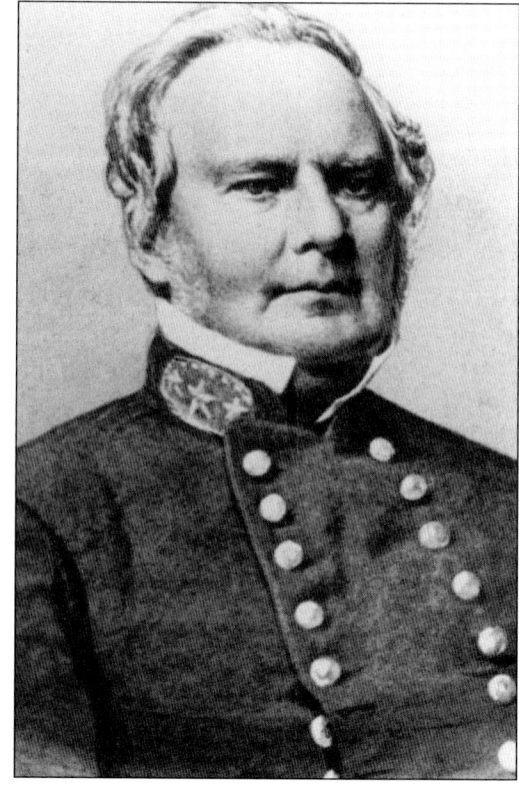

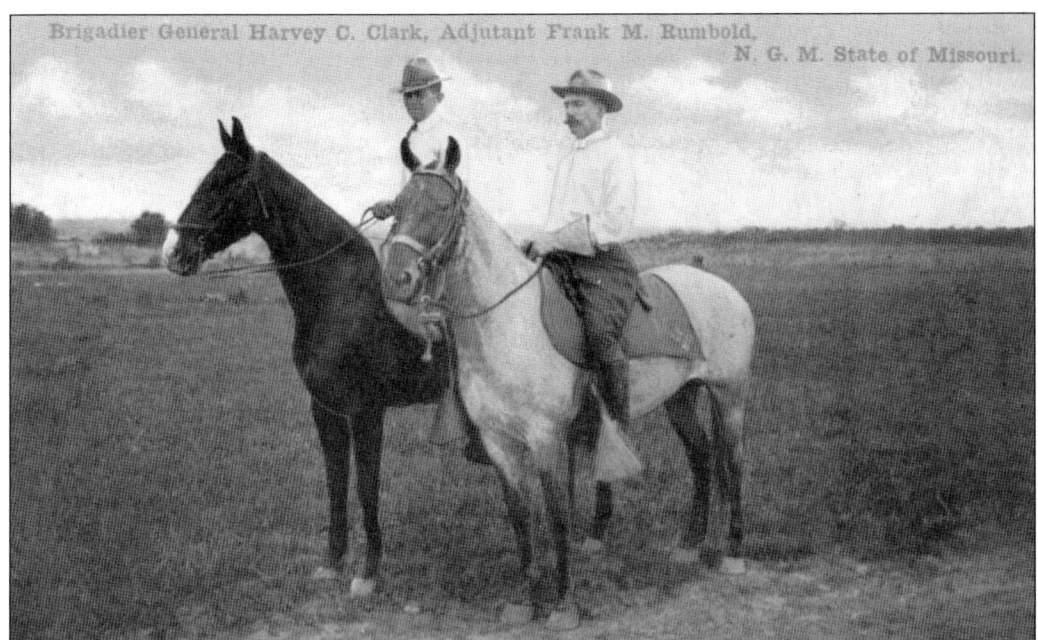

Harvey C. Clark was born in 1869 in Bates County, Missouri, and attended Wentworth Military Academy in Lexington. He became a member of the Missouri Militia (forerunner of the Missouri National Guard) in 1888 and is credited with organizing the 6th Missouri Volunteer Infantry during the Spanish-American War. Clark went on to command Missouri National Guard troops during the Punitive Expedition to Mexico and in 1918 was appointed as adjutant general of the state guard. A lawyer by trade, General Clark died from meningitis in 1921.

William A. Raupp, pictured on this real-photo postcard, was born in Ohio in 1868. His family moved to Missouri when he was two years old and settled in Pierce City. He was, for many years, associated with the 2nd Missouri Infantry, with whom he served during the Spanish-American War and later in the Punitive Expedition to Mexico. During World War I, he commanded the 56th and 60th Pioneer Infantry Regiments and in 1921 was appointed as adjutant general of the Missouri National Guard following the death of Harvey C. Clark. Raupp died in 1946 and is buried in the Pierce City Cemetery.

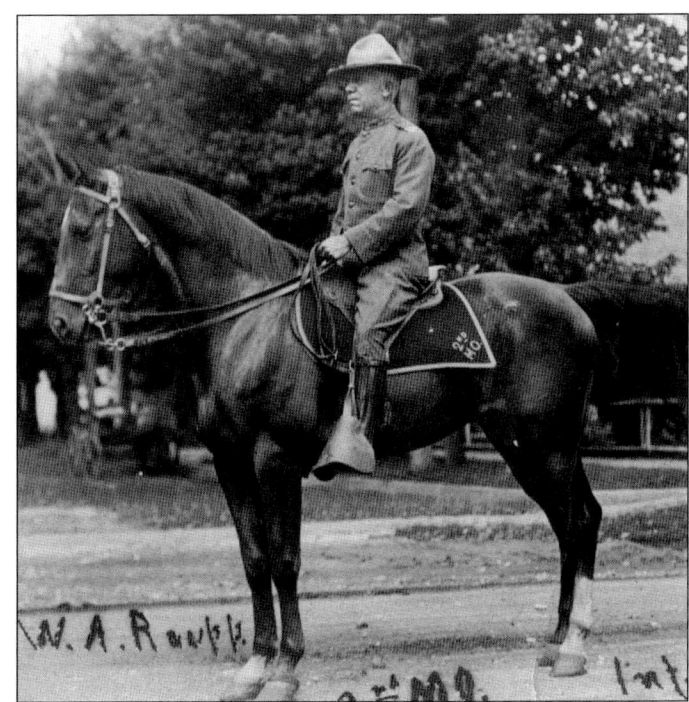

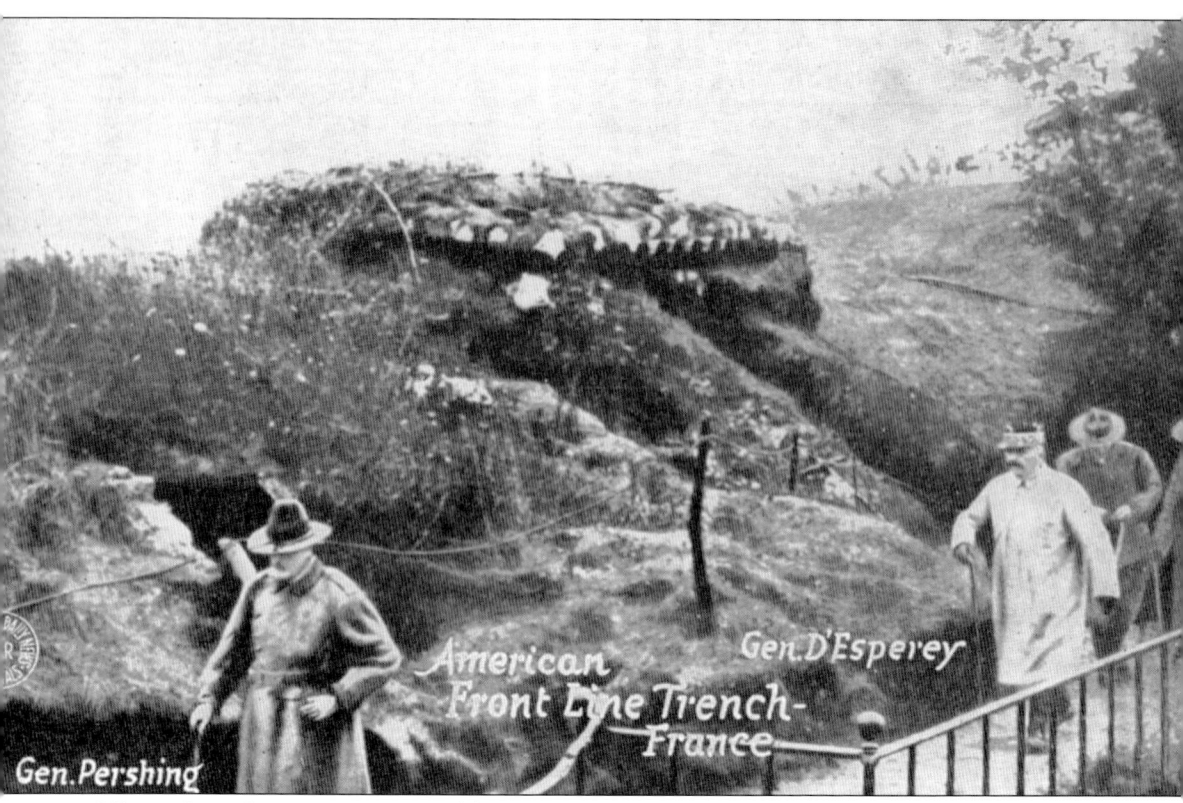

Missouri was home to many notable military leaders, including Gen. John J. Pershing. Raised in Laclede, Pershing taught school before his acceptance into the US Military Academy at West Point. He participated in several interesting military assignments during his career, which included service during the Punitive Expedition to Mexico; however, his greatest fame came from his service as commander in chief of the American Expeditionary Forces in World War I. He is seen in this real-photo postcard visiting one of the front-line trenches in France during World War I.

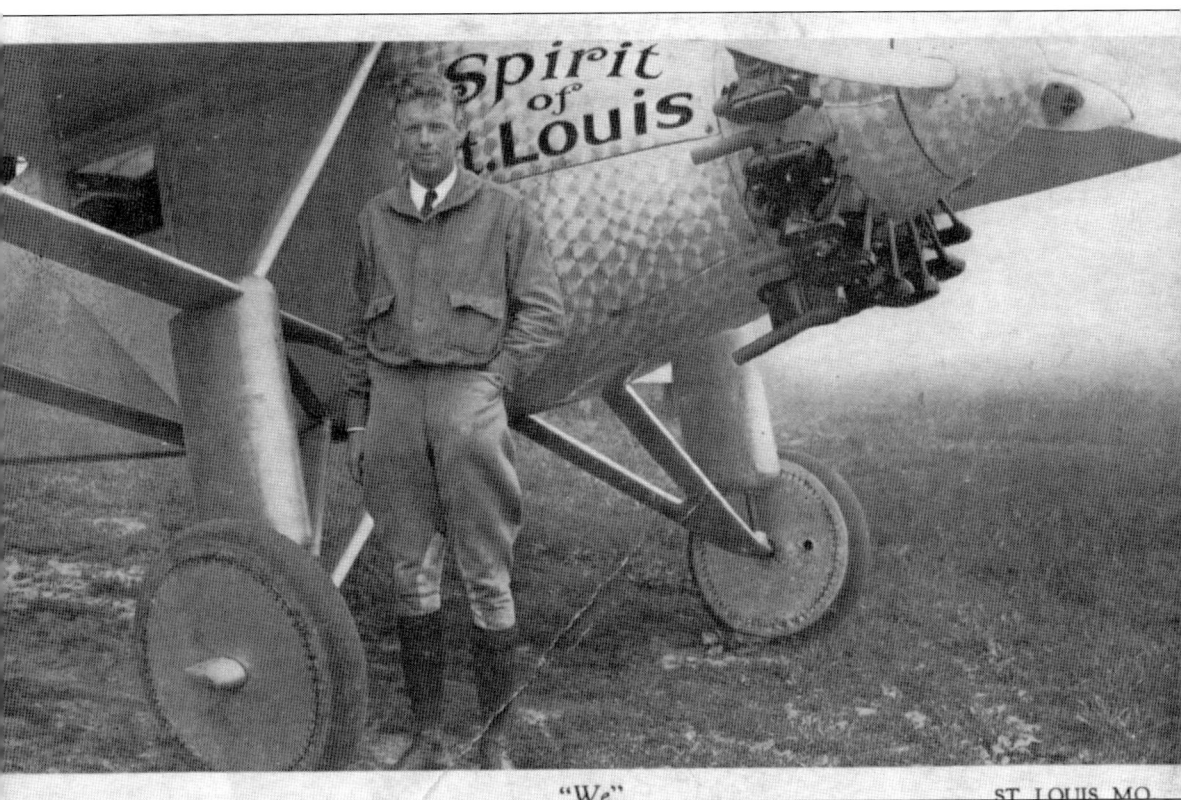

Charles A. Lindbergh is featured on this real-photo postcard standing in front of his plane, the *Spirit of St. Louis*, aboard which he made his famed transatlantic flight in 1927. Born in Detroit, Michigan, in 1902, Lindbergh moved to St. Louis in the mid-1920s and became an officer in the 110th Observation Squadron of the Missouri National Guard. The aviator had to seek permission from his commanders to make his historic flight, and after returning from the 33-hour transatlantic voyage, Lindbergh was promoted from captain to colonel by a special act of the Missouri Legislature.

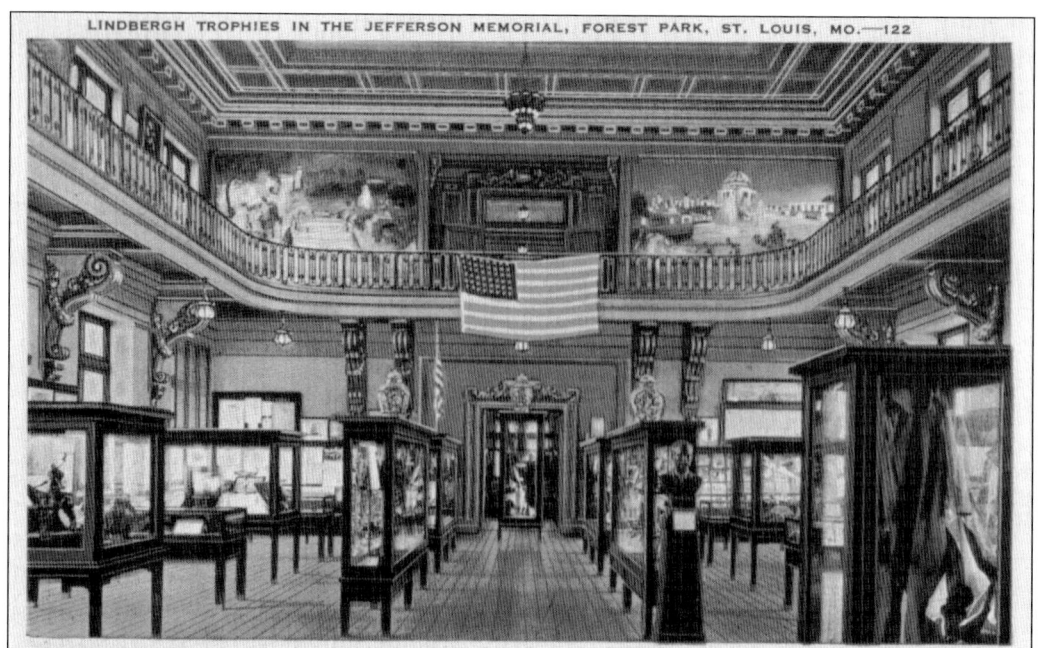

Following Colonel Lindbergh's transatlantic flight, he received trophies from nations all over the world. The Missouri Historical Society requested that Lindbergh allow them to display the trophies in Forest Park in St. Louis, to which he agreed, and they were exhibited on the first floor of the west wing of the Jefferson Memorial. The trophy room is pictured in this linen postcard with a postmark of 1940, and a few years after granting permission to display the trophies, Lindbergh deeded his collection of accolades to the historical society.

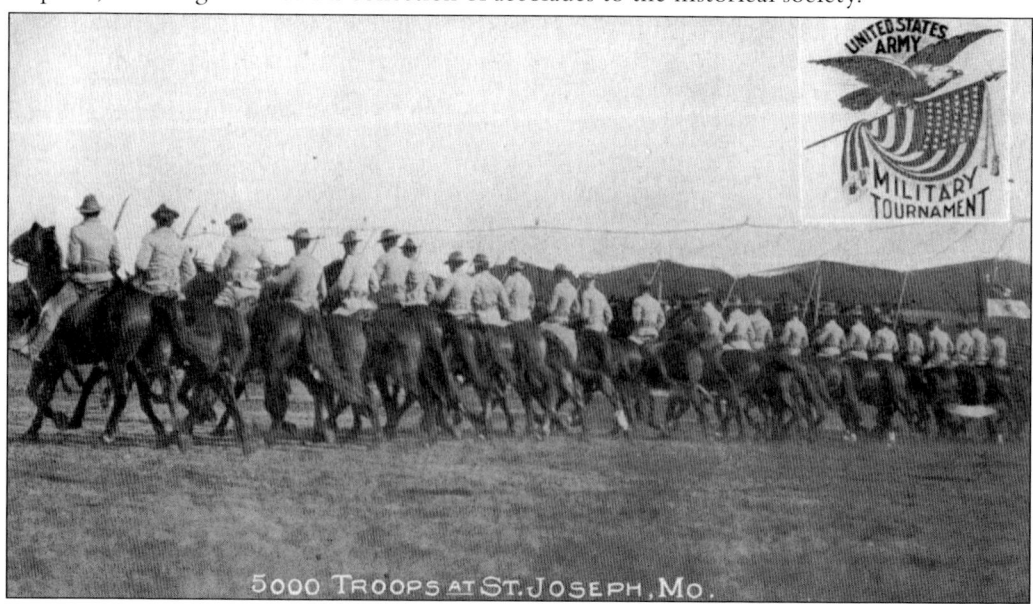

During the week of September 21–26, 1908, the city of St. Joseph became the sight of the US Army Military Tournament, during which soldiers participated in various exhibitions and competitions, such as the cavalry drill featured in this real-photo postcard. This was the second such tournament held by the US Army—the first occurred the previous fall and was also held in St. Joseph.

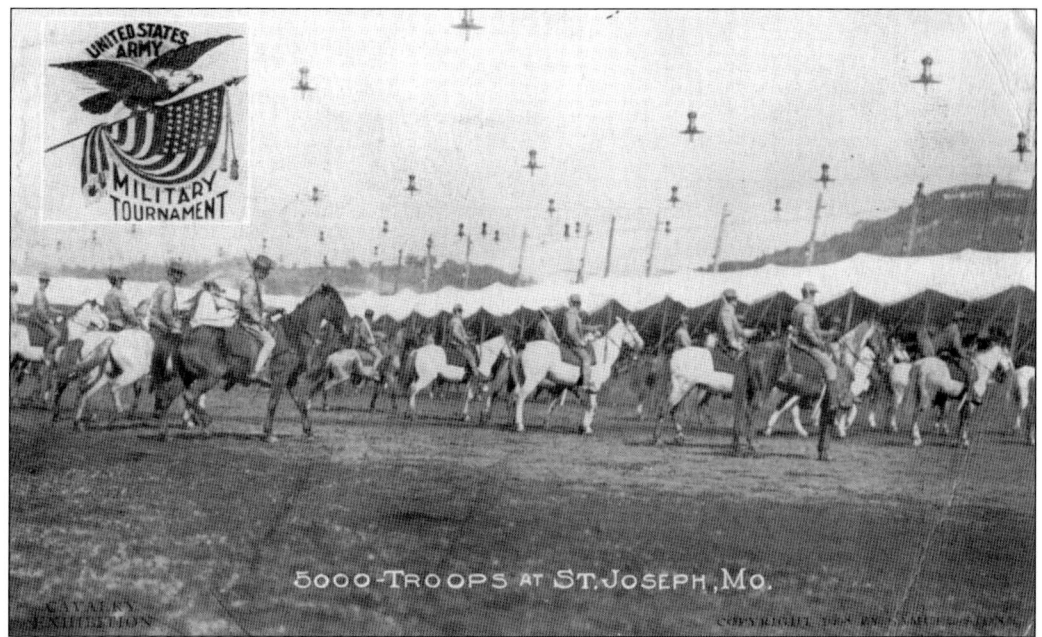

During the many events taking place at the tournament, such as the cavalry exhibition pictured here, members of the public were invited to attend and witness firsthand the capabilities of those serving in military uniform. Some local newspapers reported that there were more than 75,000 in attendance for the week's activities.

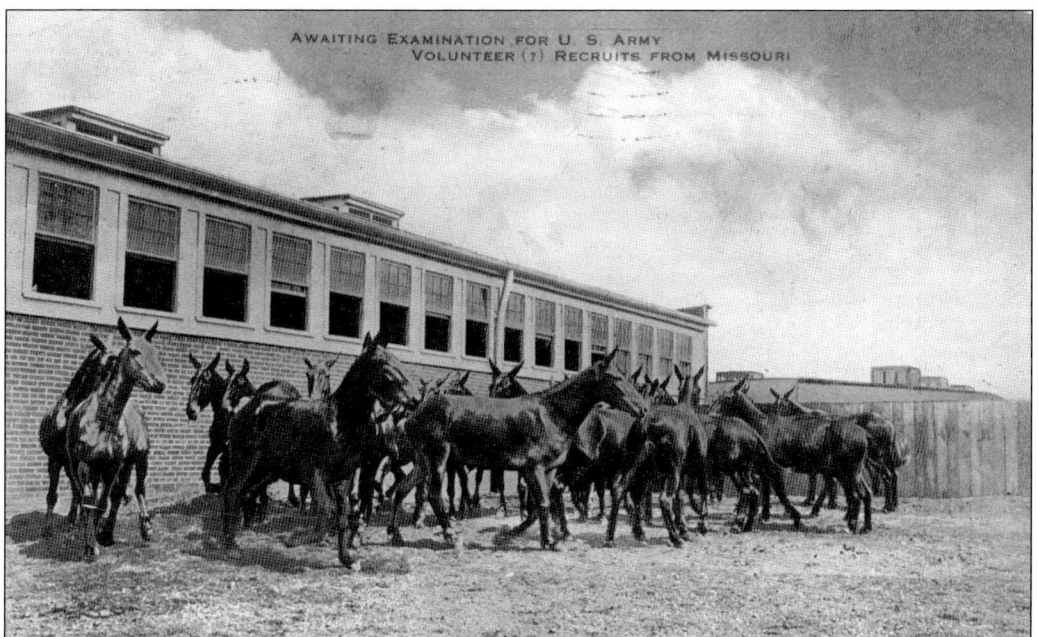

Mules have long been used by the US military to carry heavy loads over long distances. As such, Missouri continues to hold the reputation of breeding some of the best mules available and, as seen in this humorous postcard from the 1900s, was the state from where some of the most sought after military recruits were drawn.

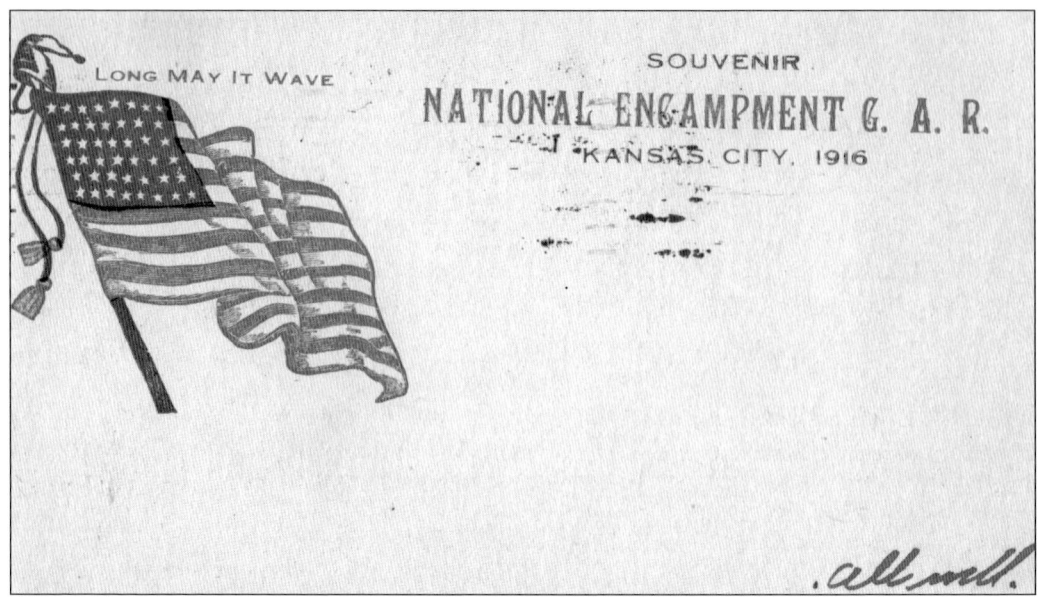

From the 50th National Encampment of the Grand Army of the Republic (GAR) in Kansas City in August 1916 came this simple souvenir postcard. The GAR was founded in Decatur, Illinois, in 1866 for honorably discharged veterans of the Union army, Navy, Marine Corps, or the Revenue Cutter Service who had served between April 12, 1861, and April 9, 1865.

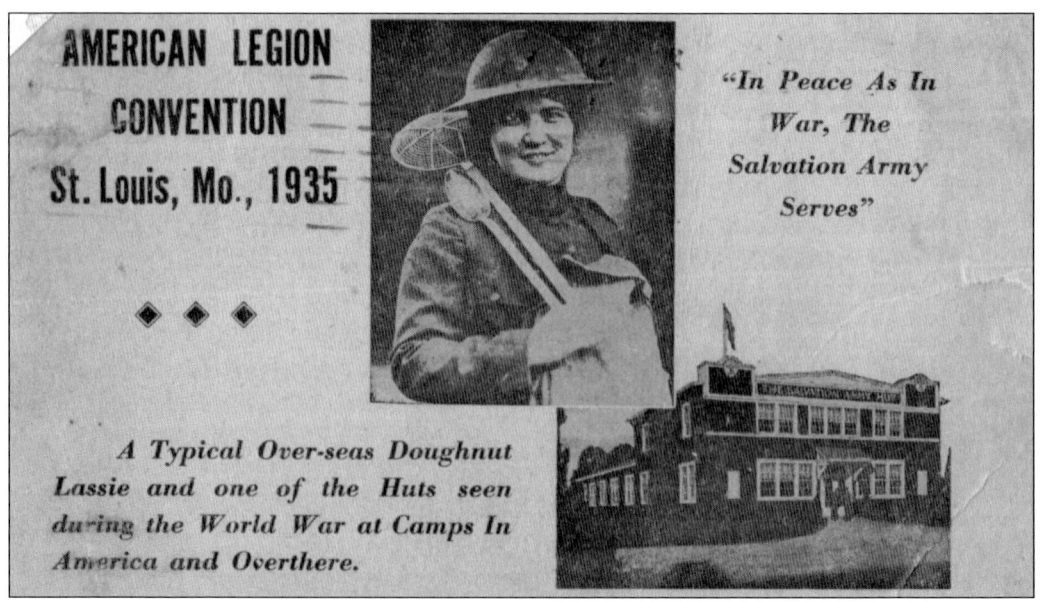

The American Legion held its 17th annual convention in St. Louis from September 23 to 26, 1935. Attendees at the event were welcomed by St. Louis mayor Bernard Dickmann and Missouri governor Guy Park. This commemorative postcard printed for the event demonstrates the appreciation that members of the American Legion maintained for the morale and welfare support provided by women of the Salvation Army during World War I.

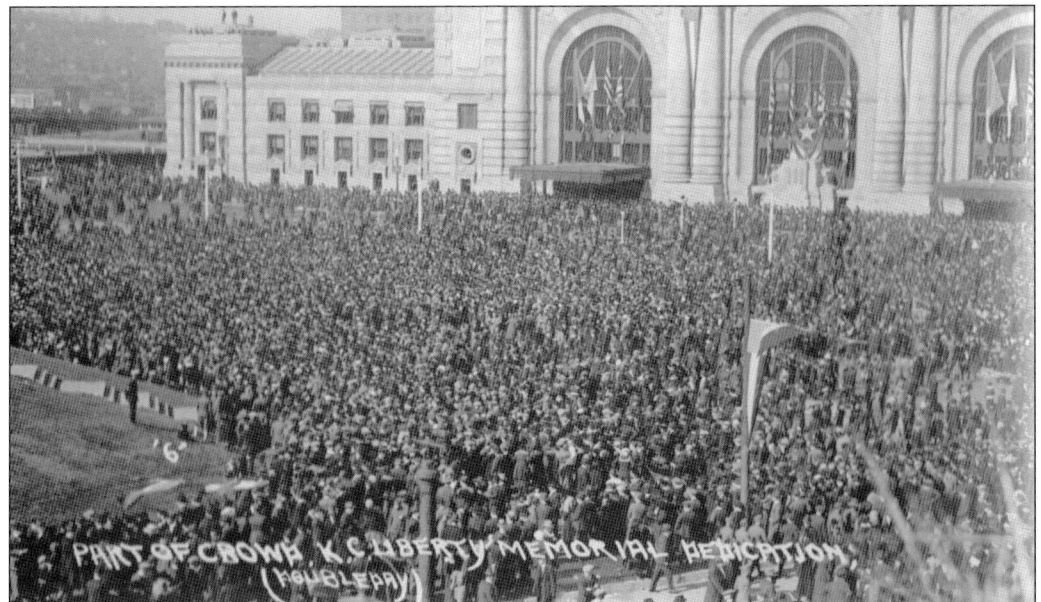

In 1921, the American Legion hosted a parade in Kansas City to dedicate the site of the Liberty Memorial that was to be built to honor those who lost their lives in World War I. Not only did members of fraternal organizations such as the American Legion, United Confederates, GAR, and Spanish-American War groups attend the event, but the streets surrounding Union Station were thronged with thousands of visitors.

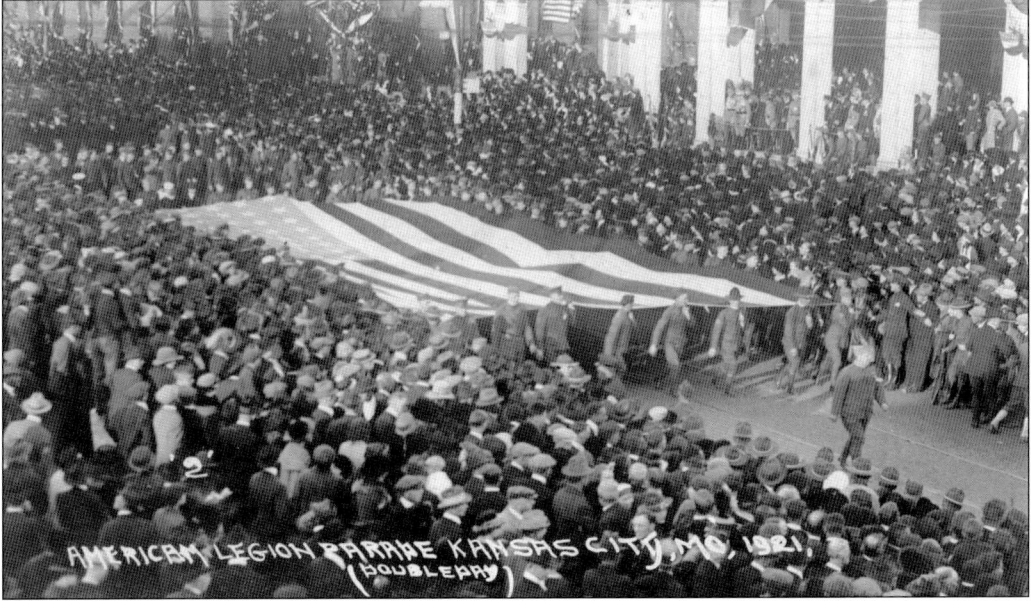

The dedication was held during the third annual convention of the American Legion and was attended by an estimated 100,000 people. Several distinguished speakers were in attendance for the ceremony, which included Lt. Gen. Baron Jacques of Belgium; Gen. Armando Diaz of Italy; Marshal Ferdinand Foch of France; Adm. David Beatty of Great Britain; and Missouri's own Gen. John J. Pershing. Pictured above is the reviewing stand before which an estimated 60,000 veterans marched in review before these five World War I leaders during the dedication parade.

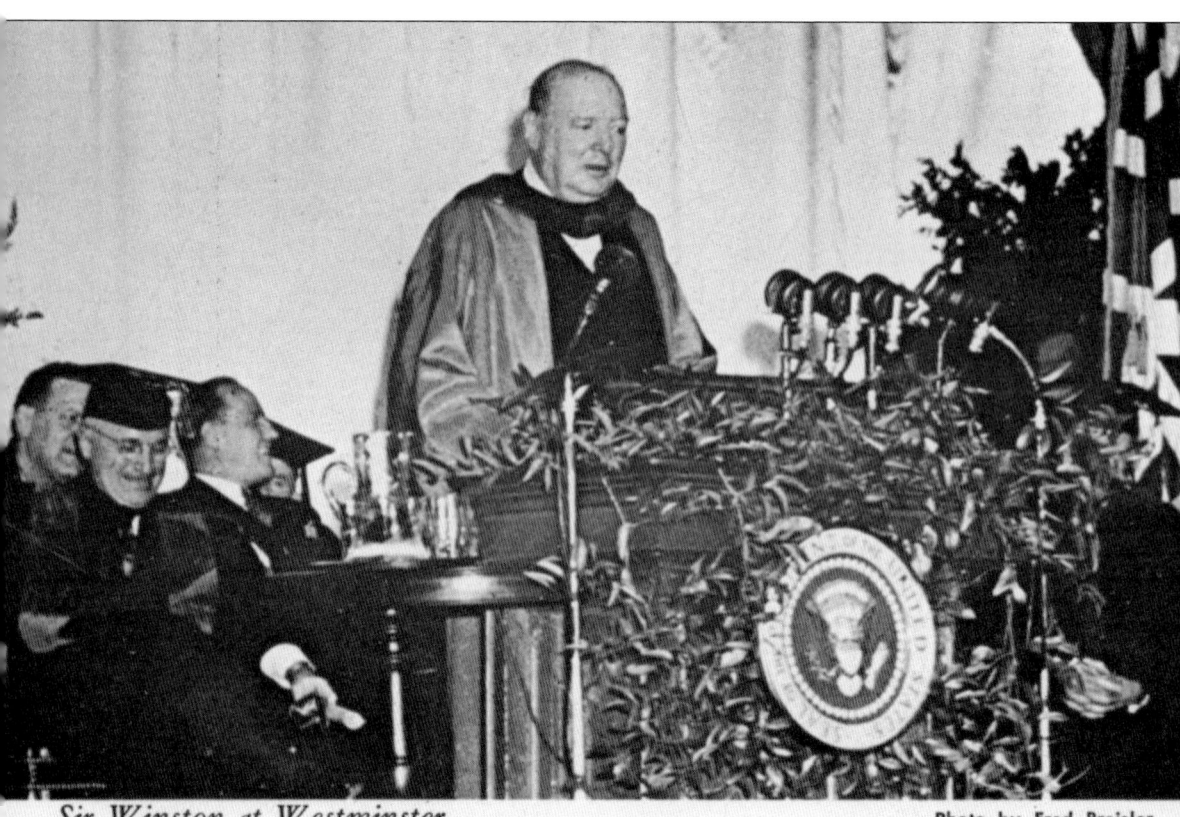

Sir Winston at Westminster — Photo by Fred Preisler

On March 5, 1946, Sir Winston Churchill visited Westminster College in Fulton, where he delivered his "Sinews of Peace" speech, which, in the annals of history, has become known as the "Iron Curtain" speech. The event was captured in this postcard by J.E. Tetrick of Kansas City and shows, seated on Churchill's right, Pres. Harry S. Truman, a Missouri native.

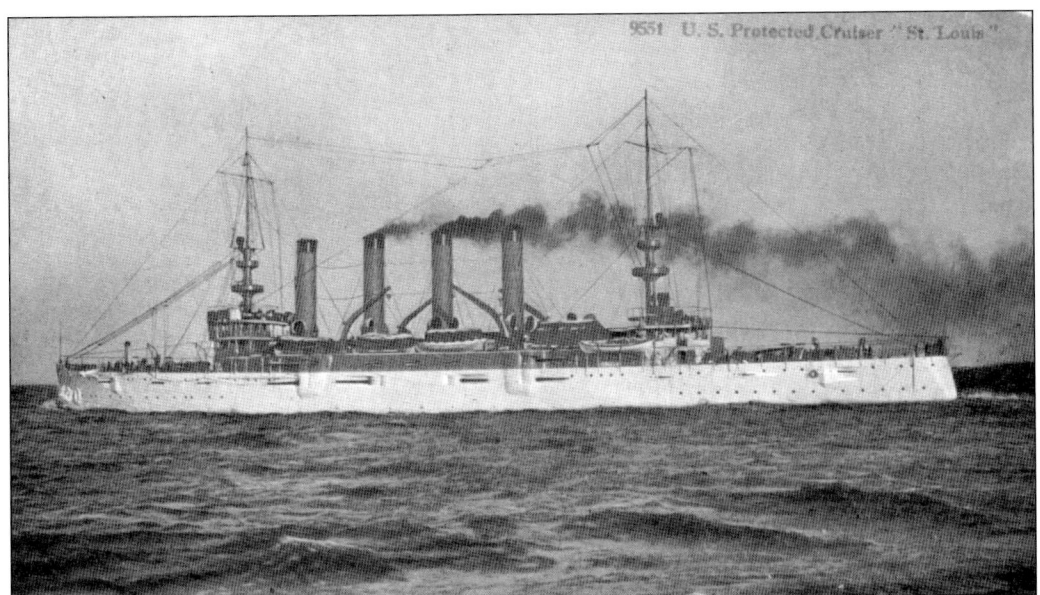

The USS *St. Louis* was one of three protected cruisers of the St. Louis class. Built by Neafie, Levy & Company in Philadelphia, Pennsylvania, the *St. Louis* was commissioned on August 18, 1906. The ship was 424 feet in length, had a displacement of 9,700 tons, and carried a crew complement consisting of 36 officers and 627 men.

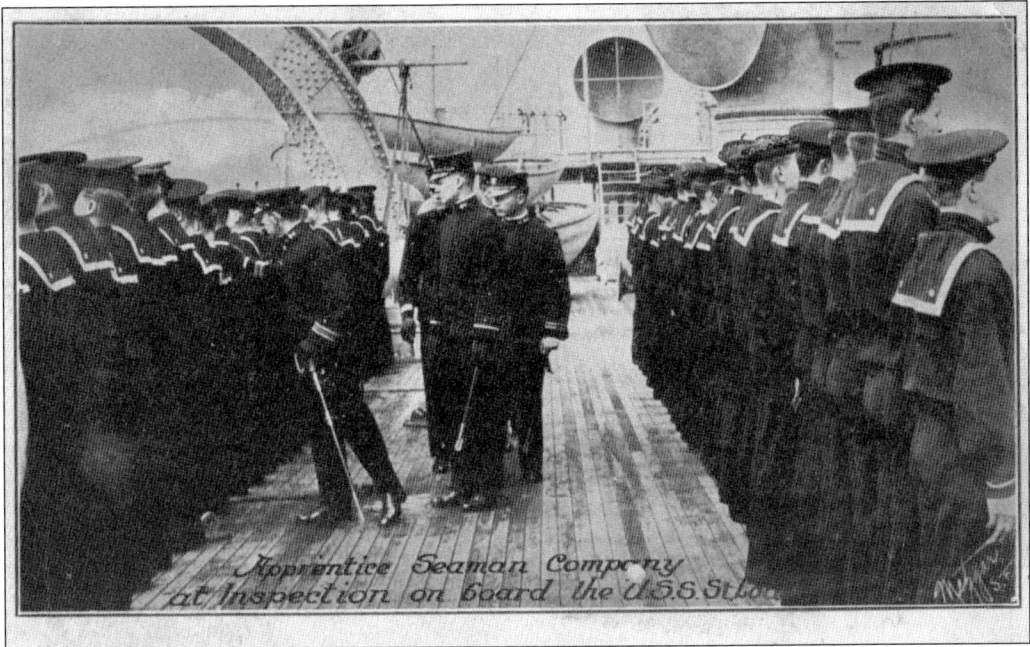

In this postcard, apprentice seaman serving aboard the USS *St. Louis* stand in formation on the deck as they undergo an inspection by naval officers. Although the ship participated in several assignments in the years following its commissioning, it remained busy during World War I transporting troops to ports in England and France. In the years after the war, the ship performed humanitarian missions but was decommissioned in 1922; eight years later, the *St. Louis* was sold and scrapped.

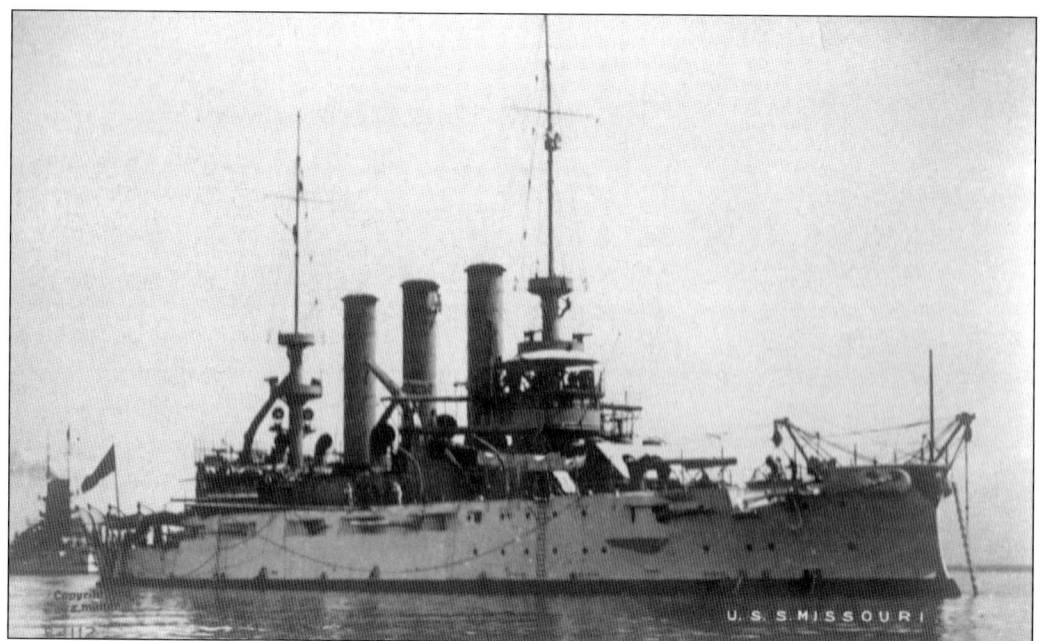

The USS *Missouri* (BB-11) was the second ship to carry the state's name. In this postcard by the Rotograph Company of New York City, the USS *Missouri* is pictured while anchored at sea. The Maine-class battleship was built by the Newport News Shipbuilding and Drydock Company in Virginia, launched in late 1901, and commissioned in December 1903.

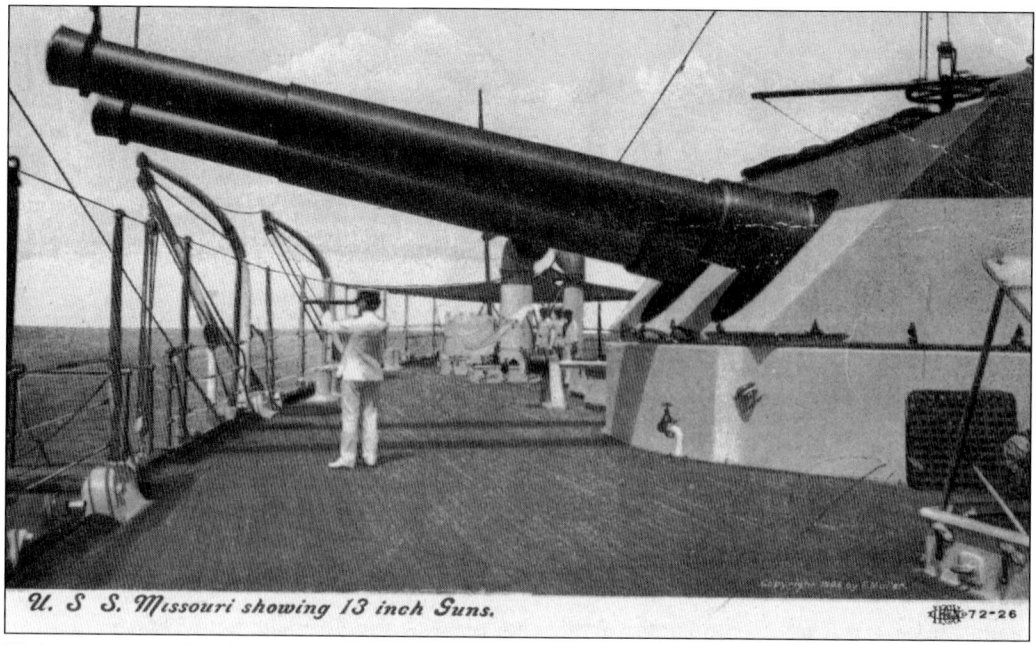

This postcard is dated 1905 and mistakenly notes that the USS *Missouri* (BB-11) was armed with 13-inch guns. However, the battleship had an armament of four 12-inch guns in addition to other smaller weapons. From December 1907 to February 1909, the ship participated in a worldwide cruise as part of the Great White Fleet—a fleet of 16 battleships sent around the world by Pres. Theodore Roosevelt as a demonstration of the naval strength of the United States.

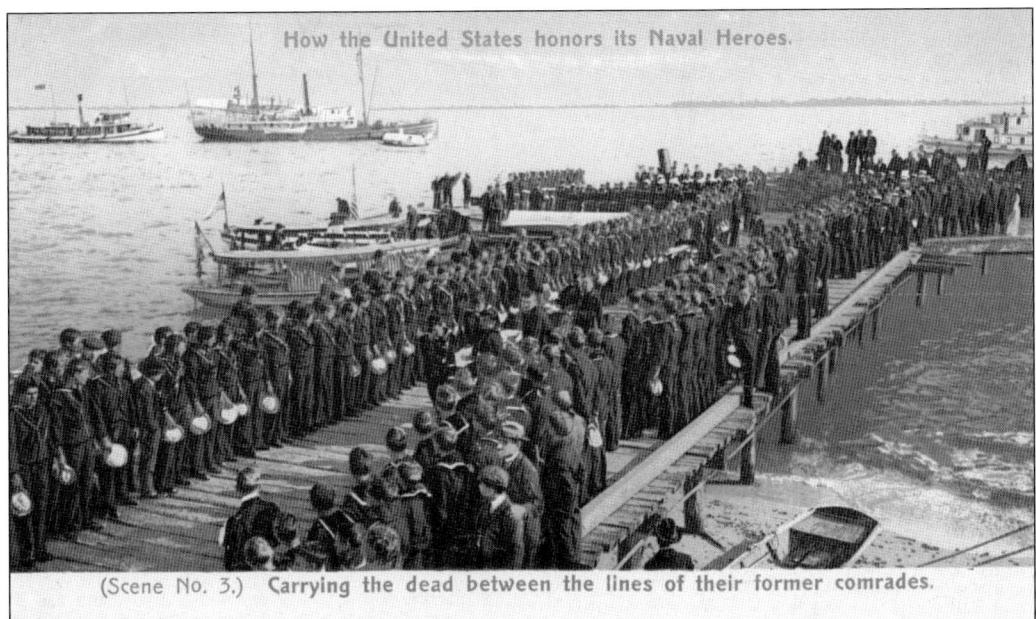

The American News Company of New York published a collection of six postcards highlighting a tragedy associated with the USS *Missouri* (BB-11). On April 13, 1904, the ship was participating in gunnery exercises when an accident with one of the 12-inch gun turrets took the lives of 36 people on board. This postcard, the third of six, features the deceased being carried along a dock between columns of sailors to their final resting spot.

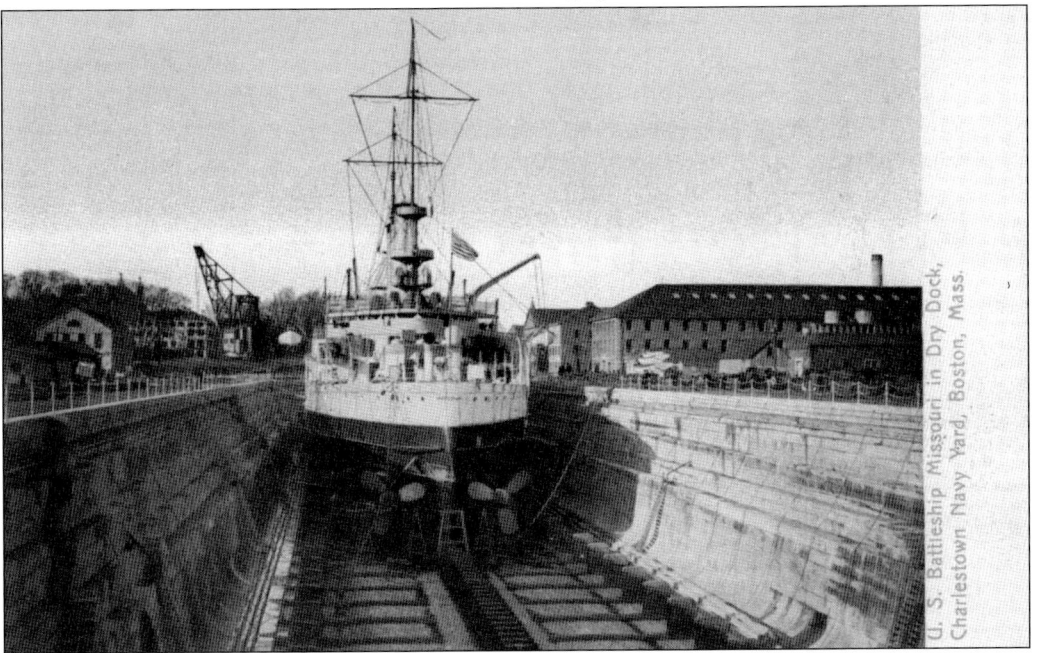

The USS *Missouri* (BB-11) is pictured in drydock at Charlestown Navy Yard in Boston, Massachusetts, sometime between 1910 and 1911. The ship was used to train sailors during World War I, and after the armistice was signed, it was employed to ferry soldiers back to the United States. In 1919, the USS *Missouri* was decommissioned and sold for scrap three years later.

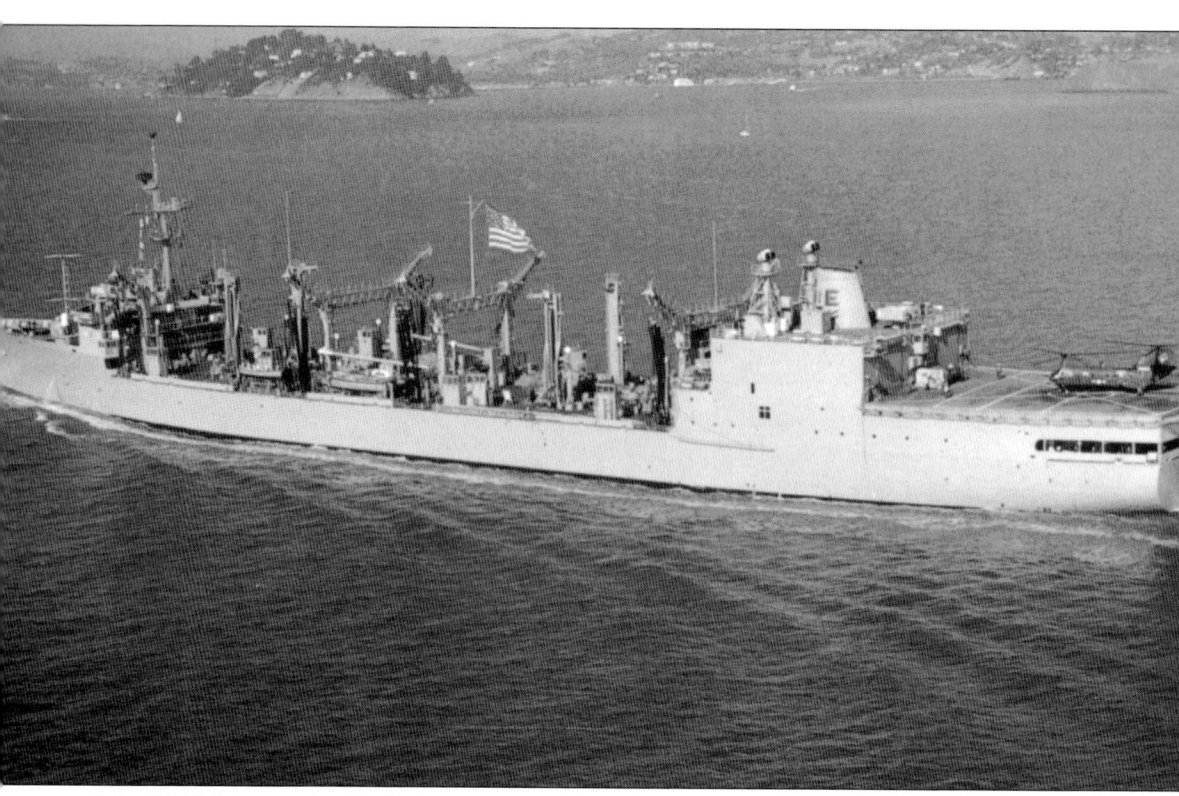

The USS *Kansas City* (AOR-3) was a Wichita-class replenishment oiler built by the Quincy Shipbuilding Division of the General Dynamics Corporation in Quincy, Massachusetts, and was launched on June 28, 1969. The ship had a crew complement of 22 officers and 398 enlisted personnel, participated in series of Western Pacific deployments, and saw service in both Vietnam and Operation Desert Storm. The ship was decommissioned on October 7, 1994, and has since been disassembled.

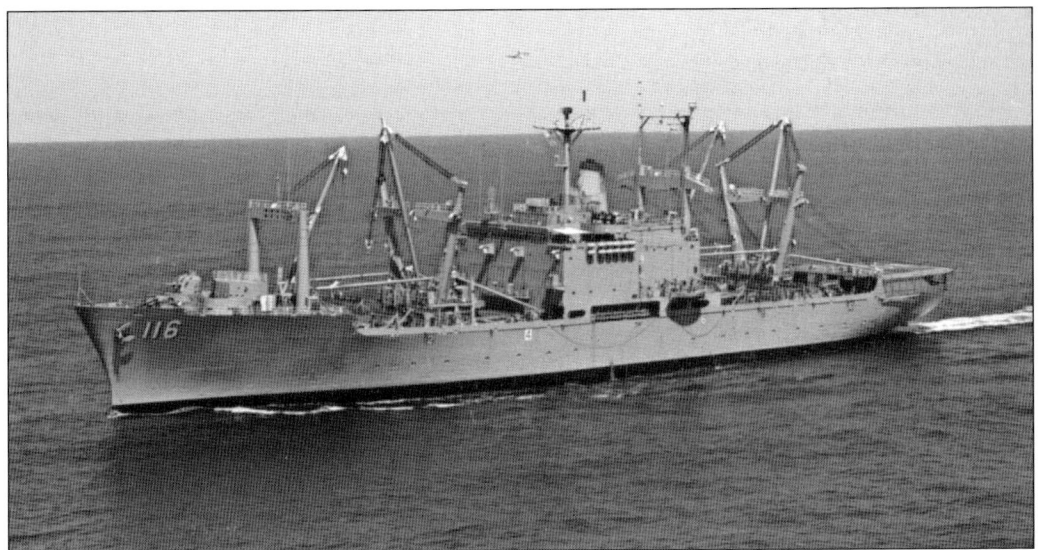

Featured on this real-photo postcard is the USS *St. Louis* (LKA-116)—an amphibious cargo ship built by the Newport News Shipbuilding Company in Virginia. Commissioned on November 22, 1969, the ship had a complement of 34 officers and 375 enlisted, went on to earn two campaign stars for service during the Vietnam War, and was decommissioned on November 2, 1992.

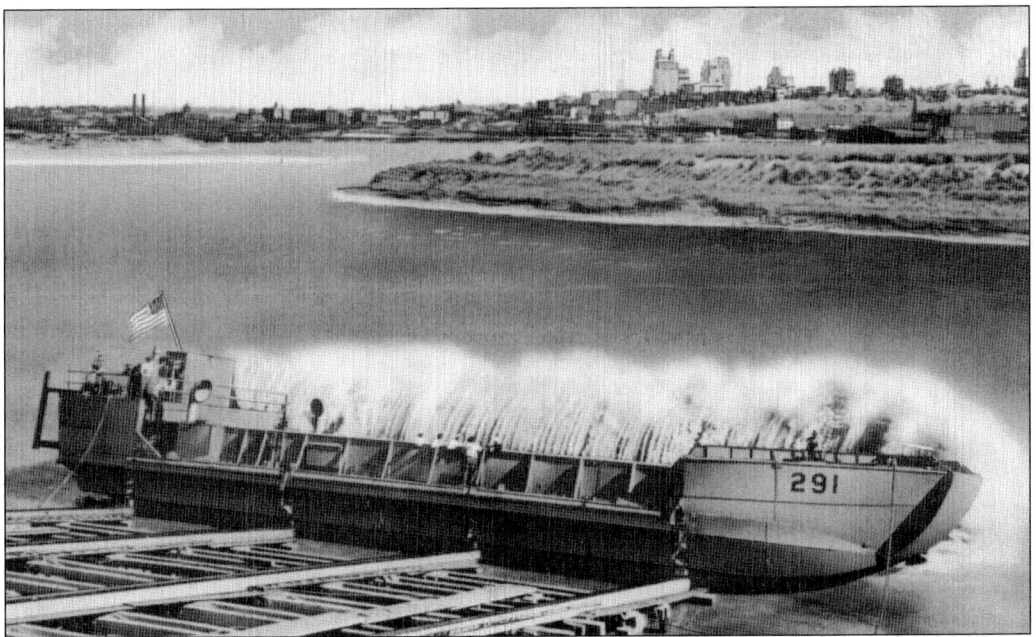

Just across the state line in Kansas City, Kansas, was the Darby Corporation. During World War II, the company produced vessels called Landing Craft Tanks (LCTs) for the US Navy in its shipyard at the junction of the Kaw and Missouri Rivers. Once completed, the vessels were launched, as featured in this postcard, and then sailed down the Missouri and Mississippi Rivers to New Orleans, where they were then prepared for entry into naval service. The company also produced locomotives, railcars, and water towers and remained in operation until closing in 1989.

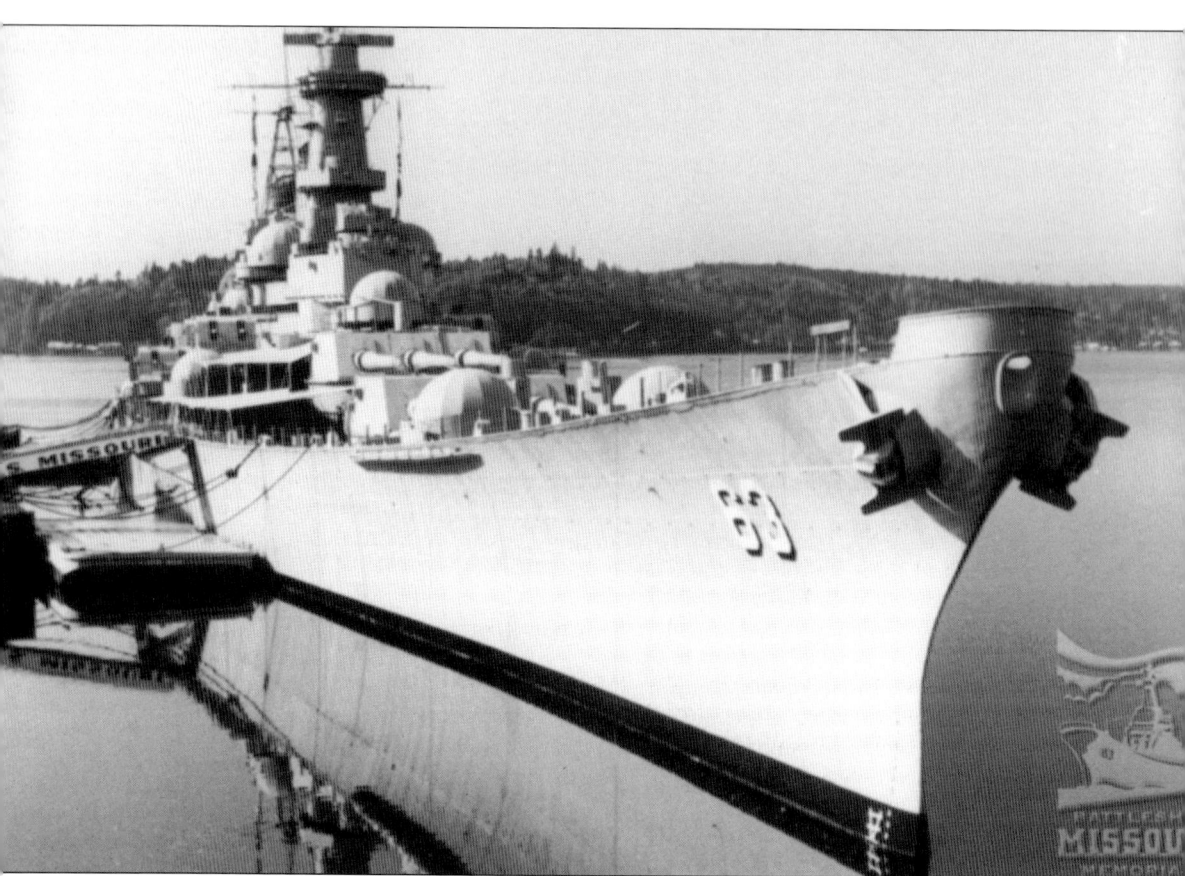

Commissioned on June 11, 1944, the USS *Missouri* (BB-63) became the third US Navy ship to carry the name of the Show-Me State. Though the ship possesses a lengthy and storied history, it gained the most notoriety during the Second World War when it hosted the surrender ceremony of Japan in Tokyo Bay on September 2, 1945. The "Mighty Mo" is now located in Pearl Harbor and continues its service as a floating museum.

BIBLIOGRAPHY

Berg, Scott. *Lindbergh*. New York, NY: GP Putnam's Sons, 1998.

Bonner, Kit and Carolyn. *USS Iowa at War*. St. Paul, MN: Zenith Press, 2007.

"Chillicothe's Armory Dedicated Thursday." *Chillicothe Constitution-Tribune*. November 8, 1940: 1.

"Coontz Armory to be Dedicated Saturday." *Palmyra Spectator*. November 1, 1939: 3.

Egan, Maurice, and John Kennedy. *The Knights of Columbus in Peace and War: Volume 1*. New Haven, CT: Knights of Columbus, 1920.

Fiedler, David. *The Enemy Among Us: POWs in Missouri During World War II*. St. Louis, MO: Missouri Historical Society Press, 2003.

"General Raupp to be Buried Today." *Joplin Globe*. May 7, 1946: 3.

Hodge, Leta. *Soldiers, Scholars, Gentlemen: The First One Hundred Years of the Missouri Military Academy*. Mexico, MO: Missouri Military Academy, 1988.

"Hyde Praises Soldiers." *St. Louis Post-Dispatch*. September 13, 1924: 11.

Johnson, Danny. "Camp Enoch H. Crowder, Missouri." Army History Center. January 28, 2015.

National Register of Historic Places Inventory: Blees Military Academy. US Department of the Interior, National Park Service. 1979.

Settle, Raymond W. *The Story of Wentworth*. Kansas City, MO: Spencer Printing Company, 1950.

Tabbert, Mark. *American Freemasons: Three Centuries of Building Communities*. New York, NY: University Press, 2005.

"Veterans Rooms to be Dedicated Today." *Joplin Globe*. November 14, 1925: 1.

Wolfenbarger, Deon. *Excelsior Springs Job Corps Center: Historic/Architectural Survey*. June 3, 1986.

DISCOVER THOUSANDS OF LOCAL HISTORY BOOKS FEATURING MILLIONS OF VINTAGE IMAGES

Arcadia Publishing, the leading local history publisher in the United States, is committed to making history accessible and meaningful through publishing books that celebrate and preserve the heritage of America's people and places.

Find more books like this at
www.arcadiapublishing.com

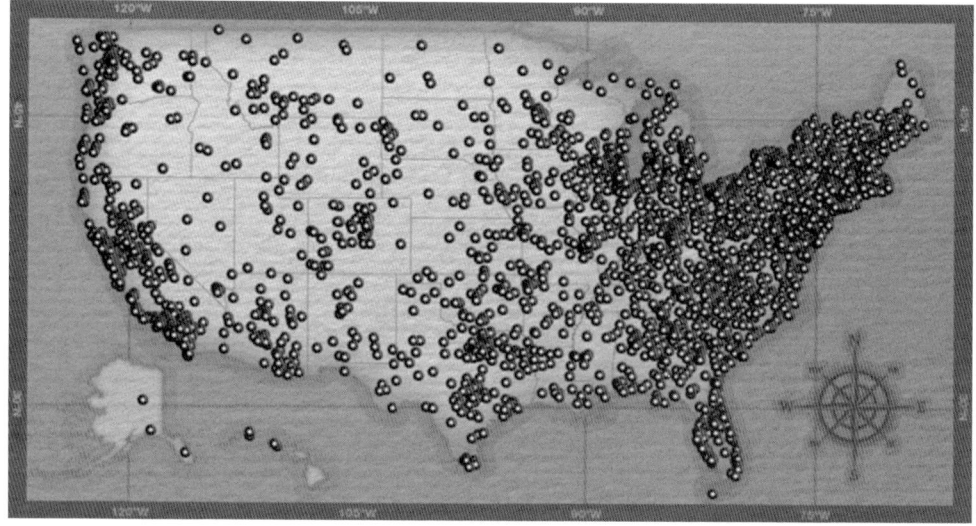

Search for your hometown history, your old stomping grounds, and even your favorite sports team.

Consistent with our mission to preserve history on a local level, this book was printed in South Carolina on American-made paper and manufactured entirely in the United States. Products carrying the accredited Forest Stewardship Council (FSC) label are printed on 100 percent FSC-certified paper.

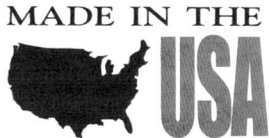